ECONOMICS IN THEORY AND PRACTICE:
AN ECLECTIC APPROACH

# Advanced Studies in Theoretical and Applied Econometrics

Volume 17

---

*For a list of volumes in this series see final page.*

# Economics in Theory and Practice: An Eclectic Approach

Essays in Honor of F. G. Adams

edited by

## Lawrence R. Klein
*Department of Economics,*
*University of Pennsylvania, U.S.A.*

and

## Jaime Marquez
*Division of International Finance,*
*Federal Reserve Board, U.S.A.*

KLUWER ACADEMIC PUBLISHERS
DORDRECHT / BOSTON / LONDON

Library of Congress Cataloging in Publication Data

```
Economics in theory and practice : an eclectic approach / edited by
  Lawrence Klein, Jaime Marquez.
       p.   cm. -- (Advanced studies in theoretical and applied
  econometrics ; 17)
    "Essays in honour of F.G. Adams."
    ISBN 0-7923-0410-1
    1. Econometric models.  2. Economics.  3. Adams, F. G.   I. Adams,
F. Gerard (Francis Gerard), 1929-   .  II. Klein, Lawrence Robert.
III. Marquez, Jaime R.   IV. Series: Advances studies in theoretical
and applied econometrics ; v. 17.
HB141.E256  1989
330--dc20                                                  89-15588
```

ISBN 0-7923-0410-1

Published by Kluwer Academic Publishers,
P.O. Box 17, 3300 AA Dordrecht, The Netherlands.

Kluwer Academic Publishers incorporates
the publishing programmes of
D. Reidel, Martinus Nijhoff, Dr W. Junk and MTP Press.

Sold and distributed in the U.S.A. and Canada
by Kluwer Academic Publishers,
101 Philip Drive, Norwell, MA 02061, U.S.A.

In all other countries, sold and distributed
by Kluwer Academic Publishers Group,
P.O. Box 322, 3300 AH Dordrecht, The Netherlands.

*Printed on acid-free paper*

# TABLE OF CONTENTS

## PART III: INDUSTRIAL ORGANISATION AND GOVERNMENT POLICY

# PREFACE

Lawrence Klein, *University of Pennsylvania*
Jaime Marquez, *Federal Reserve Board**

An examination of the economics literature over the last twenty years reveals a marked tendency towards polarisation. On the one hand, there has been a propensity to develop theoretical models which have little connection with either empirical verification or problems requiring immediate attention. On the other hand, empirical analyses are generally typified by testing for its own sake, with limited examination of the implications of the results. As a result, the number of papers confronting theory with facts towards the solution of economic problems has been on the decline for years.

To fill this growing gap in the literature, we have invited a number of authors to write papers using both theoretical and empirical techniques to address current issues of interest to the profession at large: the US trade deficit and the global implications of policies that attempt to reduce it, the international ramifications of the debt crisis, the international oil market and its implications for the US oil industry, and the development of new econometric techniques. In addressing these issues, each author has approached the subject matter from an eclectic standpoint – that is, avoiding strict adherence to a given doctrine.

These essays are grouped in three sections according to issue they address. In section I we include papers dealing with the development of new techniques for forecasting, model evaluation, and econometric modelling. Section II contains three papers examining the international debt crisis and its relation with international trade. Finally, section III is devoted to studying the issue of industrial organisation and its relation to changes in both the regulatory environment and the international oil market.

## I. FRONTIERS IN FORECASTING AND ECONOMETRIC MODELLING

For an econometric model to be useful in decision making, it must be accurate. In this regard, much has been written about the forecasting records of both time series models and structural models. However, until recently, the approaches available forced practitioners to choose one type of model or the other. *Lawrence Klein and Eduardo Sojo* develop a single forecasting model that integrates time series modelling with structural modelling. As they show, the chief advantage of this integration is the reduction in the risk associated with forecasting. This task is accomplished by combining forecasts from models that rely on data with different frequencies. For example, the forecasts of a structural quarterly model can be combined with the forecasts of a supplementary time series model that relies on monthly information.

Several advantages arise from their approach to forecasting. First, it is possible to exploit the most recent information, which is generally available in high frequencies. Second, it is possible to integrate time series and structural modelling, with the former being more accurate in the short run and the latter being more accurate in the long run. Finally, the paper by Klein and Sojo is of interest to policymakers, who often have access to a low frequency model and the high frequency data.

A particular forecast is not very useful if there is no information about its standard error. With this error, it is possible to evaluate the relative risk of the forecast, which is particularly important for making economic decisions. However, the complexity of existing econometric models precludes the computation of such standard errors in all but the simplest of models. *Roberto Mariano and Bryan Brown* develop a methodology to compute forecast standard errors for large scale models in a computationally simple way. They accomplish this task by examining the large sample properties of alternative forecasting procedures for the class of dynamic nonlinear models. Because the vast majority of econometrically estimated models fall into this class, their analysis has immediate applicability to private and public institutions for which economic forecasts are an integral part of the decision making process. Mariano and Brown recognise that the historical residuals of an econometric model can be treated as estimates of the original disturbances. These estimated residuals form the basis to generate stochastic dynamic simulations that would enable researchers to compute the standard errors associated with both model forecasts and model multipliers.

Finally, the econometric estimation of parameters of interest requires variation in the data. There are circumstances, however, in which model predictions would be improved by incorporating relations which, by their own nature, do not tend to produce data with the needed variability. An important issue is, then, whether it is possible to combine models using different methodologies for parameter estimation, and if so, what interpretation can be given to the model results.

*Walter Labys* studies these questions in the context of the world copper market. Specifically, he uses "engineering" parameter estimates along with econometric parameter estimates in a single model. The former are used to gauge technical relations which ultimately determine productive capacity and thus, long run supply. However, it is not possible to obtain data on long—run relations, and even if it were, the data would not exhibit enough variation to permit econometric estimation of the associated parameters.

By integrating two strands of commodity market modelling, Labys is able to focus on the transition from a short—run disequilibrium to a long—run equilibrium. Short—run disequilibrium is modelled in a standard commodity (econometric) model (e.g., the work of Adams, Behrman, and Labys) which is well suited for explaining supply side considerations, such as capacity formation. The model is validated and in this process, Labys is able to identify the effects of both supply and demand factors on fluctuations in copper prices.

## II. TRADE, DEBT, AND DEVELOPMENT

One of the oldest questions in economics is whether international trade is conducive to development. Although theoretical arguments lead one to believe that it does, it has been argued that international trade has increased the exposure of developing countries to price fluctuations which in turn have hampered their development process.

To address this question, *Jere Behrman, Jeffrey Lewis, and Sherif Lotfi* use a Computable General Equilibrium model to examine the extent to which fluctuations in commodity prices have affected the development process of Indonesia. As it stands, the existing literature, much of which has been written by Behrman himself, focuses on the macroeconomic consequences of lower commodity prices. However, as the paper argues, the question is not whether lower export prices affect adversely growth prospects, but whether a greater variability in these prices is responsible for lower growth rates. Furthermore, very little attention has been given to the microeconomic implications of greater price variability. Microeconomic considerations are important because they explain the degree to which the supply of both labour and goods are affected by unpredictable price paths. Finally, the effects of price increases have received less attention than the effects of price decreases. This asymmetry in price effects interacts with policy responses from both domestic and international institutions potentially obscuring the ultimate effect.

A more recent, and related issue is the degree to which many debtor countries are able to support both a sustained growth path and service their debt obligations. *Pedro Palma* studies the policy responses of debtor countries to commodity price changes, an issue of interest given that most debtor countries are currently engaged in debt rescheduling agreements the viability of which are also dependent on commodity prices. A second important issue addressed by Palma is the effect of alternative debt rescheduling agreements on the macroeconomy. Knowledge of these macro effects is of interest because it helps to determine the rescheduling package a country should adopt and the policy responses that would be required to support a given rescheduling plan if commodity prices change.

To address these questions, Palma relies on dynamic simulations of a medium size econometric model for the Venezuelan economy. Venezuela is an ideal case for addressing these questions because of the recent volatility in oil prices, the heavy reliance on oil exports as a source of export revenues, and the existence of a debt rescheduling agreement with banks. Thus fluctuations in oil prices affect not only Venezuela's growth prospects but also the country's ability to service its external obligations. The result of this analysis, besides being relevant to policy making in other debtor nations (e.g., Mexico), might shed light on questions regarding the difference between liquidity and solvency as well as the conduct of stabilisation policy in developing countries.

*Jaime Marquez* studies the design of policy responses to address international trade imbalances and the associated consequences for international trade flows. To address these issues, Marquez develops a trade model explaining bilateral trade flows in an eight region world economy (Canada, Germany, Japan, the United Kingdom, the United States, Other OECD, non—OPEC developing countries, and OPEC). A key feature of this model is that international trade imbalances add up to zero. The analysis estimates income and price elasticities for bilateral import equations, tests for the properties of the error term, for parameter constancy, and for the choice of dynamic specification.

The paper also re—examines the structural asymmetries in elasticities noted by Houthakker and Magee and tests whether the Marshall—Lerner condition holds. The reliability of the model as a whole is assessed with residual based stochastic simulations. The paper finds that changes in relative prices account for the bulk of the deterioration of the US trade account, that reliance on either foreign or domestic growth to eliminate the US external imbalances entails significant changes in real income, and that the speed with which US net exports respond to exchange rate changes is sensitive to minor changes in own—price elasticities.

## III. INDUSTRIAL ORGANISATION AND GOVERNMENT POLICY

Conventional economic theory predicts that cartels are short lived forms of organisations. Chiselling and cheating among the members of the cartel ultimately result in its elimination as a viable organisation. Yet, a closer examination of the historical record suggests that the predictions of economic theory are at variance with the actual experience of numerous cartels. Is this discrepancy between theory and practice real? If so, what factors can account for it?

To address these questions, *James Griffin* develops a model to explain the determinants of a cartel's success. Specifically, Griffin explains the Lerner index for a given cartel as a function of the Herfindahl index, the market share of the cartel, and the cartel's organisation structure. To estimate the relative importance of these determinants, Griffin relies on least squares as applied to a sample of international commodity cartels that have been active since 1900. The paper uses the statistical findings to draw implications for the future of OPEC, a cartel that (up to now) has defied a conventional characterisation of its behaviour.

A second important question in the area of industrial organisation is the degree to which existing government regulations affect an industry's flexibility to respond to changes in its external environment. *Leslie Grayson and Robert Morris* examine this question by focusing on how the disruption in the oil market in 1979 interacted with the existing regulatory system to affect the distribution of gasoline in the United States. In particular, they examine the monthly distributional patterns of gasoline across states in which the Iranian oil disruption led to shortages.

Knowledge of these interactions is important for several reasons. First, by comparing the 1979 crisis to the experience of the 1974 oil shock, it is possible to estimate the extent to which the regulatory system affected the flexibility of the price allocation system to respond to supply shocks. Second, it is clear that the behaviour of oil companies, as reflected in their adjustment of oil inventories, affects the distribution of gasoline. As a result, there might be a conflict between private and social interests, an issue that Grayson and Morris address.

Economic changes generally involve shifts in the location of economic activities and the form of their organisations — the fall of the industrial Northeast, the rise of the Sunbelt. Specifically, firms' ability to shift internationally both the location of production and investment decisions, as well as the change in the structure of production away from manufacturing and towards services, has had a number of implications for regional unemployment levels and thus for the development of macroeconomic policies. To examine these implications, *Norman Glickman* studies the degree to which regional changes in US economic activities have been influenced by international considerations (e.g. exchange rates and oil prices) and by domestic considerations (e.g. productivity and demographics). An understanding of the determinants of these regional shifts is relevant to addressing policy questions at the local level (city and state), which have been largely neglected by mainstream economics.

---

*     The views expressed in this book are solely the responsibility of the authors and should not be interpreted as reflecting those of the Board of Governors of the Federal Reserve System or other members of its staff.

PART I

**FRONTIERS IN FORECASTING AND ECONOMETRIC MODELLING**

CHAPTER 1


# COMBINATIONS OF HIGH AND LOW FREQUENCY DATA IN MACROECONOMETRIC MODELS

L.R. Klein and E. Sojo, *University of Pennsylvania*

## 1. ECONOMETRIC PRACTICE

Econometricians who try to follow and project the overall economy as closely as possible ("Economy Watchers") frequently base their main forecasts on macroeconometric models, supplemented by the frequent flow — almost daily — of indicative information. As soon as reports are prepared about some specific area of economic activity, they are released to the public. At the extreme, we have instantaneous market reports, originating with the start of the day at the international date line and moving with the sun to Tokyo, Hong Kong, Sidney/Melbourne, Singapore, Frankfurt/Paris, London, New York, Chicago, Los Angeles/San Francisco. These data cover both commodity and financial market reports.

On a monthly basis, there are national statistics for price indexes, wage rates, employment, unemployment, orders, shipments, inventories, construction, exports, imports, and many other indicators. Most macroeconometric models are based on social accounting statements that are prepared at either quarterly or annual intervals. It is possible to construct social accounts more frequently, but it has not been done on more than a fragmentary or sporadic basis. In practical sense, we should assume that quarterly models will be used for some time to come. They will use sample data from the quarterly social accounts, many of whose entries will be time aggregations of monthly or higher frequency data. The use of high frequency data will be for the construction of price deflators but also for the direct estimation of nominal (current value) entries in the accounts. The deflators of consumer spending will make use of monthly data on consumer

3

*L. R. Klein and J. Marquez (eds.), Economics in Theory and Practice: An Eclectic Approach, 3–16.*
© *1989 by Kluwer Academic Publishers.*

prices; other deflators will use monthly prices from different indexes — wholesale, producers, commodity markets with the exception of government employee compensation which is obtained implicitly (nominal/real). Personal income series are actually produced monthly, and their entries in the national income accounts are obtained from monthly tax reports, social insurance records, company dividends when issued, and monthly public sector budget reports.

On the expenditure side of the social accounts, consumer outlays are computed from monthly (weekly) retail sales reports, inventory investment from monthly inventory reports and export/import outlays from monthly trade statistics, which need to be converted to a national account basis.

The preparation of the social accounts is a major statistical activity involving the combining of many diverse pieces of information. Many of these pieces are produced at high frequency intervals, but the total articulated report is quarterly, at the best, and for many countries only annually.

In using macroeconometric models for forecasting the national economy, practitioners are tied to the time schedule for preparing and releasing the social accounts. In the United States, the main lag is approximately three weeks. After the end of a calendar quarter, the first round estimates of the completed quarter are released on about the 20th of January, April, July and October. These lack profit statistics which become available one month later. Updating of data files and preparation of the forecast typically takes about 7 to 10 days, although it could be speeded up, if necessary. During the second and third months of a quarter, forecasts are examined and revised, partly an the basis of revisions in the quarterly social accounts on about the 20th of each month and partly on the basis of high frequency data which provide new information about short run economic movements. Official data—preparing agencies use high frequency data for the estimation of quarterly totals and must frequently round out a quarter's estimates by projecting missing months within the quarter.

The econometric forecaster using a quarterly model therefore starts the projections with input data for the previous quarter (lags) and solves for the current quarter. Some things are known about the current quarter at the time the solution is initiated. The solution typically has a future horizon of some twelve quarters, or thereabouts. Should the econometric forecaster simply stand by the model result and ignore what is already known about the current quarter, or should the econometrician regard the high frequency data as added information, outside the sample? Since econometric samples are small and data are scarce, it seems sensible to make use of the added information. In practice, this is done by adjusting the constant term of relevant equations (or using a nonzero error term) in order to make the model outcome agree with the new information.

In a single equation this amounts to replacing an estimated equation value

$$y_t = f(x_t, \hat{\theta}) + 0 \tag{1}$$

where $y_t$ = dependent variable, $x_t$ = independent variable (input data), $\hat{\theta}$ = estimated parameter value

by

$$y_t = f(x_t, \hat{\theta}) + a_t \tag{2}$$

where $a_t$ = adjustment value.

The original equation, before estimation, is

$$y_t = f(x_t, \theta) + e_t \tag{3}$$

In equation (1) the value of $\theta$ is replaced by its estimate $\hat{\theta}$, which is, in a sense, a representative value from a sampling distribution. In the same sense 0 is the mean of the distribution of $e_t$. The random variable need not take on its mean value, and the high frequency data are used, to replace 0 by $a_t$. If the function f is linear, this is obviously equivalent to changing the constant term of the equation by the amount $a_t$ and leaving the zero mean of the distribution of $e_t$ in place.

This widely practiced procedure has been criticised as being informal and subjective. A defense can be made for the practical procedure but an objective procedure that can be digitally replicated is available.

It has been observed that time series analysis of high frequency data provide good forecasts of economic magnitudes for the short run, say up to six months. Some analysts may claim validity for longer horizons, but experience with many series suggests good performance in short horizons. Such performance is not generally superior to model performance, but it is as good as model performance. It has also been observed and formally rationalised that combinations of forecasts, by different procedures, reduce the risk of forecast error, and may be preferred to forecasts from one method alone. In this spirit of inquiry we propose the estimation of current quarter forecasts by time series methods, using as much high frequency data as possible, and using these forecasts as benchmarks to which to adjust a quarterly model. The time series adjusted model is then extrapolated over a lengthier horizon. This approach has been independently pursued by econometricians at the Federal Reserve Board and the University of Michigan.[1] The present paper uses different high frequency models and different econometric models than those in other studies. This is, therefore, an independent investigation along lines similar to those followed elsewhere.

The idea of combining data of different frequencies in model analysis and forecasting is not new. In quite different contexts these combinations have been frequently made. In project LINK, where macroeconometric models from 79 countries or regions are simultaneously related to one another through trade flows, we have consistently combined quarterly models of the main industrial countries with annual models of the developing and centrally planned economies. Final results are reduced to the lowest common denominator, namely, annual data, but in getting the results, we first evaluate quarterly models, add or average quarterly values into annual values and then combine the time–aggregated data with the results from the annual models. This process needs to be iterated, and in re–entering the quarterly models on the i–th iteration, we must disaggregate the final annual results obtained on the (i–1)st iteration.

In another application of mixed frequencies, we combine, at Wharton Econometrics, short term business cycle results from a quarterly model with medium term (10 years or more) results from an annual model. Careful forecasting of zigs and zags is applied to the quarterly models, and the quarterly results are aggregated (averaged). The annual model is then adjusted, as described above, to reproduce approximately the same yearly time path that the aggregated quarterly results follow. After the annual model traverses the short run business cycle span of three years, it takes a life of its own for the remainder of the simulation horizon.

## 2. THREE APPROACHES TO THE CURRENT QUARTER MODEL

To make use of monthly or weekly data in model construction, and to have a capability of generating current (and subsequent) quarter forecasts of major economic magnitudes, we approach the problem from three sides:

    (i) the expenditure side

    (ii) the income side

    (iii) through unstructured empirical indicator relations.

For case (i), we consider the main entries on the expenditure side of national income and product accounts (NIPA) and also the main data sources used by the US Department of Commerce in constructing their accounts. We estimate time series and other interrelationships among high–frequency variables and then establish empirical "bridge" equations between the entries in the national income and product accounts and the high frequency data.

Where possible, the bridge equations are estimated from monthly data on both the indicators and the NIPA components. All NIPA components, however, are not reported monthly. In such cases, we must build quarterly bridge equations by aggregating the monthly indicators into quarters and correlating those with quarterly NIPA series. Our estimated equations are designed so as to be able to extrapolate the high frequency data series to fill out the current quarter and extend beyond for one or two more quarters.

In case (ii) we do the same thing for the main entries on the income side of the national income accounts that we do in case (i) for the expenditure side. In most of the prior work done at the Federal Reserve Board and elsewhere, the emphasis has been on the expenditure side. Of course, we have the problem of reconciling the two central aggregates produced by the methods of case (i) and case (ii) in reaching a single main aggregate to represent either gross national expenditure (product) or national income.

Case (iii) has no particular accounting structure. We simply put together all the "quick" information that we can assemble at high frequency early in the quarter. Much of it is intercorrelated. We then extract the leading principal components of the quarterly aggregates (averages) of these several indicators and regress major quarterly magnitudes on the quarterly aggregates (averages) of the principal components.

Let us first consider the detailed procedures followed in case (i), the construction of the current quarter estimates of the expenditure side. The Bureau of Economic Analysis of the United States Department of Commerce makes and releases its first estimates of a quarter's National Product Accounts about 3 weeks after a quarter's end. This is a preliminary estimate and is based on monthly or weekly data, much of which are incomplete for the entire quarter being estimated. Our procedure is to use the same high frequency data that the BEA use in making the preliminary forecast. In fact, a rigorous test of a model used for forecasting is to demand that the model be as "close" to the ultimate estimate as is the preliminary figure. After all, the estimate of the official national income statisticians represents a figure that is as close as we, who do not have access to all the details, could conceivably be able to come.

We first estimate nominal GNP and its components on the expenditure side.

Some of these require a physical volume indicator and an associated price indicator. Next we estimate price deflators for categories of nominal (current value) expenditure items of the GNP. The real expenditure side estimates are obtained by deflating nominal expenditures by the estimated price deflator. The nominal GNP is built up from the following table, which lists the National Income and Product Account series on the left and the indicator series on the right hand side.

| NIPA (quarterly) | INDICATOR (monthly) |
|---|---|
| Personal Consumer Expenditures | Retail Sales of: |
| Durable goods | |
|   Autos and parts | Unit sales and CPI, autos |
|   Furniture & household equipment | Furniture, home furnishings & equipment stores |
|   Other durable goods | Durable goods less specific categories |
| Nondurable goods | |
|   Food and beverages | Food stores |
|   Clothing and shoes | Apparel and accessory stores |
|   Gasoline and oil | Gasoline service stations |
|   Other nondurable goods | Nondurable goods less specific categories |
| Services | Employment in services |
| Gross private domestic investment | |
|   Nonresidential structures | Value of new nonresidential construction put in place |
|   Producers durable equipment | |
|     Motor vehicles | Personal consumer expend., autos & parts |
|     Other equipment | Exports, machinery & transport. equip. Imports, machinery & transport. equip. Manufacturers' shipments of nondefense capital goods |
|   Residential structures | Housing starts and value of new residential construction put in place |
|   Nonfarm inventory change | |
|   Manufacturing | Book value of manufacturing inventories |
|   Retail trade | Book value of retail trade inventories |
|   Merchandise wholesalers | Book value of merch. wholesale inventories |
|   Nonmerch. wholesalers | ARIMA (autoregressive integrated moving average) |
|   Other | ARIMA |
|   Farm inventory change | ARIMA |

| | |
|---|---|
| Exports | Merchandise exports |
| Merchandise exports | Exports of goods |
| Service exports | Residual |
| Imports | Merchandise imports |
| Merchandise imports | Imports of goods |
| Service imports | Residual |
| | |
| Government purchases | |
| Federal | Net outlays, federal government |
| Federal structures | Federal government new construction put in place |
| Fed. employee compens. | Federal government employment |
| Other federal | Residual |
| State & local employee compensation | State & local government employment |
| State & local structures | State & local govt. new construction put in place |
| Other state and local | ARIMA |

| | |
|---|---|
| Deflators of the GNP | Consumer price indexes of: |
| Durable goods | Durable goods |
| Autos and parts | New cars |
| Furniture & household equipment | Furniture & bedding and household appliances |
| Other durable goods | Residual |
| | |
| Nondurable goods | Nondurable goods |
| Food and beverages | Food and beverages |
| Clothing and shoes | Apparel |
| Gasoline and oil | Motor fuel, oil, and coolant |
| Other nondurables | Residual |
| Services | Services |
| | |
| Gross private domestic investment | |
| Nonresidential structures | PPI, intermed. materials for construction |
| | |
| Producers durable equipment | |
| Motor vehicles | ARIMA |
| Other equipment | Producer price of finished goods, capital equipment |
| Residential structures | PPI, intermed. materials for construction |
| | |
| Nonfarm inventory change | |
| Manufacturing | Implicit (nominal/real) |
| Retail trade | Implicit (nominal/real) |
| Merchandise wholesalers | Implicit (nominal/real) |
| Nonmerch. wholesalers | Implicit (nominal/real) |
| Other | Implicit (nominal/real) |
| | |
| Farm inventory change | Implicit (nominal/real) |
| | |
| Merchandise exports | Unit value of exports |

| Service exports | Merchandise exports |
|---|---|
| Merchandise imports | Unit value of imports |
| Service imports | Merchandise imports |

Government purchases
| Federal employee compensation | Implicit (nominal/real) |
|---|---|
| Structures | Nonresidential structures |
| Other | Producer price index, capital equipment |
| State & local employee compens. | Implicit (nominal/real) |
| Structures | Nonresidential structures |
| Other | Producer price index, capital equipment |

The data in this table are used in two ways. First, bridge equations are estimated. These are regressions of NIPA quarterly series on quarterly aggregates of the indicator series. Where there is no appropriate indicator available, the NIPA series is estimated directly from an ARMA process. For any NIPA–type variable, $y_{it}$, we estimate a quarterly ARMA process as

$$y_{it} + \sum_{j=1}^{p} \alpha_{ij} y_{i,t-j} = \sum_{j=0}^{q} \beta_{ij} e_{i,t-j} \tag{4}$$

differencing $y_{it}$ when the autocorrelations show signs of nonstationarity. The $\alpha_{ij}$ and $\beta_{ij}$ are estimated by time series techniques, testing the random errors, $e_{i,t}$ for randomness; i.e.; we assume these random variables to be white noise errors.

In the second stage, after we have determined the regressions of the NIPA variables on indicators, where possible, we estimate monthly ARMA equations for each of the indicators. In applications of this system, we first extrapolate the indicators so that values for complete quarters (the current plus one or two ahead) can be estimated. We then put these estimated indicators on the right hand side of the bridge equations to obtain values for the NIPA variables in the current and projected quarters.

A typical equation is

$$CENGD = 0.0403 + 9.470 \ ICENGD \tag{5}$$
$$(1.01) \quad (23.84)$$
$$R^2 = 0.71 \qquad \rho_1 = -0.13$$

CENGD = Consumer expenditures on gasoline and oil in current prices and in first differences

ICENGD = Retail sales of gasoline service stations in current prices and in first differences

The correlograms of residual error is flat, near zero, and the first order serial correlation is −0.13.

The indicators are generally highly correlated with the corresponding NIPA variable. All the equations of the system are listed in an annex.

The GNP and various sub–categories are obtained from the relevant sums (or differences) of the components. The components in constant prices are estimated by dividing the estimated nominal series, listed above, by the estimated price deflators. The deflators themselves are estimated in the same way that the current value series in the GNP are estimated.

The design of calculations on the income side proceeds in an analogous way. We begin with a table of relationships between NIPA and indicator elements.

| NIPA (quarterly) | INDICATORS (monthly) |
| --- | --- |
| Gross national product | From identity |
| Less: capital consumption | Fixed investment |
| allowances | (see expenditure side) |
| Equals: net nation. product | From identity |
| Less: business transfer payments | Residual |
| Less: statistical discrepancy | Residual |
| Plus: subsidies less current surplus | Net outlays, federal government |
| | (see expenditure side) |
| Equals: national income | From identity |
| Less: corporate profits & | Industrial production |
| adjustments | Retail sales |
| Less: contributions for social insurance | |
| Personal | Wage & salary disbursements |
| Employer | Wage & salary disbursements or personal contributions for social insurance |
| Less: wage accruals less disbursement | ARIMA |
| Plus: transfer payments | |
| Government | Total transfer from monthly personal income |
| Business | Residual |
| Plus: interest paid by | Outstanding consumer installment |
| government & consumers | credit federal governmt. debt, interest rate, prime comm. paper, 6 months |
| Net interest paid by consumers | Outstanding consumer installment, credit, interest rate, prime comm. paper, 6 months |
| Net interest paid (fed) | Federal governmt. debt, interest rate, prime comm. paper, 6 months |
| Less: interest paid to foreign | Interest rate, prime comm. paper, 6 month |
| Net interest paid (state) | Residual |
| Plus: dividends | Personal dividends from monthly personal income |
| Equals: personal income | From identity |
| Personal income | From identity |
| Wage & salary disbursements | |

Commodity producing industries

| | |
|---|---|
| Manufacturing | Employment manufacturing avg. weekly hours, manufacturing average hourly earnings |
| Other | Employment, other average weekly hours, manufacturing average hourly earnings |
| Distributive industries | Employment, wholesale & retail trade avg. weekly hrs, wholesale & retail trade avg. hourly earnings |
| Services | Employment, services average weekly hours, services average hourly earnings, services |
| Government | ARIMA |

| | |
|---|---|
| Other labour income | Employment |
| Proprietor's income | |
| Farm | Prices paid by farmers Prices received by farmers |
| Business & professional | Industrial production retail sales |

| | |
|---|---|
| Rental income of persons | ARIMA |
| Personal dividends | Dividend to price ratio, stock prices |
| Personal interest income | |
| Interest paid by consumers | Outstanding consumer installment credit interest rate, prime comm. paper, 6 months |
| Other | Interest rate, prime comm. paper, 6 months |
| Transfer payments to persons | Total unemployment |
| Less: personal tax & nontax paymts. | Wage and salary disbursements |
| Equals: disposable personal income | From identity |

The income side is naturally estimated in current prices. The values could be deflated by some combination of price indexes that are simultaneously projected from the expenditure side, and the deflated values could be taken as representative of real GNP. It is, however, less speculative to confine the estimates from the income side to current values and to compare such estimates for reconciliation purposes with current value estimates obtained from the expenditure side.

In the third case, we aim to use as much high frequency data as are available in the current quarter to estimate just three magnitudes — real GNP, nominal GNP, and the GNP deflator. Since these are related by the identity

$$PDGNP * GNP = GNP (\$)$$

only two series should be computed directly from indicator data; the third should be obtained from the above definitional equation. Early readings on a number of variables are collected monthly. These are meant to be revealing about the overall economy.

Enough values are estimated for the current quarter so that we have three monthly figures (observed and projected) for each indicator variable. Leading principal components are computed from the observed set of quarterly aggregates of monthly variables. The three aggregates (PDGNP, GNP, and GNP($)) are regressed on the leading principal components. Projected values of the indicator variables for the current quarter and also for one quarter ahead are substituted into the regression on principal components in order to obtain current and future quarter forecasts of the desired aggregates.

The source data used to form indicators of PDGNP, GNP and GNP($) are listed below.

## INDICATORS (MONTHLY)

PDGNP, Price deflator of GNP

Consumer price index

Producer price index, finished goods

Producer price index, intermediate materials

Average hourly earnings

Average weekly hours

Unit value index of imports

Prices received by farmers


GNP($), Nominal gross national product

Value of shipments, manufacturing

Value of new orders, manufacturing

Value of unfilled orders, manufacturing

Nominal personal income

Money stock (M1)

Retail sales

Interest rate on 6 month CDs

Index of net business formation


GNP, Real gross national product

Value of shipments deflated by PPI intermediate materials

Value of new orders deflated by PPI intermediate materials

Value of unfilled orders deflated by PPI intermediate materials

Nominal personal income deflated by CPI

Money stock (M1) deflated by CPI

Retail sales deflated by CPI

Real interest rate (6 month CD rate less CPI inflation rate)

Industrial production index

Employment

Average weekly hours

Each indicator variable is projected ahead by an ARMA process that has been fitted to historical data on the monthly indicator values.

Each indicator is first fitted to the semilog trend formula

$\ln I = a + bT$

$I$ = quarterly aggregates of monthly indicator

$T$ = chronological time

$a, b$ = estimated regression coefficients

Detrended values are computed from

$I / \exp(a + bT)$

Principal components are extracted from the detrended variables after standardisation. Call the components $(PC)_1$, $(PC)_2$, etc.

We fit the empirical regressions

$$PDGNP^* = c_0 + \sum_i c_i (PC)_i$$

$$GNP(\$)^* = d_0 + \sum_i d_i (PC)_i$$

$$GNP^* = e_0 + \sum_i e_i (PC)_i$$

The asterisk denotes that detrended values are used for dependent variables in the three regressions.

The residuals are examined for serial correlation and well–known autoregressive corrections are used in order to isolated white noise errors from the principal component regressions.

Detrended estimates of the main variables are obtained and then transformed back to original units with trend. The mean absolute percentage errors of estimate over the sample period are

real GNP             0.28

nominal GNP          0.39

price deflator                0.21

## 3. APPLICATIONS

The use of the three different current quarter models (expenditure side, income side, and empirical indicator model) is self evident. As data become available during the first or second month of any quarter, estimates of the entire quarter and the next future quarter are made. This could be done at any time, but typically during the early days of the second month. The three models could be averaged. The expenditure and income side models could be brought close together by minimising the one reconciling item, *the statistical discrepancy.*

These estimates can be used for the early quarters of a forecast, but they can also be used for the purpose of adjusting, or calibrating, a model so that it starts from realistic values. In the process of making adjustments to the constant or error terms of equations in a model, it has been customary to bring the model into agreement with observations for period T and T–1, the latest observed periods just before the forecast projection period, T+1, T+2, T+3, ...

The values of $a_t$ in equation (2) above are the adjustment values. They can be chosen so that $y_t$, the variables that are to be forecasted, agree with the values of the current quarter model. In other words, choose $a_t$ such that

$$y_t^* = f(x_t, \hat{\theta}) + a_t$$

where

$y_t^*$ = forecast of $y_t$ from the current quarter model

$f(x_t, \hat{\theta})$ = value of $y_t$ computed from the estimated structural equation solved in a deterministic mode.

Since $y_t^*$ are computed from objective equations that can be replicated, this is an objective adjustment procedure.

Some forecasters have a tendency to adjust many equations of a model — substantially more than one–half.

Our view is that adjustment should be kept to a minimum. This means that only the equations that are mainly responsible for leading variables (like GNP) should be adjusted. The results should be scrutinised to be sure that no variable is terribly far out of line.

In principle, it would be possible to construct a loss function so that a selected number of adjustment values were chosen in order that the loss value is minimised.

$$L = \Sigma w_i (y_{it} - y^*_{it})^2 = \min.(\text{w.r.t.}, a_t)$$

subject to:

$$F(y'_t, y'_{t-1}, ..., x'_t, x'_{t-1}, ..., \hat{\theta}') = a_t$$

where F is a column vector of functions, $y_t$ is a column vector of endogenous variables (equal in number to the count of elements of F), and $x_t$ is a column vector of exogenous variables. $\hat{\theta}$ is a column of parameter estimates, and $a_t$ is a column vector of adjustment values. The weights $w_i$ in L, show the relative importance of the various elements of y that are evaluated in the current quarter model. These weights should reflect the variables for which the current quarter model shows greater possibilities of improving the econometric model and may vary with the monthly observations we have about the current quarter. The problem is to search for values of $a_t$, such that the solution of the entire system brings $y_t$ as close as possible, in the square, to $y^*_t$. Many of the elements of $a_t$ could, of course, be zero. In some models, it will be possible to bring L to zero. This is where it is possible to bring $y_t$ to their targets $y^*_t$ without violating any equations of the system. In general, however, if all the values of $y_t$ are fixed exactly at $y^*_t$, it may not be possible to find a consistent solution of the system. In this case, we seek a least–squares solution for deviation of $y_t$. In any event, if the number of nonzero elements of $a_t$ is to kept quite small, there will be fewer nonzero elements of $a_t$ than there are target values $y^*_t$ of $y_t$. In such cases, the objective will be to bring $y_t$ *near* to $y^*_t$, in the sense of minimum squared deviation.

It should also be possible to choose values of selected elements of $x_t$ in order to minimise L, leaving all $a_t = 0$. In most cases, we shall have a priori information about $x_t$ for the short run — up to six months — and will not, for the present problems, want to search for optimal values of $x_t$.

## NOTES

1.  Carol Corrado and Mark Greene (1988), "Reducing Uncertainty in Short–Term Projections: Linkage of Monthly and Quarterly Models", *Journal of Forecasting* 7, pp.77–102. Mark Greene, E. Philip Howrey, and Saul H. Hymans, "The Use of Outside Information in Econometric Forecasting", in D.A. Belsley and E. Kuh (eds.) (1986), *Model Reliability*, Cambridge: MIT. The estimation of current quarter models from high frequency data was initiated many years ago by Otto Eckstein at Data Resources, Inc.

CHAPTER 2

# STOCHASTIC SIMULATION, PREDICTION AND VALIDATION OF NONLINEAR MODELS *

Roberto S. Mariano, *University of Pennsylvania*
Bryan W. Brown, *Rice University*

## 1. INTRODUCTION

Many econometric models for forecasting and policy analysis consist of a statistically estimated dynamic system of nonlinear stochastic equations. The distinguishing feature of these models is the nonlinearity of the solution for the endogenous variables in terms of model disturbances. Additionally, they are dynamic — with lagged endogenous variables and/or serially correlated errors. Models of macroeconomic systems and limited dependent variables in a simultaneous setting are notable examples.

The widespread use of such models highlights the need for a formal analysis of forecasting and testing procedures that have been developed for these models. No such comprehensive study is available as yet. In sharp contrast, estimation of these models has been studied extensively — e.g., Amemiya (1985) and Gallant (1987).

In covering these aspects of statistical inference beyond estimation, this paper reports recent results of ours concerning the statistical properties of forecasting and testing procedures based on simulations of estimated nonlinear systems. More complete technical details are contained in Mariano and Brown (1983a, 1983b, 1985, 1988), Brown and Mariano (1984, 1987, 1988a, 1988b, 1988c), Mariano and Tabunda (1987), and Mariano and Gallo (1988). Related results, which are not surveyed here, regarding simulations of simultaneous systems are in Calzolari (1987), Baillie (1981), Schmidt (1973, 1974, 1977), and Yamamoto (1980).

*L. R. Klein and J. Marquez (eds.), Economics in Theory and Practice: An Eclectic Approach, 17–36.*
© *1989 by Kluwer Academic Publishers.*

The analysis, which is based mostly on large—sample asymptotic expansions, shows potential shortcomings in the current practice of forecasting through deterministic simulations. New methodology in forecasting and validating non-linear dynamic econometric models are developed. They are based on the idea of using calculated sample period residuals as proxies for disturbances in stochastic simulations of the model. The large—sample properties, their relative merits vis—a—vis current practice, and their applications to model validation are the main contents of this paper.

In the area of forecasting, the common practice of using deterministic solutions of the model is assessed in terms of statistical prediction efficiency as well as numerical convenience. Stochastic simulations are proposed to correct for the bias present in deterministic simulations. Among stochastic simulation procedures, we develop a new forecasting method, the residual—based stochastic predictor, which is less burdensome computationally and less sensitive to misspecification in comparison with standard Monte Carlo techniques. The paper also discusses two other important areas. The first is the use of variance—reduction techniques in the implementation of the residual—based and Monte Carlo forecasting procedures. The second goes beyond point prediction to the construction of prediction regions and the estimation of nonparametric measures such as quantiles for the endogenous variables.

For model diagnostics, simulation error analysis has a long history in the statistics and econometrics literature. With research on econometric model testing going at a vigorous pace over the past few years, various diagnostic aspects of model simulations have been discussed more recently. Some references are Chong and Hendry (1986) and Pagan (1989) for linear simultaneous equations, Mariano and Brown (1983b), Fair (1984), Fisher and Salmon (1986), and Parke (1987) for nonlinear systems. For limited dependent variables, diagnostic procedures based on residuals have been suggested, for example, in the calculation of LM test statistics in Engle (1984), residual plot analysis in Gourieroux et al (1987a, 1987b), and Chesher and Irish (1987), and specification tests in multinomial logit models in McFadden (1987).

For nonlinear simultaneous econometric models, the usual approach is to apply various specification tests in analysing each equation in the system. In terms of the performance of the model as a whole, practitioners' validation of the estimated system has proceeded, for the most part, on an informal basis. This is typically done with descriptive summary error statistics calculated from deterministic simulations of the model over a portion of the sample.

Our study of stochastic simulations in this paper naturally leads to the development of what we would call system specification tests which focus on the validation of the model as a whole. The procedures we develop look at forecast errors over the sample period — as in common practice — but are based on asymptotically valid tests of statistical significance. They utilise stochastic simulations and they have power against deterioration in the predictive performance of the model.

The model, basic assumptions, and the alternative predictors are introduced in Section 2. Section 3 summarises the large–sample properties of predictors. Section 4 considers quantile estimation and construction of prediction regions. Section 5 discusses our system specification tests. Section 6 contains some concluding remarks and briefly touches on our more recent results on the effects of data uncertainty on forecasts.

## 2. MODEL, ASSUMPTIONS, AND PREDICTORS

We consider a simultaneous system of n nonlinear stochastic dynamic equations:

$$f(y_t, y_{t-1}, x_t; \theta) = u_t; \quad t = 1, 2, ..., T \tag{1}$$

where f is n x 1, $y_t$ is n x 1, $x_t$ is m x 1, and $\theta$ is p x 1. The vector of functions, f, is completely known; $\theta$ denotes the unknown parameter vector; and the $u_t$ are unobservable disturbance terms for which we assume

$$u_t \sim \text{i.i.d. } N(0, I), \text{ for all } t. \tag{2}$$

The vector $x_t$ is exogenous and taken to be nonstochastic. The components of $y_t$ are the endogenous variables in the system. The dynamic character of the system arises from the presence of lagged endogenous variables in $f(\cdot)$.

We assume that, as a mapping from $y_t$ to $u_t$, (1) defines a locally unique inverse relationship

$$y_t = g(u_t, y_{t-1}, x_t; \theta) . \tag{3}$$

In the nonlinear model we consider here, it is usually the case that $g(\cdot)$ cannot be written in closed form and, for a given set of values of $(u_t, y_{t-1}, x_t; \theta)$, the corresponding value of $y_t$ is calculated as the numerical solution to (1) and not directly from (3).

We further assume that at least the first two moments of $y_t$ are finite. We denote these moments by

$$\gamma(x_t; \theta) = Ey_t = \gamma_t$$

$$\Omega(x_t; \theta) = E(y_t - \gamma_t)(y_t - \gamma_t)' = \Omega_t. \tag{4}$$

Given a sample $((x_t', y_t'): t = 1, 2, ..., T)$, from which $\theta$ can be estimated consistently, and given $x_*$ for some time point, $*$, outside the sample period, the main prediction problem is to predict $y_*$.

The predictors of interest can be more easily introduced in a static model, where $y_{t-1}$ is not an argument of $f(\cdot)$ in (1). In this case, we define the following predictors of $y_*$, given a consistent estimate $\hat{\theta}$ which is calculated from the available sample:

1. Closed—Form Predictor (C):

$$\hat{y}_c = \gamma(x_*; \hat{\theta}) = \int_u g(u, x_*; \hat{\theta}) \, dF(u), \tag{5}$$
$$F(\cdot) = \text{assumed distribution of } u_*.$$

2. Deterministic Predictor (D):

$$\hat{y}_d = g(0, x_*; \hat{\theta}) . \tag{6}$$

This is numerically calculated from the implicit system

$$f(\hat{y}_d, x_*; \theta) = 0 . \tag{7}$$

3. Monte Carlo Stochastic Predictor (M):

$$\hat{y}_m = \sum_{s=1}^{S} \hat{y}_{ms}/S ,$$

$$\hat{y}_{ms} = g(\tilde{u}_s, x_*; \hat{\theta}) = \hat{g}(\tilde{u}_s) , \tag{8}$$
$$\tilde{u}_s \sim \text{independent draws from } N(0, I), s = 1, 2, ... , S.$$

4. Residual—Based Stochastic Predictor (R):

$$\hat{y}_r = \sum_{t=1}^{T} \hat{y}_{rt}/T$$

$$\hat{y}_{rt} = g(\hat{u}_t, x_*; \hat{\theta}) = \hat{g}(\hat{u}_t) , \tag{9}$$

$$\hat{u}_t = f(y_t, x_t; \hat{\theta}) .$$

5. Bootstrap Predictor (B):

$$\hat{y} = \sum_{j=1}^{R} \hat{g}(w_j)/R \,, \tag{10}$$

where the $w_j$ are independent random draws (with replacement) from the empirical distribution of the calculated structural residuals $\hat{u}_t$.

6. Monte Carlo Antithetic Predictor (MA):

$$\hat{y}_{ma} = (\hat{y}_m + \hat{y}_{m'})/2$$

$$\hat{y}_{m'} = \sum_{s=1}^{S} g(-\tilde{u}_s, x_*; \theta)/S = \sum_{s=1}^{S} \hat{g}(-\tilde{u}_s)/S \tag{11}$$

7. Residual–Based Antithetic Predictor (RA):

$$\hat{y}_{ra} = (\hat{y}_r + \hat{y}_{r'})/2 \tag{12}$$

$$\hat{y}_{r'} = \sum_{t=1}^{T} \hat{g}(-\hat{u}_t)/T \,.$$

8. Monte Carlo Covariance–Corrected Control Variate Predictor (MC):

$$\hat{y}_{mc} = \sum_{s=1}^{S} [\hat{g}(\tilde{u}_s) - \hat{P}_m \tilde{u}_s - \hat{Q}_m(\tilde{u}_s \otimes \tilde{u}_s - \text{vec } I_n)]/S$$

$$\hat{P}_m = \sum_{s=1}^{S} [\hat{g}(\tilde{u}_s) \otimes \tilde{u}_s']/S \tag{13}$$

$$\hat{Q}_m = (1/2) \sum_{s=1}^{S} [\hat{g}(\tilde{u}_s)(\tilde{u}_s \otimes \tilde{u}_s - \text{vec } I_n)']/S$$

9. Residual–Based Covariance–Corrected Control Variate Predictor (RC):

$$\hat{y}_{rc} = \sum_{t=1}^{T} [\hat{g}(\hat{u}_t) - \hat{P}_r \hat{u}_t - \hat{Q}_r(\hat{u}_t \otimes \hat{u}_t - \text{vec } I_n)]/T$$

$$\hat{P}_r = \sum_{t=1}^{T} [\hat{g}(\hat{u}_t) \otimes \hat{u}_t']/T \tag{14}$$

$$\hat{Q}_r = (1/2) \sum_{t=1}^{T} [\hat{g}(\hat{u}_t)(\hat{u}_t \otimes \hat{u}_t - \text{vec } I_n)']/T$$

10. Deterministic Bias–Corrected Predictor (DD):

$$\hat{y}_{dd} = g(0, x_*; \hat{\theta}) + (1/2) \sum_{i=1}^{n} [\partial^2 g(0, x_*; \hat{\theta})/\partial u_i^2]. \tag{15}$$

In general, the integral in the closed–form predictor (5) cannot be evaluated analytically since neither $g(\cdot)$ nor $\gamma(\cdot)$ is available in closed form — so that it would have to be approximated through numerical integration techniques.

The deterministic predictor is by far the most commonly used procedure because of its numerical simplicity relative to the others. The Monte Carlo predictor has been used in practice only to a limited extent. Incidentally, this predictor can be interpreted as one way of approximating numerically the closed–form predictor under the assumption that $u_* \sim N(0, I)$.

The residual–based predictor has been proposed by us in Brown and Mariano (1984) as an alternative stochastic simulation method which reduces the computational burden and misspecification sensitivity in the Monte Carlo predictor. It differs from the Monte Carlo in that it uses the calculated sample period residuals as stochastic proxies. It can also be interpreted as a closed form predictor when the underlying distribution of $u_*$ coincides with the empirical distribution of the calculated residuals.

Both Monte Carlo and residual–based predictors are arithmetic means of what can be thought of as "pseudo" samples from the distribution of $y^*$: $\{\hat{y}_{ms}$: $s = 1, 2, ..., S\}$ for the Monte Carlo and $\{\hat{y}_{rt}$: $t = 1, 2, ..., T)$ for the residual–based. Alternative measures of central tendency can be used (e.g., sample medians, etc.) but, under squared error loss, these would be inferior to the sample means that we choose to use here.

These pseudo samples generated by the stochastic simulations contain much more information concerning the probability distribution of $y_*$ than the single calculation of the mean. We exploit this information to go beyond point prediction into the construction of prediction regions and the estimation of higher order moments and quantiles of $y_*$. This cannot be done at all with deterministic simulations.

While the residual–based predictor uses all the residuals, the bootstrap predictor, on the other hand, utilises only a random sample of the calculated residuals. This introduces additional noise to the prediction (relative to the residual–based), but it may turn out to be more feasible when sample sizes are extremely large, especially in dynamic systems.

The next four predictors (nos. 6–9) reflect the application of variance reduction techniques to improve statistical efficiency for a given number of replications. The negatives of the stochastic proxies are used as well in the antithetic predictors. For the next pair of predictors, a Taylor series expansion of $g(\cdot)$, with respect to u, up to the second order, generates the control variables; this is done in such a manner as to guarantee a reduction in the variability of the predictor. These techniques will improve prediction efficiency only through the component of efficiency due to simulation variation. It will have no impact at all on efficiency components due to endogenous variation or parameter estimation.

Finally, the deterministic predictor is modified (in no. 10) through a correction on its bias. This correction is calculated from a second–order Taylor series expansion of $g(\cdot)$ around $u_*$ equal to zero.

In the dynamic case, with (1) as the model, we consider alternative forecasts one period and two periods ahead – that is, the prediction of

$$y_{T+1} = g(u_{T+1}, y_T, x_{T+1}; \theta) \tag{16}$$

$$y_{T+2} = g(u_{T+2}, y_{T+1}, x_{T+2}; \theta)$$

$$= g[u_{T+2}, g(u_{T+1}, y_T, x_{T+1}; \theta), x_{T+2}; \theta] \,.$$

All forecasting procedures are analogous to those defined earlier for the static case – except for the residual–based predictor in multi–period forecasting. Thus, for one period ahead, the "standard" predictors of $y_{T+1}$ are

$$\hat{y}_{d,1} = g(0, y_T, x_{T+1}; \hat{\theta}), \tag{17}$$

$$\hat{y}_{c,1} = \gamma(y_T, x_{T+1}, \hat{\theta}); \; \gamma_1(y_T, x_{T+1}; \hat{\theta}) = E(y_{T+1}|y_T) \,,$$

$$\hat{y}_{m,1} = \sum_{s=1}^{S} g(\tilde{u}_s, y_T, x_{T+1}; \hat{\theta})/S \,.$$

$$\hat{y}_{r,1} = \sum_{t=1}^{T} g(\hat{u}_t, y_T, x_{T+1}; \hat{\theta})/T \,.$$

For two periods ahead, we have

$$\hat{y}_{d,2} = g(0, g(0, y_T, x_{T+1}; \hat{\theta}), x_{T+2}; \hat{\theta}) \qquad (18)$$

$$= g(0, \hat{y}_{d,1}, x_{T+2}; \hat{\theta}) ,$$

$$\hat{y}_{c,2} = \gamma_2(y_T, x_{T+1}, x_{T+2}; \hat{\theta}) , \quad \gamma_2 = E(y_{T+2}|y_T) ,$$

$$\hat{y}_{m,2} = \sum_{s=1}^{S} g[\tilde{u}_{s2}, g(\tilde{u}_{s1}, y_T, x_{T+1}; \hat{\theta}), x_{T+2}; \hat{\theta}]/S ,$$

where $\tilde{u}_{s1}$, $\tilde{u}_{s2}$ are independent draws from $N(0, I)$ for $s = 1, 2, ...., S$. Some variations of the residual–based procedure in forecasting two periods ahead are:

a. Paired Sample (with T even):

$$\hat{y}_{rp,2} = \sum_{j=1}^{T/2} g[\hat{u}_{2j}, g(\hat{u}_{2j-1}, y_T, x_{T+1}; \hat{\theta}), x_{T+2}; \hat{\theta}]/(T/2) \qquad (19)$$

b. Complete Enumeration

$$\hat{y}_{re,2} = \sum_{i=1}^{T} \sum_{j=1}^{T} g[\hat{u}_i, g(\hat{u}_j, y_T, x_{T+1}; \hat{\theta}), x_{T+2}; \hat{\theta}]/T^2 \qquad (20)$$

c. Bootstrap

$$\hat{y}_{b,2} = \sum_{r=1}^{R} g[w_{r2}, g(w_{r1}, y_T, x_{T+1}; \hat{\theta}), x_{T+2}; \hat{\theta}]/R \qquad (21)$$

where $w_{r1}$, $w_{r2}$ are independent draws (with replacement) from the uniform distribution on $(\hat{u}_t: t = 1, 2, ..., T)$.

## 3. LARGE–SAMPLE BEHAVIOUR OF PREDICTORS

For a consistent, asymptotically normal $\hat{\theta}$ and under smoothness assumptions on $g(\cdot)$, explicitly given in Mariano and Brown (1983a) and Brown and Mariano (1984), the following large–sample asymptotic results hold. (Throughout this discussion we take asymptotic moments of predictors to mean exact expectations of retained leading terms in the asymptotic expansions for the appropriate function of prediction error.)

1. The asymptotic bias is $0(1)$ for the deterministic predictor and $0(1/T)$ for the closed form and all the stochastic predictors. (For the Monte Carlo predictors, we assume that the number of basic replications, S, has the same order of magnitude as T). Because of its non–vanishing asymptotic bias, the deterministic predictor has the largest asymptotic mean–squared prediction error (AMSPE) in the group.

2. The closed–form predictor provides a lower bound AMSPE among all the predictors under consideration.

3. While the Monte Carlo and residual–based predictors are both inefficient relative to the closed–form, their AMSPEs exceed the closed–form AMSPE by only a small percentage amount. In comparing these two standard stochastic predictors with each other, the residual–based predictor would be more efficient asymptotically than the Monte Carlo when the Monte Carlo replication size is less than or equal to the sample size T. However, the AMSPEs for these two stochastic predictors do not differ from each other by much: the difference is at most $(1/T)$ or $(1/S)$ of the lower bound AMSPE.

4. Except for the residual–based antithetic, the modification through variance–reduction techniques leads to a lower AMSPE. Thus

$$AMSPE(ma) < AMSPE(m)$$
$$AMSPE(mc) < AMSPE(m)$$
$$AMSPE(rc) < AMSPE(r) ,$$

but $AMSPE(r)$ and $AMSPE(ra)$ cannot be ordered in general. The efficiency gains, however, are not of the same percentage magnitude as obtained in parameter estimation.

5. For $S \leq T$, results analogous to those described in no. 4 hold. Modified residual–based dominates its Monte Carlo counterpart:

$$AMSPE(rc) < AMSPE(mc)$$
$$AMSPE(ra) < AMSPE(ma) .$$

Explicit expressions for the asymptotic moments, on which the above comparisons are based, are given in Mariano and Brown (1983a) and Brown and Mariano (1984, 1988b). These analytical results support the residual–based procedure as a viable alternative to the Monte Carlo and deterministic predictors. In general, as long as the model is correctly specified and consistently estimated, the residual–based predictor is asymptotically unbiased like the Monte Carlo. Relative to Monte Carlo, the residual–based predictor is less sensitive to distributional assumptions about the disturbances. It draws its stochastic proxies from the empirical distribution of the actual residuals instead of what can be an erroneous pre–specified probability law.

So far the comparisons we have made are based on relative magnitudes of AMSPEs. More realistically, we must consider not only the gain in statistical prediction efficiency but also the incidence of higher computation costs. This becomes relevant, in particular, when comparing the deterministic with stochastic predictors and when considering variance reduction techniques in stochastic simulations. In Brown and Mariano (1988b), this trade–off between AMSPE and computer costs is formalised in a loss function which is quadratic in prediction error and linear in the number of model solutions, (N), and the number of stochastic draws, (R):

$$L = aN + bR + (y_* - \hat{y}_*)'W(y_* - \hat{y}_*). \tag{22}$$

In this case, asymptotic expected loss is

$$AE(L) = aN + bR + tr(W \cdot AMSPE(\hat{y}_*)) + 0(1/T) \tag{23}$$

Further reductions in computer costs through super–computer technology are captured in unit costs a and b; the weight matrix, W, reflects the relative importance of the various components of $y_*$ in the forecasting exercise.

For each stochastic predictor, we can determine the unique optimal number of replications which minimises expected loss for that predictor. Having done so, we can then compare predictors on the basis of these optimised expected losses. The results of such a comparison are summarised in Table 1 adapted from Brown and Mariano (1988b).

Table 1. Comparison of Predictors

| Comparison | AMSPE | Expected Loss |
|:---:|:---:|:---:|
| D : Any | Any | ?[1] |
| R : M | R | R |
| MA : M | MA | ? |
| RA : R | RA | ? |
| RA : MA | RA | RA[2] |
| MC : M | MC | MC |
| RC : R | RC[3] | RC[3] |
| RC : MC | RC | RC |

[1] The deterministic behaviour may be better than any of the stochastic predictors when its bias is quite small relative to the covariance matrix of the endogenous variables and computer costs are high.

[2] If the optimal replication size for RA is infeasible (bigger than T), this comparison is indefinite.

[3] If the optimal replication size for RC equals sample size, then the two predictors coincide.

Two major conclusions emerge from the last column of Table 1. In terms of minimising minimum expected loss, the choice among the stochastic predictors would be either RA or RC; thus the residual–based dominates Monte Carlo. The only qualification here is that the comparison between RA and MA would be indefinite if the optimal replication size for RA exceeds sample size. Secondly, there are situations when the asymptotically biased deterministic predictor may be preferred to all the asymptotically unbiased stochastic predictors. Reflecting the trade–off between AMSPE and computer–cost, this occurs in a case where computer costs are non–negligible and variances of endogenous variables are large relative to the deterministic prediction bias.

For the dynamic case, the asymptotic analysis is further complicated by the fact that all predictions are made conditional on the terminal sample values of the endogenous variables. Based on the way we have specified our dynamic model in (1), the only conditioning terminal sample value is $y_T$. In such a conditional analysis, we would then assume that the smoothness and regularity properties of $g(\cdot)$ and $\hat{\theta}$ apply conditional on the given value of $y_T$. Under this assumption, asymptotic expansions and comparison results, analogous to those obtained for the static case, also hold in the case of one–period–ahead prediction.

In multi–period–ahead forecasting, the asymptotic moment expressions in the static case apply to the deterministic and Monte Carlo predictors. The formulas apply as well as to the residual–based with sample–pairing – except that the effective number of calculated residuals used in the procedure is sample size divided by the length of the forecast horizon. Thus, as expected, this variation of residual–based has an AMSPE which deteriorates as the forecast horizon expands. It is shown further in Brown and Mariano (1988c) that the complete enumeration residual–based predictor is asymptotically inefficient relative to the closed form, efficient relative to the deterministic and Monte Carlo (for $S \leq T/2$) and indefinite relative to the paired–sample predictor.

The bootstrap predictor has an asymptotic bias of order $1/T$ and the same as the complete–enumeration predictor. In terms of AMSPE, the bootstrap is efficient relative to the deterministic but inefficient when compared with the closed–form, the complete enumeration, the Monte Carlo with $R \leq S$, and the paired–sample predictors (with $R \leq T/2$). As the bootstrap replication size, R, approaches infinity, the bootstrap predictor approaches the complete enumeration predictor. For a given sample size, the inefficiency property of the bootstrap predictor is counterbalanced by its robustness (when compared with the Monte Carlo predictor) and its lesser computational requirements relative to complete enumeration.

## 4. QUANTILES AND PREDICTION REGIONS

By its very nature, the deterministic predictor provides only one value – the point forecast. It does not offer any additional information concerning the probability distribution of $y_*$. The Monte Carlo and residual–based stochastic predictors, on the other hand, provide pseudo samples of $y_*$ (conditional on the given values of exogenous variables and parameter estimates). These pseudo samples are

Monte Carlo: $(\hat{y}_{ms}: s = 1, 2, ..., S)$

Residual–based: $(\hat{y}_{rt}: t = 1, 2, ..., T)$ .

The definition of $\hat{y}_{ms}$ and $\hat{y}_{rt}$ are in (8) and (9) respectively.

Both pseudo samples can be exploited to study other population attributes of $y_*$ beyond its first moment. In particular, higher order moments, the empirical cumulative distribution function (cdf), and quantiles of either pseudo sample are consistent and asymptotically normal estimates of the corresponding population characteristics of $y_*$. These results, discussed in Brown and Mariano (1984, 1987), can be utilised further with Chebychev's Inequality to construct a conservative prediction region for $y_*$ and then get a refined estimate of the probability content of the region through additional stochastic simulations.

For the estimation of the marginal cdf of a component of $y_*$ at a given scalar point, let

$y_{*1}$ = first component of $y_*$

$c_*$ = given scalar point

$$I(z; c) = \begin{cases} 1, \text{ if } z \leq c \\ 0, \text{ otherwise} \end{cases} \tag{24}$$

$$\pi(c; \theta) = \Pr(y_{*1} \leq c) = E(I(y_{*1}; c)) .$$

The Monte Carlo and residual–based estimates of $\pi$ are, respectively,

$$\hat{\pi}_m = \sum_{s=1}^{S} I(\hat{y}_{msl}; c)/S$$

(25)

$$\hat{\pi}_r = \sum_{t=1}^{T} I(\hat{y}_{rt1}; c)/T ,$$

where $\hat{y}_{msl}$ and $\hat{y}_{rt1}$ are the first components of $\hat{y}_{ms}$ and $\hat{y}_{rt}$, respectively. Note that $\hat{\pi}_m$ and $\hat{\pi}_r$ are the sample proportions of the pseudo observations on $y_{*1}$ which do not exceed the given value c.

We will assume throughout this section that the probability density function of $y_{*1}$ is strictly positive and continuous with respect to $y_{*1}$ for $-\infty < y_{*1} < \infty$ and has partial derivatives with respect to $\theta$ which are continuous in $y_{*1}$ over the whole real line. Under additional assumptions detailed in Brown and Mariano (1984), the following results hold:

1. $\sqrt{T}(\hat{\pi}_m - \pi) \xrightarrow{d} N(0, k\pi(1 - \pi) + \Pi\Psi\Pi')$, as $T \to \infty$ (26)

2. $\sqrt{T}(\hat{\pi}_r - \pi) \xrightarrow{d} N(0, \pi(1 - \pi) + \Pi\Psi\Pi' - D\Psi D')$, where $\Psi$ is the asymptotic covariance matrix of $\sqrt{T}\,(\theta - \theta)$ and

$$k = \lim T/S$$

$$\Pi = \partial\pi(c; \theta_0)/\partial\theta'$$

(27)

$$D = \bar{H}_1 - \Pi$$

$$\bar{H}_1 = \lim\Sigma(\partial EI(g_1(f(y_t, x_t; \theta_0), x_*; \theta_0) ; c)/\partial\theta')/T .$$

For quantile estimation, let $F(\cdot)$, $F_m(\cdot)$, and $F_r(\cdot)$ denote the cdf of $y_{*1}$ and the empirical cdfs of the Monte Carlo and residual–based pseudo observations on $y_{*1}$. Thus, for a given c,

$$F_m(c) = \sum_{s=1}^{S} I(\hat{y}_{msl}; c)/S$$

(28)

$$F_r(c) = \sum_{t=1}^{T} I(\hat{y}_{rt1}; c)/T .$$

For a given probability value $\pi$, the $\pi$th quantile of F is

$$\zeta = \zeta(\pi) = \inf(c: F(c) \geq \pi)$$

(29)

The Monte Carlo and residual–based estimates of $\zeta(\pi)$, with given $\pi$, are

$$\hat{\zeta}_m = \inf\{c: F_m(c) \geq \pi\} \tag{30}$$

$$\hat{\zeta}_r = \inf\{c: F_r(c) \geq \pi\} .$$

The basic results on the asymptotic behaviour of these quantile estimates, shown in Brown and Mariano (1987), are stated here without proof:

1.  $\sqrt{T}(\hat{\zeta}_m - \zeta) \overset{d}{\to} N[0, (k\pi(1 - \pi) + \Pi\Psi\Pi')/\lambda^2]$ (31)

2.  $\sqrt{T}(\hat{\zeta}_r - \zeta) \overset{d}{\to} N[0, (\pi(1 - \pi) + \Pi\Psi\Pi' - D\Psi D')/\lambda^2]$

where

$$\lambda = \text{pdf of } y_{*1} \text{ evaluated at } \zeta . \tag{32}$$

For both marginal cdf and quantile estimation, we see from (26) and (31) that the comparison results parallel those that we have outlined for prediction or estimation of first moments. The residual–based estimator is asymptotically more efficient than Monte Carlo for a similar number of replications. However, note that, as remarked in Brown and Mariano (1984), the difference in the asymptotic variance between these two estimators can be proportionately substantial.

To exploit these results in the construction of prediction regions, quantile estimates can of course be used to determine (approximate) prediction intervals for individual components of $y_*$. For the multivariate case, we can use the following multivariate version of Chebychev's Inequality:

$$\Pr((y_* - \gamma_*)'\Omega_*^{-1}(y_* - \gamma_*) \leq \kappa^2) \geq 1 - n/\kappa^2 . \tag{33}$$

where

$\kappa$ = number chosen to achieve a specific confidence level,

n = dimension of $y_*$ .

In (33), replace $(\gamma_*, \Omega_*)$ by $(\hat{y}_m, \hat{\Omega}_m)$ or $(\hat{y}_r, \hat{\Omega}_r)$ and then refine the probability statement in (33) in one of the following ways:

1.  Given $\kappa$, use stochastic simulations to obtain a more precise probability statement for the ellipsoid in (33), or

2.  Find the value of $\kappa$ corresponding to a given value of the probability content. This involves the estimation of quantiles of the quadratic form defining the ellipsoid.

## 5. SYSTEM SPECIFICATION TESTS

The common practice in validating nonlinear simultaneous systems can be summarised as follows:

1.  Apply various diagnostic procedures to assess each equation in the system separately.

2.  Simulate the estimated model deterministically over the sample period, or portion of it.

3.  Calculate summary error statistics, such as root mean square errors or mean absolute percentage errors and the like, to get an idea of how well the estimated model tracks the movements of endogenous variables over the simulation period. Here, these error statistics are descriptive in nature; no statistical tests are applied formally to determine the significance of these error statistics.

4.  Perhaps run regressions of the simulated values on actual observations and test whether or not the intercept is zero and the slope coefficient is equal to 1.

Although we do not go into the details of step 1, step 1 is a must. For steps 2, 3, and 4, the analytical results we have surveyed in the preceding sections of this paper provide directions towards a more appropriate and more rigorous approach.

Structural and reduced–form residuals are asymptotically linear trans-formations of each other in the linear case. Consequently, Pagan (1989) points out that simulating the model would be redundant. However, since this linear relationship in the residuals does not hold in nonlinear models, we argue that beyond step 1 (dealing with structural residuals) appropriate simulations of the estimated nonlinear model contain additional information. Indeed, such simulations can be used to construct significance tests which have power against model misspecification that adversely affects forecast performance. Diagnostic tests in step 1 may not have as much power in this direction.

Thus, the system approach implicit in step 2 should remain a part of our diagnostics for model validation. However, since deterministic simulations are biased, even asymptotically, we would then recommend using stochastic simulations as the basis of our diagnostics.

After this correction of step 2, instead of relying on descriptive statistics alone, we would proceed to develop significance tests which are based, generally, on the limiting distribution of appropriate test statistics. Along these lines, regression validation tests of Monte Carlo and bootstrap simulation errors over the sample period are developed in Mariano and Brown (1983b) and Mariano and Tabunda (1987).

The basic idea in these tests is that under the null hypothesis, $H_o$, of correct model specification, the "reduced–form" errors

$$v_t = y_t - \gamma(x_t; \theta) \tag{34}$$

would have mean zero. When the model is misspecified, however, $Ey_t \neq \gamma(x_t; \theta)$ and $Ev_t \neq 0$. We can then proceed to test $H_o$ vs $H_1$ by looking at the appropriate stochastic proxies for $v_t$, e.g. the Monte Carlo forecast errors

$$\hat{v}_{mt} = y_t - \hat{y}_{mt} . \tag{35}$$

For each time t, a pseudo sample on $y_t$ is generated:

$$\{\hat{y}_{mts} = g(\tilde{u}_{ts}, x_t; \theta): s = 1, 2, ..., S\} \tag{36}$$

with sample mean equal to $\hat{y}_{mt}$.

A parametric formulation of a test is in the form of an auxiliary regression model

$$\hat{v}_{mt} = Dh_t + \eta_t \tag{37}$$

where $h_t$ is is vector of observations on a selected set of nonlinear functions of $x_t$ (and possibly other variables) and $\eta_t$ has mean zero. Under $H_o$, $D = 0$ while under $H_1$, with appropriate choice of $h_t$, $D$ would be different from zero. Consequently a test can be based on, for example, the least squares regression of

$\hat{v}_{mt}$ on $h_t$. The main result derived in Mariano and Brown (1983b) is that under $H_o$, as $T \to \infty$

$$Td'W^-d \to x^2(r) , \tag{38}$$

where d is vec($\hat{D}$), $\hat{D}$ is the least squares estimate of D, $W^-$ is the generalised inverse of W, r is the rank of W and W is the asymptotic covariance matrix of $\sqrt{T}$ d under $H_o$. An explicit expression for W is

$$W = (I \otimes Q)^{-1}(\tilde{\Omega} - \tilde{\Gamma}\Psi\tilde{\Gamma}')(I \otimes Q)^{-1} \tag{39}$$

where

$$Q = \plim_t(\Sigma h_t h_t'/T) ,$$

$$\tilde{\Omega} = \lim_t \Sigma(\Omega_t \otimes h_t h_t'/T) , \tag{40}$$

$$\tilde{\Gamma} = \lim \Sigma(\Gamma(x_t; \theta) \otimes h_t/T) \,,$$

$$\Gamma(x_t \; \theta) = \partial\gamma(x_t; \theta)/\partial\theta' \,.$$

To estimate W, use

$$\tilde{\Omega}_t = \underset{s}{\Sigma}(\hat{y}_{mts} - \hat{y}_{mt})(\hat{y}_{mts} - \hat{y}_{mt})'/S$$

$$\tilde{Q} = \underset{t}{\Sigma} h_t h_t'/T \qquad\qquad\qquad (41)$$

$$\tilde{\Gamma}(x_t; \theta) = \underset{s}{\Sigma}(\partial g(\tilde{u}_{ts}, x_t; \hat{\theta})/\partial\theta)/S = \tilde{\Gamma}_t$$

$$\tilde{\Gamma} = \underset{t}{\Sigma}(\tilde{\Gamma}_t \otimes h_t)/T \,.$$

The expression in (38) suggests that auxiliary regressions like (37) have a fairly complicated error covariance structure. It is certainly far from being scalar as early attempts at regressions of forecast errors have presumed. When applied to the linear simultaneous system and $h_t = x_t$, the test based on (38) simplifies to a comparison of the restricted and unrestricted estimates of the reduced–form coefficients.

The derivation of W relies on the asymptotic results described in earlier sections. A similar development applied to the dynamic model leads to an analogous test based on one–period simulations of the estimated model. Tests based on multi–period–ahead simulations can also be constructed after the appropriate asymptotic theory is developed for multi–period stochastic predictors. With this machinery in place, we can also investigate the relationship between one–period and multi–period simulations of nonlinear systems – an issue studied by Chong and Hendry (1986) in the linear case.

Analogous tests are also developed in Mariano and Tabunda (1987) and Brown and Mariano (1988a) based on

1.  comparison of bootstrap simulations with actual observations;
2.  stochastic (residual–based or Monte Carlo) versus deterministic simulations as a way of measuring the incidence or testing the statistical significance of bias in deterministic forecasts.

A particular specialisation of item 2 leads to correction of the common practice of using the usual t–statistics in the regression of sample period forecast errors on observable endogenous variables. Furthermore, correction for heteroscedasticity in the auxiliary regression does not suffice; serial correlation is also present and must be addressed. Details are in Brown and Mariano (1988a).

Some remarks regarding the operational aspects of the test developed here are in order. In our application of this test to validate a macroeconometric model for the Philippines, we have encountered difficulties in the numerical evaluation of the asymptotic covariance matrix $\Psi$ and the derivative matrices $\tilde{\Gamma}_t$. These are both needed in the estimation of W, or more appropriately, of the covariance matrix of the least squares estimate D. Consequently, it may be useful to try semi–parametric methods, such as heteroscedasticity autocorrelation corrected (HAC) procedures to obtain an estimate of W which disregards the specific structure of W beyond the presence of heteroscedasticity and serial correlation in the auxiliary regression.

## 6. CONCLUSION

The large–sample asymptotic results we have reported regarding prediction and validation of nonlinear models highlight the use of stochastic simulations of estimated systems to

1. forecast endogenous variables
2. estimate variances and higher order moments of endogenous variables
3. estimate probability distributions and quantiles
4. construct prediction regions
5. develop more rigorous simulation procedures (asymptotically valid significance tests) to validate nonlinear systems as a whole.

The procedures suggested here for forecasting and system specification can be used in a wide range of nonlinear models and we are now in the process of investigating their numerical feasibility as we implement them in actual applications.

We remarked at the outset that our treatment of prediction analysis will assume complete certainty about future values of exogenous variables. This is a convenient starting point for our analytical study. But we realise that measurement errors and uncertainty about exogenous variables can be a major source of prediction error. The analysis that is reported here has now been extended, with preliminary results, in Mariano and Gallo (1988) to include the additional complications due to exogenous variable uncertainty.

NOTES
* Partial support from NSF Grants SES–8604219 and SES–8520969 is
gratefully acknowledged.

REFERENCES

Amemiya, T. (1985), *Advanced Econometrics*, Harvard University Press,
Cambridge, MA.
Anderson, G.J. (1987), "Prediction Tests in Limited Dependent Variable
Models", *Journal of Econometrics* 34, pp.253–26.
Andrews, D. (1987), "Heteroskedasticity and Autocorrelation Consistent
Covariance Matrix Estimation", Yale University Discussion Paper.
Baillie, R. (1981), "Prediction from the Dynamic Simultaneous Equation Model
with Autoregressive Errors", *Econometrica* 49, pp.1331–37.
Brown, B.W. and R.S. Mariano (1984), "Residual–Based Procedures for
Prediction and Estimation in a Nonlinear Simultaneous System",
*Econometrica* 52, pp.321–43.
Brown, B.W. amd R.S. Mariano (1987), "Interval and Quantile Prediction in
Nonlinear Simultaneous Systems", University of Pennsylvania and Rice
University Discussion Paper.
Brown, B.W. and R.S. Mariano (1988a), "Measures of Deterministic Prediction
Bias in Nonlinear Models", University of Pennsylvania Discussion Paper.
Forthcoming in *International Economic Review.*
Brown, B.W. and R.S. Mariano (1988b), "Reduced–Variance Prediction in
Nonlinear Models", University of Pennsylvania Discussion Paper.
Brown, B.W. and R.S. Mariano (1988c), "Predictors in Dynamic Nonlinear
Models: Large–Sample Behavior", University of Pennsylvania and Rice
University Discussion Paper.
Calzolari, G. (1987), "Forecast Variance in Dynamic Simulation of Simultaneous
Equation Models", *Econometrica* 55, pp.1473–76.
Chesher, A. and M. Irish (1987), "Residual Analysis in the Grouped and
Censored Normal Linear Model", *Journal of Econometrics* 34, pp.33–61.
Chong, Y. and D. Hendry (1986), "Econometric Evaluation of Linear
Macro–Economic Models", *Review of Economic Studies* 53, pp.671–90.
Engle, R. (1984), "Wald, Likelihood Ratio, and Lagrange Multiplier Tests in
Econometrics" in Z. Griliches and M. Intriligator (eds.), *Handbook of
Econometrics Vol. 2*, North Holland, Amsterdam.
Fair, R. (1984), *Specification, Estimation and Analysis of Macroeconometric
Models*, Harvard University Press.
Fisher, P. and M. Salmon (1986), "On Evaluating the Importance of Nonlinearity
in Large Macroeconometric Models", *International Economic Review* 27,
pp.625–46.
Gallant, R. (1987), *Nonlinear Statistical Models*, J. Wiley & Sons, New York.
Gourieroux, C. et. al. (1987a), "Generalised Residuals", *Journal of Econometrics*
34, pp.5–32.
Gourieroux, C. et. al. (1987b), "Simulated Residuals", *Journal of Econometrics*
34, pp.201–52.
Mariano, R.S. and B.W. Brown (1983a), "Asymptotic Behavior of Predictors in a
Nonlinear Simultaneous System", *International Economic Review* 24,
pp.523–36.
Mariano, R.S. and B.W. Brown (1983b), "Prediction–Based Tests for Mis-
specification in Nonlinear Simultaneous Systems" in T. Amemiya, S.
Karlin and L. Goodman (eds.), *Studies in Econometrics, Multivariate
Statistics and Time–Series Analysis*, Academic Press.

36

Mariano, R.S. and B.W. Brown (1985), "Stochastic Prediction in Dynamic Nonlinear Econometric Systems", *Annales de l'INSEE* 59/60, pp.267–78.

Mariano, R.S. and A. Tabunda (1987), "A Test for Misspecification in Nonlinear Simultaneous Systems Using the Bootstrap Predictor", University of Pennsylvania Discussion Paper.

Mariano, R.S. and B.W. Brown (1988), "Prediction in Dynamic Nonlinear Models: Finite–Sample Behaviour", University of Pennsylvania Discussion Paper.

Mariano, R.S. and G. Gallo (1988), "Prediction in Nonlinear Models with Data Uncertainty", University of Pennsylvania Discussion Paper.

McFadden, D. (1987), "Regression–Based Specification Tests for the Multinomial Logit Model", *Journal of Econometrics* 34, pp.63–83.

Pagan, A. (1989), "On the Role of Simulation in the Statistical Evaluation of Econometric Models", *Journal of Econometrics* 40, pp.125–40.

Parke, W. (1987), "Macroeconometric Model Comparison and Evaluation Techniques: A Practical Appraisal", *Journal of Applied Econometrics* 2, pp.133–44.

Schmidt, P. (1973), "Asymptotic Distribution of Dynamic Multipliers", *Econometrica* 41, pp.161–64.

Schmidt, P. (1974), "The Asymptotic Distribution of Forecasts in the Dynamic Simulation of an Econometric Model", *Econometrica* 42, pp.303–9.

Schmidt, P. (1977), "Some Small–Sample Evidence on the Distribution of Dynamic Simulation Forecasts", *Econometrica* 45, pp.997–1005.

Yamamoto, T. (1980), "On the Treatment of Autocorrelated Errors in the Multiperiod Prediction of Dynamic Simultaneous Equation Models", *International Economic Review* 21, pp.735–48.

CHAPTER 3


AN INTEGRATED EXHAUSTIBLE RESOURCE MODEL
OF COPPER MARKET DYNAMICS


Walter C. Labys, *West Virginia University*


## 1. INTRODUCTION

A longstanding problem in the modelling of resource markets in general and mineral markets in particular has been the lack of a model specification suitable for explaining long run as well as short run market adjustments. One possible solution for solving this problem considered here is to integrate relevant aspects of the rational extractions model (REM) and the standard commodity model (SCM) into a single model framework. The REM enables us to explain long run resource depletion and the possibility of rising extraction costs which would provide an incentive for establishing reserve additions. The SCM accommodates resources held in the form of above–ground materials inventories and emphasises short run market equilibrium forces such as production, consumption and inventory holding. The model framework under scrutiny thus embodies dynamic market disequilibrium where stock adjustments affect flow equilibrium in the form of below–ground reserve stocks and above–ground inventory stocks. Other factors frequently neglected, but presently included are production capacity and secondary supply.

To test the model's properties empirically, the world copper market has been selected as the basis for analysis. Descriptive data for this market are generally good and a number of modelling studies have been performed. The latter help to improve the accuracy of the model parameterisation, especially since econometric models intending to capture long run behaviour often suffer parameter instability over time. This same problem has made it necessary to employ a dynamic simulation model in preference to the conventional form of econometric model.

37

L. R. Klein and J. Marquez (eds.), Economics in Theory and Practice: An Eclectic Approach, 37–55.
© 1989 by Kluwer Academic Publishers.

Simulations have been conducted which test not only the realism of the resulting copper model but also certain long and short run hypotheses regarding its specification. The conclusions suggest potential model applications in market and policy analysis relevant for long run investment and planning decisions.

## 2. THE BACKGROUND

The incentive to perform this model analysis comes from several sources. First, there is the disillusionment with the ability of the Hotelling model to survive empirical testing. As emphasised by Pindyck (1981), even the REM descendants of this model have not led to empirical applications which would make it a useful modelling tool similar to that of the SCM. Secondly, extensions of the SCM to minerals modelling have often depended on agricultural modelling specifications (Labys and Pollak, 1984). Such extensions have concentrated typically on medium and short run market behaviour, neglecting the long run aspects inherent to resource exhaustion. Thirdly, recent attention to the supply of storage theory (Lonoff, 1982) has shown it to be useful for extending the REM to include above–ground materials inventory holding. Finally, possibilities for better linking long and short run adjustment processes can be seen in recent work on recycled scrap (Radetzki and Van Duyne, 1983a) and on investment in mine capacity (Radetzki and Van Duyne, 1983b).

Past attempts to make the Hotelling model and its REM extensions more realistic in this regard are too numerous to summarise here and readers should consult Devarajan and Fisher (1981) and Labys (1985). Researchers such as Pindyck (1981) and Frank and Babunovic (1984) have explored the difficulties of verifying the REM empirically and it would seem necessary that the strong maximisation conditions of optimal control theory underlying the REM be supplanted by the less strong maximisation conditions underlying the SCM. There also would appear to be too many assumptions in the Hotelling model that are not presently valid. Major attempts to correct this situation include that of introducing: (1) a noncompetitive market structure, e.g., Weinstein and Zeckhauser (1975), (2) heterogeneous reserve composition, e.g., Solow and Wan (1976), (3) non–constant costs over extraction levels, e.g., Fisher (1979), (4) declining costs, prices and inventory holding, e.g., Eswaren, Lewis and Heaps (1983) and Lonoff (1982), (5) introducing uncertainty, e.g., Hoel (1978) and Pindyck (1980), and (6) recycling, e.g., Schulze (1974) and Pindyck (1978a).

Past attempts to make the SCM more realistic also have been numerous and readers should consult Labys (1973) and Labys and Pollak (1984). Of most importance here is adding dynamic adjustment processes of a long run nature. The theoretical possibility for linking the long and short run dynamically based on stock and flow considerations received attention earlier from Keynes (1936) and Harrod (1964) and more recently from Hicks (1979). Particularly in the markets for extractive industries this modification can explain market adjustments where investments in exploration and in productive capacity only slowly instigate these adjustments. Examples include Frank and Babunovic (1984) who combine long and medium run adjustment phenomena into their exhaustible resource investment model. Labys (1980a,b), Richard (1978), and Wagenhals (1984) have constructed econometric models of the copper market which incorporate adjustments in mining capacity. And Charles River Associates (CRA, 1978) include reserve formation in their copper modelling study.

An appropriate model framework which would integrate both long run and short run stock adjustments has been suggested in Figure 1. Most important is that stock and flow market adjustments are represented at three levels: (1) longer term mineral reserve stocks with flow depletion and additions, (2) medium to long term stocks in the form of primary production capacity with flow depletion and additions, and (3) short term inventory of stocks finished products determined by flows of consumption and production. Scrap could also be considered a stock which leads to secondary production flows, but for simplicity, scrap and secondary production are assumed to follow a flow process.

## 3. THE THEORETICAL MODEL

To transform the above framework into a model suitable for hypothesis testing, we concentrate on the stock adjustment aspects of dynamic market equilibrium. While Hotelling (1931) thought of optimal exhaustibility as a condition of flow equilibrium in the market for ore, Solow (1974) considered it also as a condition of stock equilibrium in the asset market. Product inventories have frequently been considered in the context of stock equilibrium relevant to short run flow equilibrium. Confirmation of this approach can be reviewed in Burrows and Lonoff (1977), Labys (1973, 1980b) and elsewhere. Mineral market quantity and price adjustments are thus a consequence of simultaneous flow equilibrium adjustments in the market for the ore and the metal, and of stock equilibrium adjustments in the market for deposits and for metal inventories.

In order to integrate these various stock adjustment processes in a single

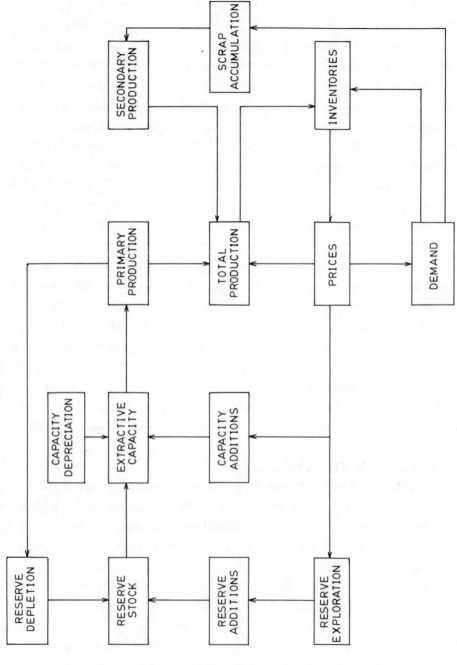

Figure 1. Exhaustible Resource Model Framework

model, it has been necessary to simplify considerably the representation of the world copper market. To begin with, copper extraction and mineral processing are assumed to represent a single production process yielding refined metal, and market exchange accordingly occurs only in refined metal. I also have chosen not to represent the formulations of the REM as the solution to an optimal reserve depletion problem based on the continuous maximum principle of optimal control theory, e.g., Clark (1976). The nature of that formulation and its implications for the theoretical specification of the equations employed in the present model can be found in a previous paper (Labys, 1985).

## 3.1 Reserves, Output and Capacity

The model specification begins with the definition of the reserve level R existing at any point in time as being equal to the initial reserve level $R_0$ minus cumulative differences between reserve additions E and mineral extraction Q.

$$R_t = R_0 + \sum_{0}^{T} (E_t - Q_t) \tag{1}$$

The theoretical background for explaining reserve additions or discoveries can be found in several sources such as Peterson (1978), Pindyck (1978b), and CRA (1978). The desired stock of reserves should be large enough to reduce uncertainty by permitting rational long term production planning. Hence, as stocks of reserves are used up in the process of extraction, producers will invest in exploration so as to maintain a desired reserve level.

Reserve additions can be postulated to depend on expected profitability $\Pi^*$ which embodies expected prices and expected costs of exploration effort, the ratio of production capacity to reserves K/R which implies that firms attempt to maintain a given relation between primary production capacity and reserves, and cumulative extraction A. The relation between prices and costs perceived in a prior period $(t-\theta)$ is an important determinant of investment in reserve additions, particularly since it reflects the declining returns which may occur as exploratory effort extends to lower quality deposits.

Reserve additions can thus be explained according to:

$$E_t = e(\Pi^*_{t-\theta}, K_t/R_t, A_t) \tag{2}$$

$$A_t = \sum_{0}^{T} Q_t \tag{3}$$

where $\dfrac{\delta \dot{E}}{\delta \Pi^*}$ and $\dfrac{\delta \dot{E}}{\delta K/R} > 0$

Profit expectations are based mainly on prices and are assumed to be of a simple lagged nature and $\theta$ represents the period required between the time of high prices and new reserve formation. Stochastic disturbance terms and additional exogenous influences have been omitted here and elsewhere to simplify presentation.

The primary output of mineral producers follows elementary production formulations such as that found in Eswaren, Lewis and Heaps (1983), Gordon (1967), and Weinstein and Zeckhauser (1975).

$$Q_t = q(P_t, K_t, R_t) \tag{4}$$

where

$$\frac{\delta Q}{\delta P}, \frac{\delta Q}{\delta K}, \text{ and } \frac{\delta Q}{\delta R} > 0 . \tag{5}$$

This function has been simplified by omitting labour and energy inputs, because the latter are of less consequence for the present analysis. While some researchers have included cumulative extraction in their supply function, the implied effect of decreasing returns can be accounted for with the included reserve variable. At the same time, the rising costs of depletion are likely to be offset by cost–reducing technological progress.

Primary production capacity adjustments can be explained on the basis of investment theories such as that of net present value or the desire of mineral producers to keep capacity in proportion to reserves. Let us begin with the definition of capacity formation

$$K_t = K_{t-1} + IN_t - \delta K_{t-1} \tag{6}$$

where $IN_t = \Delta K_t$ is investment or change in new capacity and $\delta$ is the rate of depreciation of existing capacity. Investment is explained by expanding the accelerator principle beyond production to include producer goals of profitability and of maintaining capacity in proportion to reserves.

$$IN_t = n(Y_t, \Pi^*_{t-\theta}, K_t/R_t) \tag{7}$$

where $\frac{\delta IN}{\delta Y}, \frac{\delta IN}{\delta \Pi^*}, \frac{\delta K/R}{\delta IN} > 0 .$

## 3.2 Secondary Production

It has been a common practice in constructing the SCM for metal markets to consider secondary supply and demand, e.g., Mikesell (1979). Attempts to include recycling in the REM have been made by Schulze (1974), Weinstein and Zeckhauser (1975), and Pindyck (1978b). More recently, Radetzki and Van

Duyne (1983a) have demonstrated that declining economic growth increases the importance of secondary supply and reduces the rate of growth of primary production. Among the assumptions necessary to specify the recycling component are the following: (1) all metal products are used for a number of years after which they are scrapped; (2) the proportion of scrapped products recovered and supplied to the market varies with scrap prices; (3) the market for scrap adjusts continually so that scrap demand equals scrap supply; and (4) supplies of primary and secondary metals at the finished metal stage are perfect substitutes.

The present specification states that metal products available for recycling exist in the form of a flow of recoverable material M based on past demand D, following the suggestion of Radetzki and Van Duyne (1983a).

$$M_t = \phi D_{t-\alpha} \tag{8}$$

Here $\phi$ is the recoverable share of scrap and $\alpha$ is the average age of durability of the metal products under consideration. If S represents the level of secondary supply in a given year, then it can be said to vary with the recoverable share M and with the price of scrap PS relative to that of the refined metal P.

$$S_t = s(M_t, PS_t/P_t) \tag{9}$$

Substitution for M yields secondary supply as a function of only past demand and scrap prices.

$$S_t = s(D_{t-\alpha}, PS_t) \tag{10}$$

## 3.3 Consumption

The specification of the demand relationship follows from that of the SCM. Only now resource considerations such as that suggested by Weinstein and Zeckhauser (1975) and by Pindyck (1980) are included. Demand in this case is a derived demand and depends on the consumption of the resource in its final metal product uses. That is, consumption D depends on the resource price P, industrial activity Y, (cross) commodity prices $P^C$ reflecting possible substitution from other commodities, and U representing uncertain demand influences.

$$D_t = d(P_t, Y_t, P_t^C, U_t) \tag{11}$$

where $\dfrac{\delta D}{\delta P} < 0$, $\dfrac{\delta D}{\delta P^C} > 0$, and $\dfrac{\delta D}{\delta Y} > 0$.

Since consumption is measured at the refined stage, we do not distinguish between primary or secondary sources of materials; the refined products from both are assumed to be perfect substitutes.

## 3.4 Inventories, Prices and Model Closure

The inclusion of product inventories in the REM can be justified as follows. (1) The presence of rising (or falling) marginal primary product costs gives rise to corresponding price changes and hence demand adjustments. (2) Given typically inelastic short term supply adjustability, these demand fluctuations will induce the holding of inventories. With rising demand, there is a need to increase inventories. With falling demand, there is a tendency to reduce them. (3) The cost of varying primary production capacity utilisation is high because of the deterioration of systems and equipment which would follow from the closure of these items. There will, therefore, be a tendency for firms to adjust inventories by operating in excess of consumption during recession and below consumption during prosperity. (4) The introduction of uncertainty gives rise to transactions costs, and inventories help to reduce these costs. (5) Finally, inventories can help to restore displacements from market equilibrium as is required for the adjustment process of the combined model. Eswaren, Lewis and Heaps (1983) have pointed to the importance of including inventories in the REM as a buffer to prevent discontinuous jumps in prices that would result from sudden reserve declines as reserve depletion becomes immanent. Regarding the disequilibrium specification of the present model, the existence of inventories implies that one time period is related to the next by the expectations which may occur between them or which serve to link them.

Inventory demand behaviour is normally explained by appropriate economic theories such as the "accelerator", or more recently the "supply of storage". The significance of the latter theory for describing inventory adjustments has been stated earlier. Transactions, precautionary and speculative motives are now formalised in a theory which equates marginal inventory holding costs to marginal storage costs minus insurance costs against stockout (or stockout yield) and insurance costs against over or under coverage (or coverage yield). Consumers will thus increase or decrease their inventory levels to the point where their marginal inventory holding costs equal the rate at which they expect the refined metal price to appreciate. This nonlinear relationship implies that the aggregate demand for inventories is a function of expected price changes $P^*-P$; the desired inventory size increases as the expected price difference widens.

$$I_t = i \left[ \frac{P^*_t - P_t}{h} \right] \tag{12}$$

The expected price $P$ refers to a particular horizon point in the near future, the horizon interval equalling h.

Since inventories in the SCM are often explained endogenously in the form of the closing identity given by (14), a normal procedure has been to invert equation (12) and to express resource prices as a function of the ratio between inventories and demand I/D. Since this supply of storage theory is short run, the price relationship can also integrate the long run by adding the influence of capacity utilisation Q/K.

$$P_t = p(P_t^*, I_t/D_t, Q_t/K_t) \tag{13}$$

The final equation needed to close the model is the supply of inventories and reflects the consistent differences between the total of primary and secondary supply on the one hand, and consumption on the other.

$$I_t = I_{t-1} + Q_t + S_t - D_t \tag{14}$$

## 4. THE EMPIRICAL MODEL

A major difficulty in transforming the above theoretical model into an empirical model is the selection of a methodology that would span periods from 20 to 50 years, where the capital stock of an industry including mining reserves and capacity is variable. Conventional econometric estimation of the SCM results in parameters that rarely survive the structural changes that take place in commodity markets every 5 to 10 years. An experimental dynamic simulation methodology has thus been adopted which combines econometric parameter estimation with extraneous information regarding the long run parameter values. Such a simulation which is evolutionary over time is based on related long run simulations conducted by researchers such as Barsotti (1979), Lonoff (1982), Gordon et al. (1987), Leontief et al (1983), Nordhaus and Yohe (1983), and Pindyck (1978a). It reflects recent attempts to extend conventional econometric models to long run analysis. The idea of forecasting commodity market behaviour into the next century is not a sound one, but this study makes no attempt to do that. Rather it attempts to analyse "if–then" statements, conditional about sets of assumptions about underlying economic conditions.

The copper market has been selected for this particular model application and validation, because the descriptive data are generally good and a number of modelling studies have already been performed. The market also features the sequential nature of production, extending from mining, concentrating and refining through semi–fabricating and final manufacturing. In addition to primary supply, scrap or secondary supply also plays a major role in market adjustments. Copper consumption at the refined or price making stage is a derived demand stemming from a number of industries: electrical, construction, machinery, transportation, and ordinance.

Copper price adjustments reflect above—ground inventory holding as well as capacity stock limits. Different categories of holders exist including producers, merchants, fabricators and the LME. While these inventories are dependent on prices and their expectations, the stocks of the different categories of holders do not necessarily move together. Inventories held by producers and the LME have tended to decline during periods of rising prices. Fabricators, however, adjust their inventories to influences in addition to prices such as expectations of strikes, sales contracts, demand and future market movements. Capacity affects prices mostly when demand requires that the industry operate at near capacity limits.

Since most copper transactions take place in the form of refined metal, the refined or wire bar price is the most important one for explaining market adjustments. In the US market, the producers set the refined price on what appears to be medium term demand and supply, although short run influences have tended to predominate more recently. This price is closely linked to the refined price reached on the London Metal Exchange. Although the limited volume of transactions on the LME makes it a "marginal" market compared to total copper transactions, the price reached is regarded as the international reference and provides a basis for contract negotiation in many countries.

Among the attempts to model economic activity in the copper market, the more well—known ones include that of Adams (1973), Dammert and Palaniappan (1985), Fisher, Cootner and Bailey (1972), Kovisars (1975), Richard (1978), Staloff (1977), US Bureau of Mines (1977), Pobukadee (1979), Taylor (1979), and Wagenhals (1984). The existence of this econometric history improves our perception of the nature of dynamic adjustments in the copper market. In particular, Fisher, Cootner and Bailey (1972) have explained demand and supply adjustments with dynamic mechanisms of the partial adjustment type. Staloff (1977) has advanced the dynamics of price adjustment by means of a more comprehensive analysis of both recycling and inventories. And as stated earlier, Labys (1980a), Richard (1978), and Wagenhals (1984) has added capacity formation to the dynamic adjustment process and CRA (1978) has included reserve formation.

The equations provided below which constitute the empirical structure of the model are based on data describing the world copper market. The data comprising the basic market balance are shown in Table 1 and refer to western countries only. Other important data include LME copper prices deflated by the World Bank MUV price index, mine capacity obtained from *Metal Analysis Outlook*, and reserves estimated from the US Bureau of Mines. The years of estimation, 1971–1985, represent the most recent period of stable market structure which is that of relative excess supply (Lonoff, 1982).

Table 1. Western Countries Copper Balances

| Year | PRIPRD | SECPRD | TOTPRD | CONSMT | CHGINV | INVEN |
|------|--------|--------|--------|--------|--------|-------|
| 1960 | 3512 | 675 | 4187 | 3857 | 330 | 0 |
| 1961 | 3622 | 650 | 4272 | 4130 | 142 | 130 |
| 1962 | 3969 | 677 | 4373 | 4143 | 230 | 272 |
| 1963 | 3783 | 655 | 4448 | 4430 | 18 | 502 |
| 1964 | 3974 | 774 | 4748 | 4902 | −154 | 520 |
| 1965 | 4136 | 907 | 5043 | 5025 | 18 | 366 |
| 1966 | 4145 | 1024 | 5169 | 5215 | −46 | 384 |
| 1967 | 3830 | 947 | 4777 | 4895 | −118 | 338 |
| 1968 | 4310 | 1085 | 5395 | 5180 | 215 | 220 |
| 1969 | 4751 | 1128 | 5877 | 5746 | 131 | 435 |
| 1970 | 4976 | 1158 | 6134 | 5835 | 299 | 566 |
| 1971 | 4875 | 962 | 5837 | 5733 | 104 | 865 |
| 1972 | 5406 | 987 | 6393 | 6265 | 128 | 969 |
| 1973 | 5646 | 1062 | 6708 | 6927 | −219 | 1097 |
| 1974 | 5780 | 1170 | 6950 | 6460 | 490 | 878 |
| 1975 | 5380 | 896 | 6276 | 5424 | 852 | 1368 |
| 1976 | 5686 | 961 | 6649 | 6428 | 221 | 2220 |
| 1977 | 5856 | 979 | 6835 | 6881 | −46 | 2241 |
| 1978 | 5856 | 1035 | 6891 | 7274 | −383 | 2395 |
| 1979 | 5820 | 1189 | 7009 | 7536 | −527 | 2012 |
| 1980 | 5742 | 1289 | 7081 | 7147 | −66 | 1485 |
| 1981 | 6217 | 1122 | 7339 | 7158 | 81 | 1419 |
| 1982 | 5941 | 1159 | 7099 | 6757 | 342 | 1500 |

SECPRD = Copper recovery from scrap in West
TOTPRD = Production of refined copper in West
PRIPRD = TOTPRD − SECPRD
CONSMT = Consumption of refined copper in West
CHGINV = TOTPRD − CONSMT
INVEN = World stocks of refined copper in West plus
      net CHGINVEN estimating backwards from 1982

Source:    *Metal Statistics* from Metallgesellschaft Aktiengesellschaft except for inventories 1982 which are from *World Metal Statistics*, The World Bureau of Metal Statistics.

*Consumption*

$$D_t = 1.03 + 13.35 \, \Delta A_t - 0.39 \, P_t + 0.88 \, D_{t-1}$$

where $A_t$ is OECD industrial activity which has grown at approximately 4% annually.

*Primary Production*

$$Q_t = 1.10 + 0.31 \, P_t + 0.56 \, K_t$$

*Primary Consumption*

$$K_t = -0.18 + 0.15 \, A_t + 0.05 \, P_{t-6}$$

This equation has been simplified to allow capacity to expand but to limit it to grow in industrial demand.

*Secondary Production*

$$S_t = 0.08 \, P_t + 0.15 \, D_{t-1}$$

Current lagged demand has been found to serve as a reasonable surrogate for past lagged demand of up to 25 years. The generation of such a long lag structure would unduly complicate the present model. Scrap prices are also omitted as a computational simplification.

*Total Production*

$$TQ_t = Q_t + S_t$$

*Reserves*

$$R_t = R_o + \Sigma(E_t - Q_t)$$

*Reserve Additions*

$$E_t = 7.0 \, P_{t-6} + 50 \, K_t / R_t$$

Changes in reserve additions have been erratic and data are incomplete. This relation provides a surrogate for additions which would reflect the basic investment forces acting on the market.

*Inventories*

$$I_t = I_{t-1} + TQ_t - D_t$$

*Prices*

$$P_t = -2.81 + 0.02 \, P_{t-1} - 1.00 \, (I_t/D_t) + 5.39 \, (Q_t/K_t)$$

Prices are primarily stock determined not only by the inventory/demand ratio but also by the proxy for capacity utilisation.

## 5. DYNAMIC SIMULATIONS

The purpose of the dynamic simulations is to evaluate the realism and policy potential of the present model which integrates long and short run market adjustment processes. The method adopted follows that of Barsotti (1979), Gordon et.

al. (1987), Lonoff (1982), Nordhaus and Yohe (1983), and Pindyck (1978a) who have constructed long term evolutionary commodity models. This has required formulating the above model as a simultaneous equation system and imbedding it in a Gauss–Seidel simulation framework which also incorporates the possibility of resource exhaustion. The simulation also contains a routine which causes growth in economic activity to vary cyclically and thus to emulate international economic cycles. To facilitate the interpretation of results, prices and activity (in real terms) as well as other variables have been normalised.

The validation of models of this type is not easy. The methods of validation reported in Labys and Pollak (1984) pertain mostly to models of a short or medium run nature where parametric and nonparametric tests are more relevant. The validation test which would appear to be most valid in the present circumstances involves the spectral analysis of the actual compared to the simulated cyclical response of the model's endogenous variables. This approach, however, requires a large number of observations over the historical period, as might be provided by quarterly or monthly model simulations. In the present case, model simulation conducted over the sample period (1971–1985) has shown the major endogenous variables such as prices, primary production or consumption to generate cycles of the frequency and duration associated with copper market adjustments over that period. In addition, validation can be made using classical prediction theory in the sense of Nordhaus and Yohe (1983). Following this approach, the percentage difference found between actual and estimated values of the endogenous variables over the more recent period 1971–1985 proved to be reasonably low. In future analysis, the performance of the model will be checked using out–of–sample forecasts relating to past periods.

An equally important measure of the model's performance is the cyclical response and stability exhibited by the "base case" simulation extending from 1988 to 2036. The assumptions underlying this simulation reflect the most likely evolution of the copper market. The simulations are thus not forecasts but rather conditional simulations based on the estimated parametric structure of the model and certain underlying economic assumptions. The most important of these are that demand increases exogenously according to the growth rate of world economic activity set at 3.0 percent. Changes in primary capacity are assumed to follow past average growth rates. No changes are expected in the rate of inventory adjustments. The planning horizon is 50 years from 1986 to 2036.

The resulting "base case" simulation values are reported in terms of price movements only, as shown in Figure 2. However, the simulation values for the remaining variables were stable over the horizon period with total copper supply and demand remaining in equilibrium. Copper inventory changes are slight with only a gradual drift towards inventory accumulation. Real copper prices follow an oscillatory pattern downwards. This pattern features cycles that can be considered representative of copper market behaviour in the past. The downward drift follows the tendency of copper primary capacity to increase gradually. The increase in capacity is likely due to expectations of rising economic growth; however, it is probably tempered by the relative slow growth in demand which reflects the expansion of "materials" substitutes for copper. This increase in copper investment would agree with the results achieved in the modelling exercise of Dammert and Palaniappan (1985).

Sensitivity analysis of the copper market's responses to long run and short run stock adjustments has been performed first with respect to copper primary capacity and secondly with respect to refined copper inventories. Copper capacity adjustments have been based on parameter adjustments in the capacity equation. The activity coefficient in that equation is set at 0.15. Sensitivity simulations are based on increasing and decreasing the coefficient by approximately 50 percent. Figure 2 also shows the results of increasing producer response to changing economic activity to be a sharp decline in prices. The capacity simulation values also increased but the percentage changes in capacity diminish as the end of the horizon period approaches. In the case of reducing this response, Figure 2 shows that prices increase sharply relative to the base case and capacity declines fairly regularly. Reserves do increase continuously because of the now higher prices. Figure 2 also shows that the amplitude of the cyclicality of copper prices is more highly pronounced with overcapacity conditions.

The lagged price coefficient in the capacity equation is varied also by an increase and decrease of 50 percent in each direction around the coefficient 0.05. Again the response to the parameter increase results in lower prices and higher capacity. The opposite response can be seen to the parameter decrease. Figure 3 shows the price response in which the oscillatory pattern remains similar but the amplification higher under the low response case and lower under the high response case.

The second or short run refined copper inventory sensitivity analysis is more difficult to perform, because stock holding of this type is often unintended. In addition there is no explicit stock equation in the model. However, there is an

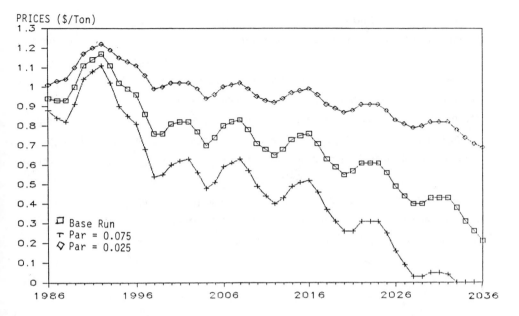

Figure 2. Copper Price Sensitivity
Capacity Adjustment to Activity Parameter

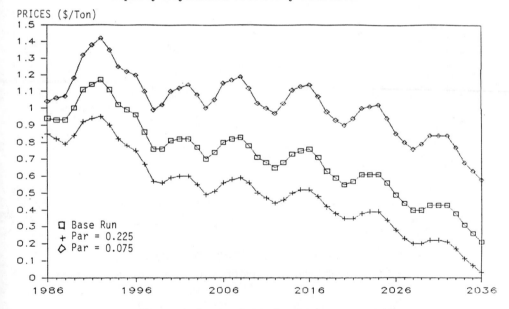

Figure 3. Copper Price Sensitivity
Capacity Adjustment to Price Parameter

implicit stock equation in the form of the copper price equation, where copper inventory coverage appears as an explanatory variable. The sensitivity analysis is thus performed by lowering the coefficient of −1.0 on this variable to −0.1 and by increasing it to −2.0. This variation is equivalent to making the inventory–price response less strong (as might occur during periods of high inventories) and more strong (as might occur during periods of low inventories). The resulting impact on prices is shown in Figure 4. The price response is more varied than for the capacity stock adjustment. When the inventory response is lessened, the cyclical pattern of copper prices not only diminishes making copper prices relatively higher, but the amplitude and frequency of the price change as well. When the inventory response is increased, the peaks and troughs of copper prices become lower as well as higher than for the base case.

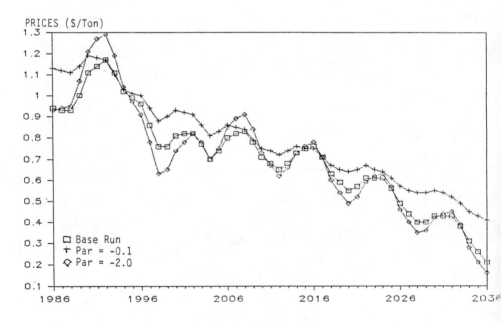

Figure 4. Copper Price Sensitivity.
Price Adjustment to Inventory Coverage Parameter

## 6. CONCLUSIONS

The performance and potential applicability of this modelling approach has been evaluated here only in a preliminary fashion. It is obvious that a more thorough evaluation employing probabilistic scenario analysis in a more systematic fashion is necessary. One noticeable weakness is that the price cycles shown in Figures 2–4 are somewhat synchronous, because the demand sector of the model was operated without, for example, Monte Carlo variations imposed on economic activity.

Sensitivity analysis of specific uncertainties could also be performed, such as that suggested by Gordon et. al. (1987). For example, will aluminium or futuristic engineering materials replace copper in most uses? Will new products and processes generate new uses that increase copper demands? Or will environmental constraints on mining eventually provide a major obstacle to copper extraction?

The present results, however, stress the importance of integrating long and short run stock adjustment behaviour in the copper market and the need for more harmonised planning of copper producing capacity and of inventories. It is well known that excesses and shortages of copper capacity have led to wide price swings in the market. The present modelling effort for the first time provides a more closer perception as to the likely nature of these swings. The price–destabilising effect of fluctuations in refined inventories is also well known. Although the present results do not evaluate the effectiveness of an international copper buffer stock, the results do suggest a strong relationship between inventory adjustments, stable price behaviour and investment–price signals.

### NOTES
* The dynamic simulation model employed in this study was constructed by Felix Londono and Paul Labys. This research has been supported in part by the Jacob Wallenberg Foundation.

### REFERENCES
Adams, F.G. (1973), "The Impact of Copper Production from the Ocean Floor: Application of an Econometric Model", Economics Research Unit, University of Pennsylvania for the United Nations Conference on Trade and Development, Philadelphia.

Barsotti, A.F. (1979), "Resource and Energy Constraints on Regional and Global Availability of Aluminium, Copper and Iron, 1975–2000", Ph.D. Dissertation, Case Western University.

Burrows, J.C. and M.J. Lonoff (1977), "Models of Metal Markets", Ford Foundation Conference on Stabilising World Commodity Markets, Airlie, VA.

Charles River Associates (CRA) (1978), "The Economics and Geology of Mineral Supply: An Integrated Framework for Long Run Policy Analysis", CRA Report No. 327, Charles River Associates, Boston, MA.

Clark, C.W. (1976), *Mathematical Bioeconomics: The Optimal Management of Renewable Resources*, John Wiley and Sons, New York.

Dammert, A. and S. Palaniappan (1985), "*Modelling Investments in the World Copper Sector*, University of Texas Press, Austin.

Devarajan, S. and A.C. Fisher, (1981), "Hotelling's Economics of Exhaustible Resources: Fifty Years Later", *Journal of Economic Literature* 19, 65–73.

Eswaren, M., T.R. Lewis and T. Heaps (1983), "On the Nonexistence of Market Equilibria in Exhaustible Resource Markets with Decreasing Costs", *Journal of Political Economy* 91, 154–67.

Fisher, A.C. (1979), "Measures of Natural Resource Scarcity", in V.K. Smith (ed.), *Scarcity and Growth Reconsidered*, John Hopkins University Press, Baltimore, MD.

Fisher, F.M., Cootner, P.H. and Bailey, M. (1972), "An Econometric Model of the World Copper Industry", *Bell Journal of Economics and Management Science*, 3, 568–609.

Frank, J. and M. Babunovic (1984), "An Investment Model of Natural Resources Markets", *Economica* 51, 83–95.

Gordon, R.B., Koopmans, T.C., Nordhaus, W.B. and B.J. Skinner (1987), "Toward a New Iron Age?", Harvard University Press, Cambridge.

Gordon, R.L. (1967), "A Reinterpretation of the Pure Theory of Exhaustion", *Journal of Political Economy* 75, 274–86.

Harrod, R.F., (1964), *Towards a Dynamic Economics*, MacMillan, London.

Hicks, J., (1979), *Causality in Economics*, Basic Books, Inc., New York.

Hoel, M., (1978), "Resource Extraction, Uncertainty, and Learning", *Bell Journal of Economics* 9, 642–45.

Hotelling, H., (1931), "The Economics of Exhaustible Resources", *Journal of Political Economy* 39, 137–75.

Keynes, J.M. (1936), *The General Theory of Employment, Interest and Money*, MacMillan, London.

Kovisars, L. (1975), "Copper Trade Flow Model", World Mineral Availability, SRI Project MED 3742–74, Stanford Research Institute, Palo Alto.

Labys, W.C. (1973), *Dynamic Commodity Models: Specification, Estimation and Simultation*, Heath Lexington Books, Lexington, MA.

Labys, W.C. (1980a), "A Model of Disequilibrium Adjustments in the Copper Market," *Materials and Society* 4, 153–64.

Labys, W.C. (1980b), "Dynamics of Market Adjustment and Stabilization in the Minerals Industry", Report submitted to the National Science Foundation under Grant No. DAR 78–08810, Department of Mineral and Energy Resource Economics, West Virginia University, Morgantown.

Labys, W.C. (1985), "An Integrated Market Model of Exhaustible Resource Behaviour", Working Paper No. 97a, Department of Mineral and Energy Resource Economics, West Virginia University, Morgantown.

Labys, W.C. and P. Pollak, (1984), *Commodity Models for Forecasting and Policy Analysis*, Croom–Helm, London.

Leontief, W., J. Koo, S. Nasar and I. Sohn, (1983), *The Future of Nonfuel Minerals in the U.S. and World Economy*, Heath Lexington Books, Lexington, MA.

Lonoff, M. (1982), "Economics Aspects of the Copper Market", Ph.D. Dissertation, Massachusetts Institute of Technology, Cambridge.

Mikesell, R.F. (1979,) *The World Copper Industry*, Johns Hopkins University Press, Baltimore, MD.

Nordhaus, W.D. and G.W. Yohe, (1983), "Future Carbon Dioxide Emissions from Fossil Fuels", in *Changing Climate*, National Academy of Sciences, Washington, D.C.

Peterson, F.M. (1978), "A Model of Mining and Exploring for Natural

Resources", *Journal of Environmental Economics and Management* 5, 236–51.

Pindyck, R.S. (1981), "Models of Resource Markets and the Explanation of Resource Price Behaviour", *Energy Economics* 3, 130–39.

Pindyck, R.S. (1978a), "Gains to Producers from the Cartelization of Exhaustible Resources", *Review of Economics and Statistics* 60, 238–51.

Pindyck, R.S. (1978b), "The Optimal Exploration and Production of Non–Renewable Resources", *Journal of Political Economy* 86, 841–61.

Pindyck, R.S. (1980), "Uncertainty and Exhaustible Resource Markets", *Journal of Political Economy* 88, 1203–225.

Pobukadee, J. (1979), "An Econometric Analysis of the World Copper Market", Wharton Econometric Forecasting Associates, Philadelphia.

Radetzki, M. and C. Van Duyne (1983a), "The Demand for Scrap and Primary Metal Ores after a Decline in Secular Growth", Seminar Paper No. 246, Institute for International Economics Studies, Stockholm.

Radetzki, M. and C. Van Duyne (1983b), "The Response of Mining Investment to a Decline in Economic Growth: The Case of Copper in the 1970's", Research Memo No. 86, Williams College, Williams, MA.

Richard, D. (1978), "A Dynamic Model of the World Copper Industry", *IMF Staff Papers* 25, 779–833.

Schulze, W.D. (1974), "The Optimal Use of Non–Renewable Resources: The Theory of Extraction", *Journal of Environmental Economics and Management* 1, 53–74.

Solow, R.M. (1974), "The Economics of Resources or the Resources of Economics", *American Economic Review* 64, 1–14.

Solow, R.M. and F.Y. Wan (1976), "Extraction costs in the Theory of Exhaustible Resources", *Bell Journal of Economics* 7, 359–70.

Staloff, S.J. (1977), "A Stock–Flow Analysis of Copper Markets", Ph.D. Thesis, University of Oregon, Eugene.

Taylor, C.A. (1979), "A Quarterly Domestic Copper Industry Model", *Review of Economics and Statistics* 61, 410–22.

U.S. Bureau of Mines (1977), Joint Aluminium/Copper Forecasting and Simulation Model, Final Report and Appendices A and B, Open File Report No. 114 (2)–1977. Prepared by Synergy Inc for US Dept. of the Interior, Washington, DC.

Wagenhals, G. (1984), *The World Copper Market*, Lecture Notes in Economics and Mathematical Systems No 233, Springer Verlag, Berlin.

Weinstein, M.C. and R.J. Zeckhauser (1975), "The Optimal Consumption of Depletable Natural Resources", *Quarterly Journal of Economics* 89, 371–92.

# PART II

# TRADE, DEBT, AND DEVELOPMENT

CHAPTER 4

# THE IMPACT OF COMMODITY PRICE INSTABILITY: EXPERIMENTS WITH A GENERAL EQUILIBRIUM MODEL FOR INDONESIA

Jere R. Behrman, *University of Pennsylvania*
Jeffrey D. Lewis and Sherif Lofti, *Harvard University*

## 1. INTRODUCTION

Fluctuations in international commodity prices long have been claimed to have deleterious effects on the producing countries. This claim has lead to considerable efforts to introduce international policies that might mitigate such effects, particularly by UNCTAD most notably in its Integrated Commodity Program and by the IMF in its Compensating Financing Facility. It also has led to a number of studies of its validity, primarily using cross–sectional data, but also, in fewer cases, using economy wide models for case studies.[1] Little work has been undertaken, however, in evaluating the impact of commodity price instability within the theoretically consistent economy wide framework of computable general equilibrium (CGE) models, though such models have been used to explore related questions, such as the impact of an one way movement in the terms of trade and of policy options to such a movement (e.g., Dick, Gupta, Mayer, and Vincent, 1983; Gelb, 1985).

This paper uses a CGE model of Indonesia to explore the impact of price fluctuations in international markets for primary products on the Indonesian economy. Comparative statics experiments are undertaken with the model to analyse macroeconomic, sectoral and distributional consequences of price instability, under alternative hypotheses about economic behaviour and institutions.

Section 2 summarises the features of our CGE model. Section 3 describes the Indonesian economy in 1980 as it is represented in the model. Section 4 outlines

*L. R. Klein and J. Marquez (eds.), Economics in Theory and Practice: An Eclectic Approach, 59–100.*

the general results of the alternative experiments that have been undertaken. Section 5 focuses on the impact of primary commodity price instability. The two appendices give model equations and the data sources.

## 2. DESCRIPTION OF OUR INDONESIAN CGE MODEL

### 2.1 Model Overview

The chief characteristic of a CGE model is that it simulates the working of a market system in which prices adjust in the markets for factors, products, and foreign exchange in response to changes in supply and demand conditions.[2] Economic performance is seen as the outcome of decentralised optimising decisions made by producers and consumers in response to market conditions, which in turn are influenced by government policies, international economic conditions, and other exogenous forces. Within each period, the model reaches a static equilibrium solution in which markets are modelled as clearing subject to specified behavioural rules and parameter values, fixed factors, and constraints on markets. The CGE model thus concentrates on the determination of relative prices among sectors and on the structure of real variables in the economy. The selection of a *numeraire* or price normalisation rule exogenously fixes the absolute price level, so that a solution to the model yields sectoral prices relative to the aggregate price level. The real focus of the model is further reflected in the complete absence of financial markets or monetary variables. Just as the prices of outputs in all sectors are relative prices, further, the exchange rate is a relative price. The real exchange rate is defined as the relative price of tradeables and nontradeables. Since we use an index of domestic prices as numeraire, variations in the "nominal" exchange rate directly affect the ratio of the price — in Indonesian rupiah — of imports and exports to the price of domestic sales, and so represent a change in the real exchange rate. In many simulations, the nominal exchange rate is fixed, and external balance is achieved through endogenous movements in foreign exchange reserves. The idea of markets responding to changing economic conditions does not imply that markets are "perfect". Instead, the model takes account of rigidities and distortions in the economy, and attempts to model them formally. For example, capital already in place in each sector is fixed, with the capital stock modified only through the allocation of new investment; labour is segmented by skill category; and sectoral wages for each type of labour are required to conform to an exogenously specified pattern embodying wage "distortions".

## 2.2 Our Indonesian CGE Model

This section provides a verbal description of our static CGE model of Indonesia. A more complete algebraic presentation can be found in Appendix A.

### 2.2.1 Product Markets and Factor Supplies

There are 12 sectors or product markets.[3] Domestic prices affect supply and demand decisions in all sectors. Technological conditions and behavioural rules influence supply decisions in response to changing prices. Technological constraints are given by sectoral production functions which allow for substitution between labour and capital inputs. Fixed input–output coefficients determine intermediate input use. Sectoral capital stocks are fixed in the period, under the assumptions that the time period of analysis precludes new capital investments becoming effective due to gestation lags and that capital market imperfections and putty–clay capital characteristics prevent the reallocation of capital across sectors once installed. Within the time period of the simulations, therefore, even if investment is induced to fluctuate widely, productive capacity remains fixed. Four labour types are identified: two types (paid workers and unpaid proprietors) appear only in the two agricultural sectors, and two types (blue collar and white collar) in all sectors. Profit maximising behaviour given exogenous (to the firm) prices and wages is assumed. The firm's decision to hire a new worker depends on a comparison between the market wage (which includes a sector specific differential) and the marginal value product of that worker. Aggregate demand for labour of each type is obtained by summing over the individual sectoral demands. The supplies of each labour type are fixed exogenously during each period. Wages adjust to clear the labour markets in our initial simulations. Finally, the *domestic* price level is set exogenously and is given by a weighted index of sectoral prices for domestic output.

### 2.2.2 Foreign Trade

Since most of these markets are for tradeable goods and our focus in this paper is on primary tradeable goods, the model's specification of export and import behaviour is important. Domestically produced goods and imports are assumed to be imperfect substitutes. For each sector, a "composite" good is defined by a CES aggregation function of the domestic good and the imported substitute. Elasticities of substitution vary across sectors, with smaller elasticities reflecting greater differences between the domestic and imported good, and hence greater difficulty in substituting one for the other in response to changes in their relative prices. The elasticity used in agriculture is quite high, those for the consumer goods sectors more moderate (e.g. food processing and textiles), and those for intermediate inputs, capital goods, and petroleum quite low. Assuming that users of a good seek to minimise the cost of acquiring it, this formulation implies that the desired ratio of the imported substitute to the domestically produced good is a function of the ratio of their prices. Following the small country assumption, the world price of the imported substitute is assumed to be given by world market conditions over which Indonesia has no influence. The domestic price of the import is determined by the world price, the tariff rate, and the exchange rate.

Sectoral exports also are assumed to be different from output sold domestically, reflecting explicit differences (such as quality) as well as a range of barriers preventing the costless reallocation of output between domestic and foreign markets (such as market penetration costs). Because of these barriers, the domestic price of output need not equal the export price, which (as with imports) under the small country assumption is determined by the world price, export subsidies, and the exchange rate. Producers maximise revenue given their output level by selling so that the ratio of exports to domestic sales is a function of their price ratio.

Total foreign exchange available for imports depends not only on export earnings, but also on foreign capital inflows: net remittance inflows, net factor service income, foreign borrowing net of amortisation and interest payments, and changes in official foreign exchange holdings.

Sectoral imports depend on the relative price of imports and imperfect domestic substitutes. With a flexible exchange rate, the market for foreign exchange would clear, so that total expenditures on imports would be equal to the sum of total exports, net foreign capital flows, and reserve changes. In Indonesia, however, the exchange rate is fixed by the government and changed only periodically, so that there is no guarantee that at the official exchange rate, import demand does not exceed export earnings and capital inflows. Therefore, the basic specification in our Indonesian model is that foreign reserves adjust to equilibrate demand and supply for foreign exchange.[4]

## 2.2.3 Income and Product Demand

The model contains an elaborate set of accounting and behavioural rules to determine how value added or factor income is distributed among three different classes of income recipients: firms, households, and the government. Basically, the distribution of value added in each sector depends on: (1) the size of the wage portion in total value added; (2) decisions by capitalists about the distribution of their net income between savings and consumption; and (3) taxes that influence the distribution of value added between the private and government sectors.

To obtain components of demand for output, saving and expenditure behaviour are specified for each type of income recipient. The income remaining with firms after they have distributed wages to labour households is distributed to capitalist households, who are the owners of capital (including land). The income flowing into the government sector from various taxes and from its share of foreign borrowing is used to finance government expenditures on the output of the productive sectors and to finance investment. Households save a fraction of their disposable income and spend the rest on goods.

Savings—investment balance is assured by setting total investment equal to available savings. Investment allocation shares are exogenously set equal to the existing structure of the capital stock. These shares specify the distribution of investment demand by sector of destination. Investment demand by sector of origin is obtained from investment activity by sector of destination using a capital coefficients matrix.[5] Fixed input—output coefficients determine intermediate input demand. The sectoral allocation of private and government consumption reflects fixed expenditure shares.

*2.2.4 Market Clearing Conditions*

The static CGE model finds wages and prices such that labour and product markets clear and the demand for foreign exchange equals supply. A solution represents an economy wide equilibrium in labour, product, and foreign exchange markets, given exogenously specified market constraints and sectoral capital availabilities. The model solution is not a perfectly competitive equilibrium; instead, it represents a market equilibrium solution constrained by behavioural and institutional specifications believed to represent a realistic picture of Indonesia. The base year, in fact, incorporates "disequilibrium" elements: intersectoral wage and profit differentials, external imbalances, and divergences between international and domestic prices. Thus the notion of "general equilibrium" embodied in the current model is more identifiable with Malinvaud (1977, Chapter 1) than with the neoclassical Arrow—Debreu economy. The equilibrium concept is best described as a situation in which, given price rigidities and institutional features, individual decisions have adjusted so as to be mutually consistent.

## 3. THE INDONESIAN ECONOMY IN 1980

### 3.1 Data Requirements for the Model

A data base for a CGE model requires a comprehensive "snapshot" of the economy for a single period.[6] In this paper, the 1980 Social Accounting Matrix (SAM) of Indonesia provides the starting point for a series of experiments that focus on the general equilibrium effects of external price shocks in the two most important tradeable sectors, petroleum and traded agriculture.

This section highlights selected aspects of the CGE model and data. Emphasis is placed on features that are important in the experiments presented in the next section, particularly regarding the distribution of income and the features of the petroleum and traded agriculture sectors.

### 3.2 Labour and Income Distribution

The experiments presented below consider the differential impact on labour and household groups of external shocks in primary commodity prices. In the model, four different types of labour are distinguished: (1) Agricultural workers, including both smallholders (owning less than one—half hectare) and landless labourers; (2) Agricultural proprietors, who are landowners with more than one—half hectare; (3) Low wage workers, composed only of manual and service labourers; and (4) High wage workers, which includes those classified in professional, managerial, clerical and sales positions. The distribution of income by households is generated by mapping the income by labour type into four households, and specifying the distribution of capital and other income as well: (1) Agricultural worker households, whose only source of income are wage payments to agricultural workers; (2) Agricultural owner households, who receive the (imputed) wage income of agricultural proprietors and the profit or rental income from ownership of the capital stock in the two agricultural sectors; (3) Urban worker households, who receive the wage income from low wage labourers; and (4) Urban owner households, who receive the wage payments to high wage labourers, the profits (net corporate income) generated in all non—agricultural sectors, and net remittances from abroad. Tables 1 and 2 show the distribution of income across the four households, and employment by sector

Table 1. Household Income Distribution

|  | Income | Consumption | Savings | Taxes |
|---|---|---|---|---|
| Agricultural Workers | 3.846 | 3.701 | 0.079 | 0.065 |
| Agricultural Owners | 7.829 | 6.808 | 0.841 | 0.180 |
| Urban Workers | 5.984 | 5.443 | 0.410 | 0.132 |
| Urban Owners | 11.299 | 9.649 | 1.378 | 0.271 |
| Total | 28.958 | 25.601 | 2.709 | 0.648 |

Table 2. Employment by Sector and Labour Type

|  | Agri. Workers | Agri. Propri. | Low Wage Workers | High Wage Workers | Total |
|---|---|---|---|---|---|
| Food Agriculture | 15.723 | 7.136 | 0.107 | 0.036 | 23.002 |
| Traded Agriculture | 3.184 | 0.837 | 0.223 | 0.061 | 4.305 |
| Mining and Petroleum |  |  | 0.404 | 0.034 | 0.438 |
| Food Industries |  |  | 1.582 | 0.069 | 1.651 |
| Textiles |  |  | 1.228 | 0.044 | 1.272 |
| Wood Products |  |  | 1.073 | 0.043 | 1.116 |
| Chemicals and Refining |  |  | 0.254 | 0.043 | 0.297 |
| Metal Industries |  |  | 1.160 | 0.092 | 1.252 |
| Utilities |  |  | 0.058 | 0.022 | 0.080 |
| Construction |  |  | 2.420 | 0.069 | 2.489 |
| Trade and Transport |  |  | 2.708 | 9.591 | 12.299 |
| Services |  |  | 5.354 | 3.003 | 8.357 |
| Total | 18.907 | 7.973 | 16.571 | 13.107 | 56.558 |

Table 3. Consumption Shares by Households (Percent)

| Sector | Agri. Workers | Agri. Owners | Urban Workers | Urban Owners |
|---|---|---|---|---|
| Food Agriculture | 35.1 | 29.0 | 12.8 | 7.4 |
| Traded Agriculture | 11.5 | 7.6 | 4.8 | 3.9 |
| Mining and Petroleum | 0.2 | 0.1 | 0.0 | 0.0 |
| Food Industries | 33.5 | 26.7 | 22.5 | 18.7 |
| Textiles | 3.2 | 3.8 | 2.3 | 3.7 |
| Wood Products | 0.3 | 0.5 | 0.8 | 1.1 |
| Chemicals and Refining | 1.3 | 4.0 | 5.9 | 5.2 |
| Metal Industries | 2.6 | 3.3 | 4.4 | 4.6 |
| Utilities | 0.0 | 0.3 | 0.6 | 0.9 |
| Construction | 0.0 | 0.0 | 0.0 | 0.0 |
| Trade and Transport | 5.4 | 12.0 | 29.4 | 38.7 |
| Services | 6.9 | 12.8 | 16.4 | 15.7 |
| Total | 100.0 | 100.0 | 100.0 | 100.0 |

and labour group. Household consumption decisions are based on Cobb–Douglas expenditure elasticities. Table 3 gives consumption patterns for each household type.

## 3.3 The Petroleum Sector

With the OPEC induced rise in oil prices in the 1970s, the Indonesian economy's dependence on the petroleum sector increased substantially. This dependency peaked around 1980, when oil sector income accounted for 68 percent of government revenues, 70 percent of export revenues, and 25 percent of GDP.

This increased oil dependence raised the vulnerability of the economy to changes in world market conditions. Oil income accrues to the government through a complex set of contractual agreements with international oil companies operating in Indonesia, which effectively channel a fixed proportion (between 70–85%) of the net export revenues to the government. However, since this percentage is applied to oil exports *after* oil companies are paid *in kind* for qualifying operating costs (the so–called "cost oil"), the actual government share of revenue from oil exports is lower. In the model, this flow is represented as a tax on the total profit income of the petroleum sector. The tax rate of 52.3 percent yields the actual government oil revenues in 1980, and remains unchanged in all experiments. Because of the strong link between the petroleum sector and the government budget, changes in oil export revenues affect the economy directly through their strong impact on government revenues and (thus) spending. Changes in oil revenues have other effects as well, as lower oil sector influence urban household income.

## 3.4 The Traded Agricultural Sector

The traded agricultural sector, which includes most of Indonesia's major agricultural export products (rubber, vegetable oils, coffee, tea, lumber, fish), was the second largest source of export revenues for Indonesia in 1980, accounting for approximately 12 percent of exports. The sector represented around 10 percent of GDP, and employed 17 percent of the agricultural workers, 10 percent of the agricultural proprietors and small numbers of urban labourers. Unlike the petroleum sector, traded agriculture has no strong link to the government budget, so that changes affecting this sector's export revenues have little direct fiscal effect – the only government revenue received directly from the sector is from the sales tax, with a rate of less than 1 percent. But changed export performance strongly influences rural household incomes for both workers and owners, and thereby has very different distributional consequences from oil sector shocks.

## 3.5 The Government Budget and Balance of Payments

Government expenditure shares are divided exogenously into consumption and investment. Government investment is added to private investment. There are five sources of government revenues in the model: (1) The most important is oil revenues, representing 70 percent of total government revenues, and calculated as an *ad valorem* tax on petroleum sector profits; (2) Personal income taxes are collected on income received by households, with tax rates ranging from 1.7 to 2.4 percent; (3) Corporate income taxes are calculated as a fixed percentage of corporate revenues, which include capital income from the non—agricultural sectors plus net private borrowing from abroad; (4) Import tariffs combine elements of the Indonesian customs duties and certain excise taxes that are levied only on imported goods; and (5) Indirect taxes combine the effect of excise taxes levied on domestic sales net of certain specific sectoral subsidies (fertilizers, oil refining, and others). In 1980, these subsidies exceeded sectoral excise taxes, so the net revenue was in fact negative.

The expenditure and revenue components used in the model are shown in Table 4. The constitutional prohibition on financing deficits through domestic borrowing means that, in practice, the budget is balanced through government borrowing from abroad. For our experiments, the amount of government foreign borrowing is exogenous, so that domestic revenues changes force equivalent expenditure changes.

The balance of payments accounts in 1980 are shown in Table 5. In 1980, at

Table 4. Components of the Government Budget (trillion rupiah)

| Revenues | 9.315 | Expenditures | 9.317 |
|---|---|---|---|
| Oil Revenues | 6.321 | Routine | 5.148 |
| Household Tax | 0.648 | Development | 4.169 |
| Corporate Tax | 0.739 | | |
| Indirect Tax | −0.374 | | |
| Tariff | 0.583 | | |
| Government Borrowing | 1.398 | | |

the height of the oil boom, exports exceeded imports by a substantial margin. Government borrowing was positive, but private capital flows (here labelled remittances and private borrowing) were negative, largely because of repatriation of oil profits and other related capital movements.

Table 5. Balance of Payments Accounts (billion US$)

| | |
|---|---:|
| Oil Exports | 18.073 |
| Non—Oil Exports | 7.705 |
| Total Exports | 25.778 |
| Oil Imports | 1.113 |
| Non—Oil Imports | 14.656 |
| Total Imports | 15.769 |
| Trade Balance | 10.010 |
| Remittances | −3.764 |
| Current Account | 6.246 |
| Government Borrowing | 2.229 |
| Private Borrowing | −3.247 |
| Capital Account | −1.018 |
| Changes in Reserves | −5.228 |
| Exchange Rate | 627 RP/$ |

## 4. THE EFFECTS OF EXTERNAL PRICE SHOCKS

This section reports on comparative statics experiments undertaken to examine the adjustment of the Indonesian economy to a series of external one—way price shocks for its most important export commodities: petroleum and traded agricultural products. The economy adjusts to the new equilibrium in one "period", with the length of the period reflecting specification assumptions (e.g., fixed capital stocks, extent of market clearing and of substitution). We analyse the implication of alternative specifications of foreign exchange and labour markets: fixed versus flexible exchange rates, and fixed versus flexible wages for skilled labour.

## 4.1 External Price Shocks Under Fixed Exchange Rates

In the first set of experiments we examine separately the impact of 20 percent and 50 percent increases and decreases in the world price of oil and traded agricultural products. Employment in each labour category is fixed, implying that all wages are flexible. However, in keeping with Indonesian policy throughout the 1970s and 1980s to date, the exchange rate is controlled by the government as an instrument of trade policy.

### 4.1.1 Macroeconomic Impact of the Shocks

Table 6 summarises the broad impact of the external shocks on the economy. Although the magnitudes of the shocks are quite large, the effect on real GDP is small due to fixed sectoral capital stocks and total employment for each labour type so that the economy operates at "full employment" regardless of the shock. The only real effect on GDP comes from the reallocation of effects of labour moving among sectors, a relatively small effect.

The results clearly suggest that, in a fixed exchange rate regime, the shocks must be absorbed primarily through offsetting changes in foreign savings (changes in reserves), which in turn permit a sizeable adjustment in the balance of trade. In Table 6, the first row shows the "impact" effect of the shock — the loss of export earnings from the initial change in price, assuming no change in the quantity exported.[7] It is interesting that in all scenarios, the loss in the shocked sector's exports after all adjustment has occurred (labelled "Change in Sec Exp") is *greater* in magnitude than the impact effect because the initial impact of the shock is compounded by the price—responsiveness of export supply. Furthermore, aggregate incentives to export and import from other sectors are unchanged, so that there is broad based response to offset the shock. In each case, aggregate exports change by *more* than that occurring in the sector experiencing the price shock, indicating the absence of any offsetting export response; aggregate imports actually rise, compounding the need for adjustment.

Despite broad similarities, the traded agriculture price shocks evoke a different pattern of adjustment than do the oil shocks. The traded agriculture shocks all are magnified much more by the induced export quantity response. The "Change in Sec Exp" for the oil price shocks averages only about 5 percent more than the impact value, while for traded agriculture, the total change is on average 70 percent larger. This difference in part reflects the differing supply elasticities of the two sectors: petroleum production is less responsive to changes

Table 6. The Macroeconomic Impact of Price Shocks: Fixed Exchange Rates

| Variable | Oil Shocks | | | | Traded Agriculture Shocks | | | |
|---|---|---|---|---|---|---|---|---|
| | -20% | -50% | +20% | +50% | -20% | -50% | +20% | +50% |
| Size of Shock (\$) | -3.615 | -9.037 | 3.615 | 9.037 | -0.622 | -1.556 | 0.622 | 1.556 |
| Change in Sec Exp (\$) | -3.820 | -9.401 | 3.906 | 9.943 | -1.064 | -2.377 | 1.152 | 2.998 |
| Change in Tot Exp (\$) | -4.224 | -10.385 | 4.340 | 11.044 | -1.344 | -2.971 | 1.480 | 3.900 |
| Change in Tot Imp (\$) | 0.528 | 1.234 | -0.652 | -1.836 | 0.521 | 1.111 | -0.598 | -1.667 |
| Change in For Sav (\$) | 4.791 | 11.637 | -4.992 | -12.880 | 1.854 | 4.073 | -2.078 | -5.567 |
| Change in For Sav (Rp) | 3.004 | 7.296 | -3.129 | -8.080 | 1.163 | 2.554 | -1.302 | -3.491 |
| Change in Gov Rev (%) | -14.5% | -36.9% | 14.9% | 37.4% | 0.2% | 0.5% | -0.2% | -0.7% |
| Change in Invest (%) | 11.4% | 27.3% | -12.1% | -31.9% | 11.6% | 25.7% | -12.7% | -33.6% |
| Change in GDP (%) | 0.0% | -0.3% | -0.3% | -1.0% | -0.2% | -1.3% | -0.3% | -1.4% |
| Change in CPI (%) | 2.7% | 6.9% | -2.6% | -6.3% | 0.1% | 0.3% | -0.1% | -0.3% |

Table 7. Household Income With Fixed Exchange Rates (Percentage Change From Base)

| Household Type | Oil Shocks | | | | Traded Agriculture | | | |
|---|---|---|---|---|---|---|---|---|
| | -20% | -50% | +20% | +50% | -20% | -50% | +20% | +50% |
| 1 Agricultural Workers | 2.1% | 5.6% | -1.9% | -4.3% | -10.6% | -23.7% | 11.3% | 29.2% |
| 2 Agricultural Owners | 1.7% | 4.6% | -1.6% | -3.6% | -12.9% | -29.0% | 13.8% | 35.4% |
| 3 Urban Workers | 9.5% | 24.4% | -9.1% | -21.4% | 8.0% | 18.6% | -8.1% | -19.7% |
| 4 Urban Owners | 2.8% | 7.5% | -2.3% | -4.8% | 5.3% | 12.2% | -5.4% | -13.3% |
| 5 Total Households | 3.8% | 10.0% | -3.5% | -7.8% | -1.2% | -2.6% | 1.5% | 4.2% |

Table 8. Cost of Living by Households With Fixed Exchange Rates (% Change From Base)

| Household Type | Oil Shocks | | | | Traded Agriculture | | | |
|---|---|---|---|---|---|---|---|---|
| | -20% | -50% | +20% | +50% | -20% | -50% | +20% | +50% |
| 1 Agricultural Workers | 3.1% | 8.2% | -3.0% | -6.9% | -4.3% | -9.7% | 4.5% | 11.8% |
| 2 Agricultural Owners | 3.4% | 8.8% | -3.2% | -7.5% | -2.6% | -6.0% | 2.8% | 7.4% |
| 3 Urban Workers | 3.9% | 10.2% | -3.8% | -8.9% | -0.1% | -0.2% | 0.2% | 0.7% |
| 4 Urban Owners | 4.2% | 10.0% | -4.0% | -9.6% | 0.8% | 2.0% | -0.8% | -1.9% |
| 5 Total Households | 3.8% | 9.8% | -3.6% | -8.5% | -0.9% | -1.6% | 1.3% | 3.9% |

Table 9. Real Consumption by Households With Fixed Exchange Rates (% Change from Base)

| Household Type | Oil Shocks | | | | Traded Agriculture | | | |
|---|---|---|---|---|---|---|---|---|
| | -20% | -50% | +20% | +50% | -20% | -50% | +20% | +50% |
| 1 Agricultural Workers | -0.9% | -2.4% | 1.1% | 2.8% | -6.5% | -15.5% | 6.5% | 15.6% |
| 2 Agricultural Owners | -1.6% | -3.9% | 1.7% | 4.3% | -10.6% | -24.5% | 10.6% | 26.0% |
| 3 Urban Workers | 5.4% | 13.0% | -5.5% | -13.7% | 8.1% | 18.9% | -8.3% | -20.2% |
| 4 Urban Owners | -1.4% | -3.0% | 1.8% | 5.3% | 4.4% | 10.1% | -4.6% | -11.6% |
| 5 Total Households | 0.0% | 0.2% | 0.1% | 0.6% | -0.4% | -1.0% | 0.3% | 0.5% |

in the world price because of the unimportance of variable production costs and the low substitution elasticity.

The fiscal impact of the shocks varies as well. The government budget is virtually unaffected by the price changes for traded agriculture (changes of less than 1 percent), but 50 percent changes in world oil prices cause swings of 37 percent in government revenues. Such swings in government finance, together with the substantial adjustment in foreign savings, lead to questions about the viability of the fixed exchange rate policy with shocks of this magnitude.

In addition to pressures on the government budget and the balance of trade, the oil shocks induce sizeable changes in the overall (CPI) price level.[8] It is interesting that a 20 percent *decline* in oil world prices induces an *increase* in the CPI (of 2.7 percent), despite the downward pressure on domestic oil prices. This indicates that the other sectoral effects are large enough to counteract this downward pressure, as is discussed more fully below.

### 4.1.2 Changes in Sectoral Performance

The major sectoral changes are driven by the channels through which the shock is felt. For example, oil shocks primarily directly affect the government budget, so that government consumption (which is mainly services) drops; correspondingly, with a fixed exchange rate, much of the adjustment comes through increased foreign savings channeled through the capital account into higher investment, which raises demand for investment goods (primarily construction and machinery). Therefore, with a 50 percent oil price decrease, value added in construction rises by over 60 percent and value added in the machinery sector by over 35 percent.

The shocks in traded agriculture are smaller relative to the rest of the economy, and have almost no direct impact on government finance. Instead, the major impact is in the agricultural sectors: traded agriculture becomes less profitable, so rural labour changes to food agriculture, where the resulting supply increase depresses profitability there as well. A negative price shock of 50 percent induces over 15 percent of labourers working in traded agriculture to move to food agriculture. As with the oil price experiment, however, the shocks are financed mostly through foreign savings, so that investment rises and demand for construction and machinery along with it. But the industrial sectors that are downstream from the traded agriculture sector (food, beverages and tobacco, wood and paper, textiles) are most affected by these shocks, with negative price shocks benefitting downstream users, and vice versa. Therefore, those who derive their income from these sectors are most affected as well.

### 4.1.3 Distributional Impact

Urban worker households benefit the most under *negative* oil price shocks. The gain experienced by urban owners reflects the across—the—board increase in the profitability of oil using industrial production as a result of lower domestic oil prices induced by lower world prices. Agricultural and service sectors are far less affected by the lower oil price. The wage bill increases in most industrial sectors, due mostly to the rise in wage rates from increased labour demand; because of the small employment in the oil sector itself, and the low elasticity of supply, there is relatively little labour reallocation from oil to other sectors. In the aggregate, cost of living decreases nearly match incomes falls, so that real consumption is unaffected.[9].

The shocks in the traded agriculture sector reveal a more distinct rural—urban dichotomy. Since negative price shocks lower rural wages and returns to capital for both agricultural sectors, rural workers and owners are both worse off. The income loss is offset to some extent by the drop in the cost of living for rural groups, reflecting the higher share of (cheaper) agricultural products in their consumption bundle. Urban capitalists experience the largest income increase with an adverse shock, but because of different consumption patterns, urban worker households in percentage terms benefit the most in consumption terms.

### 4.2 External Price Shocks Under Flexible Exchange Rates

We now consider the impact of the same set of shocks on the economy under the assumption that foreign savings are fixed at the initial level, and the exchange rate is free to adjust to a new equilibrium.

### 4.2.1 Broadening the Adjustment Base: The Macroeconomic Picture

Because of the economy wide impact of exchange rate changes, permitting the exchange rate to adjust has a profound impact on the macroeconomic and sectoral pattern of adjustment. Table 10 summarises the macroeconomic performance of the experiments.

Exports and imports react differently with a flexible than with a fixed exchange rate. With the flexible exchange rate, the *total* response of exports in the sector experiencing the shock is reduced. While the *impact* effect of the shock

Table 10. The Macroeconomic Impact of Price Shocks With Flexible Exchange Rates

| Variable | | Oil Shocks | | | | Traded Agriculture Shocks | | | |
|---|---|---|---|---|---|---|---|---|---|
| | | -20% | -50% | +20% | +50% | -20% | -50% | +20% | +50% |
| Size of Shock | ($) | -3.615 | -9.037 | 3.615 | 9.037 | -0.622 | -1.556 | 0.622 | 1.556 |
| Change in Sec Exp | ($) | -3.660 | -9.155 | 3.643 | 9.051 | -0.887 | -2.142 | 0.896 | 2.233 |
| Change in Tot Exp | ($) | -1.901 | -4.677 | 2.001 | 5.340 | -0.454 | -1.049 | 0.485 | 1.259 |
| Change in Tot Imp | ($) | -1.932 | -4.694 | 2.000 | 5.338 | -0.444 | -1.041 | 0.486 | 1.260 |
| Change in For Sav | ($) | -0.031 | 0.018 | 0.001 | 0.002 | -0.009 | -0.009 | -0.001 | -0.001 |
| Change in For Sav | (Rp) | -0.523 | -1.422 | 0.476 | 1.108 | -0.209 | -0.518 | 0.193 | 0.465 |
| Change in Nom ER | (%) | 15.9% | 43.4% | -14.5% | -33.8% | 6.4% | 15.8% | -5.9% | -14.2% |
| Change in Real ER | (%) | 3.6% | 10.1% | -3.3% | -7.3% | 4.7% | 11.6% | -4.2% | -9.9% |
| Change in Gov Rev | (%) | -4.8% | -20.1% | 1.0% | -3.0% | 5.2% | 13.1% | -5.0% | -11.8% |
| Change in Invest | (%) | -12.8% | -40.3% | 8.8% | 15.8% | 3.2% | 8.3% | -3.0% | -6.9% |
| Change in GDP | (%) | -0.7% | -3.3% | -0.1% | -1.9% | -0.3% | -1.5% | 0.0% | -0.4% |
| Change in CPI | (%) | 2.9% | 9.0% | -2.1% | -4.2% | 0.1% | 0.1% | 0.0% | -0.2% |

is the same, the subsequent price endogenous response is lessened, because the exchange rate adjustment offsets a portion of the relative price change. This is especially evident with the traded agriculture shocks: with a fixed exchange rate, the total change in traded agricultural exports averaged around 70 percent more than the initial impact; with the flexible exchange rate, this drops to around 40 percent. With the lower responsiveness of oil exports, the exchange rate movement is sufficient to eliminate virtually any price induced export change.

The real divergence from the fixed exchange rate experiments is evident when the movement in aggregate exports and imports is examined. With a flexible exchange rate, foreign savings (in dollars) is unchanged, and since no other components of the capital account adjust, the balance of trade also must stay fixed. Consequently, *the exchange rate adjustment must force sufficient change in aggregate exports and imports to restore the original trade balance.* In Table 10 the total adjustment is split approximately evenly between exports and imports. For example, with a 20 percent decline in oil prices, oil exports decline by around $3.7 billion, which must be matched by a net increase of the same magnitude in the *non—oil* balance of trade. This is accomplished through a *reduction* in total imports of $1.9 billion and an *increase* in non—oil exports of $1.8 billion. This near balance between import and export adjustment is maintained across *all* shocks, both oil and traded agriculture, pointing to another conclusion: with a flexible exchange rate, the sectoral *origin* of the shock is far less important, since movements in the exchange rate spread the adjustment throughout the economy.

As measured by changes in exports, the oil shocks are bigger than the traded agriculture shocks, so it is not surprising that the nominal exchange rate changes required to restore equilibrium are larger for the oil shocks. However, when one adjusts for the underlying world price change (in other words, for the world "inflation" or "deflation") using Indonesian trade weights, the resulting *real* depreciation story is quite similar.

The exchange rate flexibility also affects government revenues and total investment. With the oil shocks, the flexible exchange rate *reduces* significantly the change in government revenues, since exchange rate adjustments dampen the *rupiah* denominated change in oil sector earnings; the percentage swing in revenues is only −20 to +1 percent, as compared to −37 to +37 percent with a fixed exchange rate. However, with traded agriculture shocks, the flexible exchange rate increases the variability of government revenues; the nearly constant government revenues of the fixed exchange rate simulations are replaced by revenue swings of −12 to +13 percent. Note, however, that the fiscal policy swings are countercyclical: a price *decline* in traded agriculture is offset by an *increase* in government revenue, as the exchange rate depreciation raises the rupiah value of oil revenues.

### 4.2.2 Sectoral Trade and Value Added with Flexible Exchange Rates

Tables 11, 12, and 13 summarise the implications for exports, imports, and value added of the external price shocks with both fixed and flexible exchange rates. To reduce the amount of data presented, only the experiments with the 50 percent increase and 50 percent decrease in world prices are shown for each sector.

The pattern of export responses with fixed exchange rates has already been discussed. The biggest changes are in the sectors experiencing the shocks. In other sectors, while there is substantial change in exports compared to the base, the notable feature is that the response in most sectors *reinforces* the shock. Thus, with a 50 percent decline in oil prices, oil exports drop by 52 percent, and exports from all other sectors except chemicals and refining (the major downstream user) drop as well. With a 50 percent fall in traded agriculture prices, the exports of all sectors except food agriculture and food and beverages (again a downstream user) decline. Trade does not reduce the magnitude nor change the direction of the shock.

With flexible exchange rates, this conclusion is reversed. With declines in world prices, the induced exchange rate depreciation evokes an export surge in *all* other sectors, which works to offset the shock. In terms of aggregate export growth, the exchange rate adjustment reduces the impact of the shocks by around 70 percent. With negative oil price shocks, the big winners are the oil using industrial sectors, while with negative traded agriculture shocks, the big winners (in percentage terms) are the food agriculture and food industries sectors.

The data on imports show a parallel story. With fixed exchange rates and a 50 percent oil price decline, imports in all sectors except oil actually rise, and the total import bill increases by $1.3 billion. With a flexible exchange rate, however, imports in all sectors decline, and total imports decrease by $4.7 billion. With a traded agriculture price decline, the fixed exchange rate pattern is mixed, with the largest import sectors (metals industries) experiencing increases, but those sectors linked to agriculture showing falling imports; the aggregate increase in imports is $1.1 billion. With the flexible exchange rate, though, all sectors

Table 11. Sectoral Value of Exports (Billion US$)

| Sectors | Base | Oil Shocks | | | | Traded Agriculture Shocks | | | |
|---|---|---|---|---|---|---|---|---|---|
| | | Fixed ER | | Flexible ER | | Fixed ER | | Flexible ER | |
| | | -50% | +50% | -50% | +50% | -50% | +50% | -50% | +50% |
| Food Agriculture | 0.070 | 0.062 | 0.078 | 0.104 | 0.037 | 0.105 | 0.048 | 0.148 | 0.038 |
| Traded Agriculture | 3.112 | 2.821 | 3.399 | 4.008 | 1.923 | 0.735 | 6.110 | 0.970 | 5.345 |
| Mining & Petroleum | 18.073 | 8.672 | 28.017 | 8.918 | 27124 | 17.954 | 18.258 | 18.123 | 18.011 |
| Food Industries | 0.167 | 0.137 | 0.201 | 0.279 | 0.075 | 0.193 | 0.140 | 0.281 | 0.104 |
| Textiles | 0.126 | 0.099 | 0.159 | 0.228 | 0.054 | 0.115 | 0.140 | 0.164 | 0.094 |
| Wood Products | 0.249 | 0.187 | 0.335 | 0.537 | 0.096 | 0.233 | 0.265 | 0.367 | 0.169 |
| Chemicals & Refining | 1.172 | 1.195 | 1.094 | 1.782 | 0.662 | 1.091 | 1.290 | 1.278 | 1.053 |
| Metal Industries | 0.641 | 0.544 | 0.750 | 1.150 | 0.324 | 0.544 | 0.791 | 0.716 | 0.557 |
| Utilities | - | - | - | - | - | - | - | - | - |
| Construction | - | - | - | - | - | - | - | - | - |
| Trade & Transport | 2.118 | 1.640 | 2.724 | 3.998 | 0.805 | 1.797 | 2.571 | 2.624 | 1.628 |
| Services | 0.049 | 0.037 | 0.065 | 0.097 | 0.018 | 0.040 | 0.064 | 0.059 | 0.038 |
| All Sectors | 25.777 | 15.393 | 36.822 | 21.101 | 31.118 | 22.807 | 29.677 | 24.729 | 27.037 |

Percentage Change From Base

| Sectors | Oil Shocks | | | | Traded Agriculture Shocks | | | |
|---|---|---|---|---|---|---|---|---|
| | Fixed ER | | Flexible ER | | Fixed ER | | Flexible ER | |
| | -50% | +50% | -50% | +50% | -50% | +50% | -50% | +50% |
| Food Agriculture | -11.4% | 11.4% | 48.6% | -47.1% | 50.0% | -31.4% | 111.4% | -45.7% |
| Traded Agriculture | -9.4% | 9.2% | 28.8% | -38.2% | -76.4% | 96.3% | -68.8% | 71.8% |
| Mining & Petroleum | -52.0% | 55.0% | -50.7% | 50.1% | -0.7% | 1.0% | 0.3% | -0.3% |
| Food Industries | -18.0% | 20.4% | 67.1% | -55.1% | 15.6% | -16.2% | 68.3% | -37.7% |
| Textiles | -21.4% | 26.2% | 81.0% | -57.1% | -8.7% | 11.1% | 30.2% | -25.4% |
| Wood Products | -24.9% | 34.5% | 115.7% | -61.4% | -6.4% | 6.4% | 47.4% | -32.1% |
| Chemicals & Refining | 2.0% | -6.7% | 52.0% | -43.5% | -6.9% | 10.1% | 9.0% | -10.2% |
| Metal Industries | -15.2% | 17.0% | 79.4% | -49.5% | -15.1% | 23.4% | 11.7% | -13.1% |
| Utilities | - | - | - | - | - | - | - | - |
| Construction | - | - | - | - | - | - | - | - |
| Trade & Transport | -22.6% | 28.6% | 88.8% | -62.0% | -15.2% | 21.4% | 23.9% | -23.1% |
| Services | -24.5% | 32.7% | 98.0% | -63.3% | -18.4% | 30.6% | 20.4% | -22.4% |
| All Sectors | -40.3% | 42.8% | -18.1% | 20.7% | -11.5% | 15.1% | -4.1% | 4.8% |

Table 12. Sectoral Value of Imports (Billion US$)

| Sectors | Base | Oil Shocks | | | | Traded Agriculture Shocks | | | |
|---|---|---|---|---|---|---|---|---|---|
| | | Fixed ER | | Flexible ER | | Fixed ER | | Flexible ER | |
| | | -50% | +50% | -50% | +50% | -50% | +50% | -50% | +50% |
| Food Agriculture | 0.239 | 0.254 | 0.229 | 0.199 | 0.323 | 0.211 | 0.273 | 0.183 | 0.301 |
| Traded Agriculture | 0.292 | 0.321 | 0.264 | 0.224 | 0.435 | 0.269 | 0.336 | 0.217 | 0.389 |
| Mining & Petroleum | 1.111 | 0.572 | 1.506 | 0.545 | 1.609 | 1.128 | 1.073 | 1.115 | 1.103 |
| Food Industries | 1.046 | 1.154 | 0.958 | 0.756 | 1.682 | 0.977 | 1.144 | 0.783 | 1.363 |
| Textiles | 0.184 | 0.200 | 0.170 | 0.135 | 0.287 | 0.178 | 0.192 | 0.147 | 0.229 |
| Wood Products | 0.246 | 0.295 | 0.196 | 0.152 | 0.403 | 0.271 | 0.213 | 0.213 | 0.289 |
| Chemicals & Refining | 3.611 | 3.844 | 3.336 | 2.943 | 4.574 | 0.748 | 3.406 | 3.395 | 3.871 |
| Metal Industries | 7.364 | 8.575 | 5.696 | 4.764 | 9.611 | 8.372 | 5.841 | 7.134 | 7.649 |
| Utilities | - | - | - | - | - | - | - | - | - |
| Construction | - | - | - | - | - | - | - | - | - |
| Trade & Transport | 0.488 | 0.530 | 0.447 | 0.364 | 0.662 | 0.518 | 0.450 | 0.451 | 0.531 |
| Services | 1.188 | 1.255 | 1.129 | 0.991 | 1.520 | 1.208 | 1.174 | 1.088 | 1.305 |
| All Sectors | 15.769 | 17.002 | 13.931 | 11.074 | 21.106 | 16.879 | 14.102 | 14.727 | 17.030 |

Percentage Growth From Base

| Sectors | Oil Shocks | | | | Traded Agriculture Shocks | | | |
|---|---|---|---|---|---|---|---|---|
| | Fixed ER | | Flexible ER | | Fixed ER | | Flexible ER | |
| | -50% | +50% | -50% | +50% | -50% | +50% | -50% | +50% |
| Food Agriculture | 6.2% | -4.2% | -16.7% | 35.1% | -11.7% | 14.2% | -23.4% | 25.9% |
| Traded Agriculture | 9.9% | -9.6% | -23.3% | 49.0% | -7.9% | 15.1% | -25.7% | 33.2% |
| Mining & Petroleum | -48.5% | 35.6% | -50.9% | 44.8% | 1.5% | -3.4% | 0.4% | -0.7% |
| Food Industries | 10.3% | -8.4% | -27.7% | 60.8% | -6.6% | 9.4% | -25.1% | 30.3% |
| Textiles | 8.7% | -7.6% | -26.6% | 56.0% | -3.3% | 4.3% | -20.1% | 24.5% |
| Wood Products | 19.9% | -20.3% | -38.2% | 63.8% | 10.2% | -13.4% | 13.4% | 17.5% |
| Chemicals & Refining | 6.4% | -7.6% | -18.5% | 26.7% | 3.8% | -5.7% | -6.0% | 7.2% |
| Metal Industries | 16.4% | -22.7% | -35.3% | 30.5% | 13.7% | -20.7% | -3.1% | 3.9% |
| Utilities | - | - | - | - | - | - | - | - |
| Construction | - | - | - | - | - | - | - | - |
| Trade & Transport | 8.6% | -8.4% | -25.4% | 35.87% | 6.1% | -7.8% | -7.6% | 8.8% |
| Services | 5.6% | -5.0% | -16.6% | 27.9% | 1.7% | -1.2% | -8.4% | 9.8% |
| All Sectors | 7.8% | -11.7% | -29.8 | 33.8% | 7.0% | -10.6% | -6.6% | 8.0% |

Table 13. Sectoral Value Added (Trillion Rupiah)

| Sectors | Base | Oil Shocks | | | | Traded Agriculture Shocks | | | |
|---|---|---|---|---|---|---|---|---|---|
| | | Fixed ER | | Flexible ER | | Fixed ER | | Flexible ER | |
| | | -50% | +50% | -50% | +50% | -50% | +50% | -50% | +50% |
| Food Agriculture | 7.247 | 7.761 | 6.860 | 8.329 | 6.963 | 6.060 | 8.746 | 5.861 | 8.415 |
| Traded Agriculture | 4.568 | 4.633 | 4.506 | 6.491 | 3.299 | 2.515 | 7.025 | 2.653 | 6.037 |
| Mining & Petroleum | 12.427 | 5.398 | 19.528 | 8.388 | 12.323 | 12.310 | 12.541 | 14.535 | 10.519 |
| Food Industries | 1.503 | 1.756 | 1.284 | 1.337 | 1.826 | 1.791 | 1.231 | 1.632 | 1.444 |
| Textiles | 0.564 | 0.628 | 0.511 | 0.596 | .614 | 0.576 | 0.552 | 0.551 | 0.583 |
| Wood Products | 0.445 | 0.523 | 0.371 | 0.517 | 0.446 | 0.529 | 0.345 | 0.539 | 0.390 |
| Chemicals & Refining | 1.336 | 2.108 | 0.675 | 2.688 | 0.811 | 1.401 | 1.247 | 1.472 | 1.220 |
| Metal Industries | 1.484 | 2.038 | 0.888 | 1.262 | 1.489 | 1.851 | 1.013 | 1.646 | 1.353 |
| Utilities | 0.230 | 0.272 | 0.192 | 0.203 | 0.282 | 0.256 | 0.201 | 0.228 | 0.237 |
| Construction | 2.456 | 3.989 | 1.118 | 0.893 | 3.958 | 3.704 | 1.175 | 2.586 | 2.395 |
| Trade & Transport | 9.313 | 10.536 | 8.278 | 9.889 | 10.260 | 10.310 | 8.221 | 9.959 | 8.938 |
| Services | 7.141 | 8.148 | 6.276 | 7.056 | 7.980 | 7.642 | 6.615 | 7.130 | 7.244 |
| All Sectors | 48.714 | 47.791 | 50.487 | 47.651 | 50.251 | 48.945 | 48.912 | 48.792 | 48.775 |

Percentage Composition

| Sectors | Base | Oil Shocks | | | | Traded Agriculture Shocks | | | |
|---|---|---|---|---|---|---|---|---|---|
| | | Fixed ER | | Flexible ER | | Fixed ER | | Flexible ER | |
| | | -50% | +50% | -50% | +50% | -50% | +50% | -50% | +50% |
| Food Agriculture | 14.8% | 16.2% | 13.6% | 17.5% | 13.9% | 12.4% | 17.9% | 12.0% | 17.3% |
| Traded Agriculture | 9.4% | 9.7% | 8.9% | 13.6% | 6.6% | 5.1% | 14.4% | 5.4% | 12.4% |
| Mining & Petroleum | 25.5% | 11.3% | 38.7% | 17.6% | 24.5% | 25.1% | 25.6% | 29.8% | 21.6% |
| Food Industries | 3.1% | 3.7% | 2.5% | 2.8% | 3.6% | 3.7% | 2.5% | 3.3% | 3.0% |
| Textiles | 1.2% | 1.3% | 1.0% | 1.3% | 1.2% | 1.2% | 1.1% | 1.1% | 1.2% |
| Wood Products | 0.9% | 1.1% | 0.7% | 1.1% | 0.9% | 1.1% | 0.7% | 1.1% | 0.8% |
| Chemicals & Refining | 2.7% | 4.4% | 1.3% | 5.6% | 1.6% | 2.9% | 2.5% | 3.0% | 2.5% |
| Metal Industries | 3.0% | 4.3% | 1.8% | 2.6% | 3.0% | 3.8% | 2.1% | 3.4% | 2.8% |
| Utilities | 0.5% | 0.6% | 0.4% | 0.4% | 0.6% | 0.5% | 0.4% | 0.5% | 0.5% |
| Construction | 5.0% | 8.3% | 2.2% | 1.9% | 7.9% | 7.6% | 2.4% | 5.3% | 4.9% |
| Trade & Transport | 19.1% | 22.0% | 16.4% | 20.8% | 20.4% | 21.1% | 16.8% | 20.4% | 18.3% |
| Services | 14.7% | 17.0% | 12.4% | 14.8% | 15.9% | 15.6% | 13.5% | 14.6% | 14.9% |
| All Sectors | 100.0% | 100.0% | 100.0% | 100.0% | 100.0% | 100.0% | 100.0% | 100.0% | 100.0% |

80

(except oil) show declining imports, with a drop in the total of $1.1 billion.

The data on value added reinforce an earlier point: a flexible exchange rate allows the adjustment to external shocks to be more evenly distributed across sectors in the economy. Looking at the data on oil shocks in Table 13, *aggregate* value added is not affected very much by the exchange rate specification. However, the sectoral pattern of value added is affected: with the fixed exchange rate, almost all of the structural change occurs in the share of the petroleum sector in the total, which falls to 11 percent and rises to 39 percent from its initial share of 26 percent. Most other sectors change their shares by only a few percentage points in order to compensate. With a flexible exchange rate, the swings in oil sector value added are nearly eliminated, and the sectors which benefit the most (with an oil price decline) are the other big export sectors – traded agriculture and chemicals and refining.

### 4.2.3 Distributional Implications of Flexible Exchange Rates

The switch from fixed to flexible exchange rates has a significant effect on distribution as well. Because exchange rate movements have such far reaching effects on the domestic economy in terms of output, exports, trade, and relative prices, many of the earlier distributional results with the fixed exchange rate are modified or reversed.

Tables 14, 15, and 16 contain information on household income, cost of living, and consumption for the flexible exchange rate experiments. The most striking result is that the pattern of winners and losers is altered. With negative oil sector shocks and a fixed exchange rate, nominal incomes for all household groups rise. In consumption terms, low wage workers gain, other groups lose, and there is little aggregate effect. With a flexible exchange rate, urban households (workers and owners) lose, rural households gain, and overall there is a 1 percent increase in nominal incomes. In consumption terms, urban households lose significantly (over 20 percent with a 50 percent price drop), rural households gain, and overall, real consumption drops by 8 percent. In macroeconomic terms, this decline comes because foreign savings remain fixed so that (unlike the fixed exchange rate experiments) the outside world does not finance the earnings loss associated with the shock.

With traded agriculture shocks, the distributional consequences are much more similar to the corresponding experiments with the fixed exchange rate. The pattern of winners and losers is unchanged: with negative price shocks, rural

Table 14. Household Income With Flexible Exchange Rate (Percentage Change From Base)

| Household Type | Oil Shocks | | | | Traded Agriculture | | | |
|---|---|---|---|---|---|---|---|---|
| | -20% | -50% | +20% | +50% | -20% | -50% | +20% | +50% |
| 1 Agricultural Workers | 7.2% | 22.0% | -5.4% | -10.1% | -9.7% | -25.0% | 8.8% | 20.3% |
| 2 Agricultural Owners | 9.2% | 27.0% | -7.3% | -14.5% | -11.3% | -29.3% | 10.1% | 23.2% |
| 3 Urban Workers | -6.4% | -12.4% | 7.6% | 19.5% | 1.7% | 4.9% | -1.3% | -2.5% |
| 4 Urban Owners | -7.2% | -16.0% | 8.1% | 20.7% | 1.4% | 4.2% | -1.0% | -1.9% |
| 5 Total Households | 0.7% | 1.3% | 2.0% | 6.9% | -3.4% | -8.6% | 3.3% | 7.7% |

Table 15. Cost of Living by Households With Flexible Exchange Rates (% Change From Base)

| Household Type | Oil Shocks | | | | Traded Agriculture | | | |
|---|---|---|---|---|---|---|---|---|
| | -20% | -50% | +20% | +50% | -20% | -50% | +20% | +50% |
| 1 Agricultural Workers | 4.4% | 14.4% | -3.1% | -5.4% | -4.4% | -11.3% | 3.9% | 9.0% |
| 2 Agricultural Owners | 3.8% | 12.9% | -2.5% | -4.1% | -3.0% | -7.7% | 2.7% | 6.2% |
| 3 Urban Workers | 2.6% | 9.7% | -1.3% | -1.4% | -1.0% | -2.4% | 0.9% | 2.2% |
| 4 Urban Owners | 2.0% | 8.1% | -0.7% | 0.1% | -0.3% | -0.6% | 0.3% | 0.8% |
| 5 Total Households | 3.0% | 11.0% | -1.6% | -1.9% | -1.7% | -3.9% | 1.6% | 3.9% |

Table 16. Real Consumption by Households With Flexible Exchange Rates (% Change From Base)

| Household Type | Oil Shocks | | | | Traded Agriculture | | | |
|---|---|---|---|---|---|---|---|---|
| | -20% | -50% | +20% | +50% | -20% | -50% | +20% | +50% |
| 1 Agricultural Workers | 2.7% | 6.6% | -2.4% | -4.9% | -5.5% | -15.4% | 4.7% | 10.3% |
| 2 Agricultural Owners | 5.2% | 12.5% | -4.9% | -10.8% | -8.5% | -23.4% | 7.3% | 16.1% |
| 3 Urban Workers | -8.8% | -20.2% | 9.0% | 21.2% | 2.6% | 7.5% | -2.1% | -4.6% |
| 4 Urban Owners | -9.1% | -22.3% | 8.9% | 20.6% | 1.7% | 4.9% | -1.3% | -2.7% |
| 5 Total Households | -3.6% | -8.4% | 3.6% | 8.7% | -1.8% | -5.0% | 1.7% | 3.8% |

households lose (about the same amount), urban households gain (not nearly as much), and aggregate income is subject to wider swings. As with the oil sector shocks, real consumption declines, again because foreign savings is not available to finance the earnings loss from negative price shocks.

## 4.3 Wage Rigidities and External Shocks

It is frequently argued that the process of adjustment to external shocks is complicated by the existence of wage rigidities, most frequently in the formal or highly skilled categories. To explore this issue, we present simulations in which for the high wage labour category the nominal wage is fixed and aggregate employment in this category can vary. We limit our examination of wage rigidities to the flexible exchange rate case, and only consider the response to oil sector shocks, because these are larger and affect the high wage labour more directly than similar shocks in the traded agriculture sector.

### 4.3.1 Macroeconomic Adjustment

The basic effect of wage rigidity is to make other aspects of the economy adjust more, both positively and negatively, than otherwise would be required. The adjustment is forced particularly onto employment of high wage labour, the wages of other labour groups, and the income accruing to capital.

Table 17 summarises certain features of the fixed wage experiments, and compares them to the corresponding flexible wage results presented earlier. From the macroeconomic perspective, the major difference between the two is in the high wage employment and wage rates; there is relatively little movement in other aggregate indicators such as GDP, exports, or imports, although in the 50 percent price rise experiment, there is a 1.6 percent GDP effect. An unusual asymmetric response occurs in the flexible wage experiments: regardless of the direction or size of the shock, real GDP declines, suggesting that under certain conditions, any type shock can be detrimental.

### 4.3.2 Sectoral Employment Adjustment to Wage Rigidities

The trade and transport and service sectors account for nearly all of the high wage employment, and it is employment in these sectors that is affected most by the fixed wage specification (Tables 18 and 19). With the 50 percent positive shock, for example, total high wage employment rises by around 1.2 million workers, with .85 million added to trade and transport, and .32 million added to

Table 17. The Macroeconomic Impact of Price Shocks With Fixed Wages

|  |  | Oil Shocks | | | | Oil Shocks | | | |
|  |  | Flex. Exchange Rate, Flex. Wage | | | | Flex. Exchange Rate, Fixed Wage | | | |
| Variable |  | -20% | -50% | +20% | +50% | -20% | -50% | +20% | +50% |
|---|---|---|---|---|---|---|---|---|---|
| Size of Shock | ($) | -3.615 | -9.037 | 3.615 | 9.037 | -3.615 | -9.037 | 0.622 | 1.556 |
| Change in Sec Exp | ($) | -3.660 | -9.155 | 3.643 | 9.051 | -3.659 | -9.158 | 3.641 | 9.049 |
| Change in Tot Exp | ($) | -1.901 | -4.677 | 2.001 | 5.340 | -1.909 | -4.555 | 2.061 | 5.500 |
| Change in Tot Imp | ($) | -1.932 | -4.694 | 2.000 | 5.338 | -1.939 | -4.574 | 2.060 | 5.498 |
| Change in GDP | (%) | -0.7% | -3.0% | -0.1% | -1.9% | -0.7% | -2.6% | 0.3% | -0.3% |
| Changes in: |  |  |  |  |  |  |  |  |  |
| High Wage Employ | (%) | 0.0% | 0.0% | 0.0% | 0.0% | -0.4% | 5.0% | 2.6% | 8.9% |
| High Wage Rate | (%) | -0.0% | 4.6% | 2.9% | 10.4% | 0.0% | 0.0% | 0.0% | 0.0% |
| Low Wage Rate | (%) | -4.7% | -7.8% | 6.1% | 16.3% | -4.7% | -7.2% | 6.4% | 16.9% |

85

Table 18. Low Wage Employment by Sector (Million Workers)

| Sectors | Base | Oil Shocks - Flexible Wage | | | | Oil Shocks - Fixed Wage | | | |
|---|---|---|---|---|---|---|---|---|---|
| | | -20% | -50% | +20% | +50% | -20% | -50% | +20% | +50% |
| Food Agriculture | 0.107 | 0.118 | 0.134 | 0.098 | 0.089 | 0.117 | 0.134 | 0.099 | 0.090 |
| Traded Agriculture | 0.223 | 0.269 | 0.343 | 0.182 | 0.138 | 0.269 | 0.342 | 0.183 | 0.142 |
| Mining & Petroleum | 0.404 | 0.388 | 0.296 | 0.391 | 0.345 | 0.388 | 0.294 | 0.393 | 0.352 |
| Food Industries | 1.582 | 1.559 | 1.532 | 1.611 | 1.647 | 1.559 | 1.536 | 1.612 | 1.657 |
| Textiles | 1.228 | 1.290 | 1.412 | 1.184 | 1.151 | 1.290 | 1.415 | 1.187 | 1.159 |
| Wood Products | 1.073 | 1.162 | 1.357 | 1.004 | 0.927 | 1.161 | 1.365 | 1.011 | 0.947 |
| Chemicals & Refining | 0.254 | 0.349 | 0.556 | 0.189 | 0.133 | 0.349 | 0.557 | 0.191 | 0.137 |
| Metal Industries | 1.160 | 1.162 | 1.069 | 1.115 | 1.001 | 1.161 | 1.085 | 1.126 | 1.040 |
| Utilities | 0.058 | 0.057 | 0.055 | 0.059 | 0.061 | 0.057 | 0.056 | 0.059 | 0.061 |
| Construction | 2.420 | 1.868 | 0.954 | 2.877 | 3.354 | 1.865 | 0.985 | 2.905 | 3.470 |
| Trade & Transport | 2.708 | 2.848 | 3.119 | 2.618 | 2.566 | 2.848 | 3.134 | 2.610 | 2.524 |
| Services | 5.354 | 5.501 | 5.745 | 5.242 | 5.150 | 5.507 | 5.668 | 5.196 | 4.993 |
| All Sectors | 16.571 | 16.571 | 16.572 | 16.570 | 16.572 | 16.571 | 16.571 | 16.572 | 16.572 |

Table 19. High Wage Employment by Sector (Million Workers)

| Sectors | Base | Oil Shocks - Flexible Wage | | | | Oil Shocks - Fixed Wage | | | |
|---|---|---|---|---|---|---|---|---|---|
| | | -20% | -50% | +20% | +50% | -20% | -50% | +20% | +50% |
| Food Agriculture | 0.036 | 0.038 | 0.040 | 0.034 | 0.031 | 0.037 | 0.042 | 0.035 | 0.035 |
| Traded Agriculture | 0.061 | 0.071 | 0.083 | 0.052 | 0.040 | 0.070 | 0.087 | 0.054 | 0.046 |
| Mining & Petroleum | 0.034 | 0.032 | 0.022 | 0.034 | 0.031 | 0.031 | 0.023 | 0.035 | 0.035 |
| Food Industries | 0.069 | 0.065 | 0.059 | 0.072 | 0.076 | 0.064 | 0.062 | 0.074 | 0.084 |
| Textiles | 0.044 | 0.045 | 0.045 | 0.044 | 0.044 | 0.044 | 0.047 | 0.046 | 0.049 |
| Wood Products | 0.043 | 0.045 | 0.048 | 0.042 | 0.039 | 0.044 | 0.051 | 0.043 | 0.044 |
| Chemicals & Refining | 0.043 | 0.057 | 0.084 | 0.033 | 0.024 | 0.057 | 0.088 | 0.034 | 0.027 |
| Metal Industries | 0.092 | 0.088 | 0.075 | 0.091 | 0.084 | 0.088 | 0.080 | 0.095 | 0.096 |
| Utilities | 0.022 | 0.020 | 0.018 | 0.023 | 0.024 | 0.020 | 0.019 | 0.023 | 0.027 |
| Construction | 0.069 | 0.051 | 0.024 | 0.085 | 0.101 | 0.051 | 0.026 | 0.088 | 0.116 |
| Trade & Transport | 9.591 | 9.647 | 9.762 | 9.565 | 9.572 | 9.609 | 10.288 | 9.824 | 10.441 |
| Services | 3.003 | 2.951 | 2.848 | 3.033 | 3.043 | 2.943 | 2.947 | 3.097 | 3.271 |
| All Sectors | 13.107 | 13.110 | 13.108 | 13.108 | 13.109 | 13.058 | 13.760 | 13.448 | 14.271 |

services. The only other sizeable change is in construction, where the investment effect noted earlier leads to a 70 percent increase in high wage employment, and a similar percentage rise in low wage employment.

The fixed wage also has implications for the allocation of low wage labour. In the higher oil price cases, the increase in high wage labourers in trade and services lowers the demand by these sectors for the low wage substitute, so that additional low wage labourers are released for employment in other sectors.

### 4.3.3 Distributional Consequences of Wage Rigidities

The pattern of distributional adjustment across households changes little with a fixed wage (Table 20). Urban workers do a little worse with an oil price drop, and most others do a little better than with flexible wages. Both household incomes and real consumption adjustment patterns are similar. The mix of income sources to the urban owner household changes somewhat (with capital income declining less and wage income increasing more), as does how much each worker within these households receives.[10]

## 5. IMPACT OF COMMODITY PRICE FLUCTUATIONS

The previous section considers the impact of one—way movements in world oil or traded agriculture prices on various dimensions of the performance of the Indonesian economy. Some of these effects are considerable, though of course they depend on details of scenario specification, particularly exchange rate policy. But that does *not* necessarily mean that there are high costs to primary commodity instability to Indonesia. Losses and gains in an international primary commodity price bust might be offset during a boom. To see if commodity price fluctuations are likely to be costly in terms of observed variables, we must consider the impact over a cycle with equal price increases and price decreases from the underlying secular path.[11]

Therefore we reconsider the simulations discussed in Section 4 by asking to what extent the impact of oil and traded agriculture price booms and busts offset each other. To the extent that they do, conditional on the model specification, there are less likely to be high costs to international primary commodity fluctuations. To explore this question, following Adams and Behrman's (1982) analysis of macroeconomic models, we compare the effects for downward and upward price shocks to see whether one or the other dominates in absolute magnitude, without concern about which direction of shock occurs first since we

Table 20. Distributional Impact of Shocks With Fixed Wages

|  | Oil Shocks | | | | Oil Shocks | | | |
|  | Flex. Exchange Rate, Flex. Wage | | | | Flex. Exchange Rate, Fixed Wage | | | |
| Variable | -20% | -50% | +20% | +50% | -20% | -50% | +20% | +50% |
|---|---|---|---|---|---|---|---|---|
| Agricultural Workers (%) | 7.2% | 22.0% | -5.4% | -10.1% | 7.2% | 22.9% | -4.8% | -7.9% |
| Agricultural Owners (%) | 9.2% | 27.0% | -7.3% | -14.5% | 9.1% | 27.8% | -6.7% | -12.3% |
| Urban Workers (%) | -6.4% | -12.4% | 7.6% | 19.5% | -6.5% | -11.8% | 7.9% | 20.5% |
| Urban Owners (%) | -7.2% | -16.0% | 8.1% | 20.7% | -7.2% | -15.4% | 8.0% | 20.0% |
| Capital Income (%) | -18.3% | -48.0% | 16.6% | 38.3% | -18.3% | -46.8% | 17.1% | 39.1% |
| Wage Income (%) | -0.9% | 2.2% | 3.3% | 10.7% | -0.9% | 2.4% | 2.8% | 9.1% |
| Total Households (%) | -0.7% | 1.3% | 2.0% | 6.9% | -0.7% | 2.1% | 2.3% | 7.7% |

are interested in the expected impact of both a boom and a bust in whatever order. To focus on the impact of fluctuations, we assume that the secular price trend is known, so that we can abstract from errors in identifying that trend which might cause commitment to policies (and therefore an economic structure) inappropriate to the actual trend.

For the fixed exchange rate flexible wage case a 50 percent oil price cycle is simulated to reduce GDP by −1.3 percent and investment by −4.6 percent, and to increase government revenues by 0.5 percent, foreign reserves by $1.2 billion, the CPI by 0.6 percent, and real consumption by 0.8 percent (with urban worker households losing −0.7 percent, but the others gaining). A 50 percent traded agriculture price cycle is simulated to reduce GDP by −2.7 percent, investment by −7.9 percent, government revenues by −0.2 percent, real consumption by −0.5 percent (with all urban households losing) and to increase foreign reserves by $1.0 billion, with no impact on the CPI.

For the flexible exchange rate flexible wage case, a 50 percent oil price cycle is simulated to reduce GDP by −5.2 percent, investment by −24.5 percent, and government revenue by −23.1 percent and to increase real household consumption by 0.3 percent (with urban owners the only losers) and the nominal exchange rate by 9.6 percent. A 50 percent traded agriculture cycle is simulated to reduce GDP by −1.9 percent, the CPI by −0.1 percent, household real consumption by −1.2 percent (with agriculture households losing and urban households gaining), and to increase investment by 1.4 percent and government revenue by 1.3 percent.

For the flexible exchange rate fixed high wage rate case, a 50 percent oil price cycle is simulated to reduce GDP by −2.9 percent, the exchange rate by −2.4 percent, and investment by −0.8 percent and to increase employment by 1.1 percent and real household consumption by 9.8 percent (with all households gaining).

These simulations suggest five summary remarks about the impact of primary commodity price instabilities on Indonesia. First, in some important ways these simulations understate the costs (e.g., by ignoring adjustment costs and risk aversion) and in some ways they overstate the costs (e.g., by ignoring smoothing over the cycle by inventory holdings and by understating smoothing through capital markets), but we have no way of knowing which of these effects is bigger. Second, they suggest that there are some measurable impacts in terms of observed variables,[12] which seems to support the possibility of legitimate concern about such instabilities more than do many earlier studies reviewed in Behrman (1987). Perhaps the explicit specification of production relations, labour supply constraints, and limited substitutability in production and in transformation between goods for domestic versus international markets leads to effects that might be obscured in more ad hoc macroeconometric models, though we are not aware of the use of such models for exploring this question for Indonesia. Third, this impact results from asymmetries in expanding versus reducing output due to fixed sectoral capital stocks, fixed aggregate labour supplies, and limited substitution possibilities in production and in use. In the fixed wage simulation there is an added asymmetry due to the rigid wage for high wage workers, which results in a larger impact of price fluctuations on some important outcomes (e.g., GDP). Fourth, in no case is the price instability impact only good or only bad. Usually GDP and investment are reduced, but usually real consumption and foreign reserves (with a fixed exchange rate) are increased. Therefore one has to make tradeoffs in assessing whether the outcomes are preferable with or without more stable prices. Fifth, though fixed versus flexible exchange rates (with our concomitant assumptions about foreign savings) lead to different outcomes due to the price cycles, there is not a clear cut indication that one dominates in this regard. For the oil price shock cycle, the fixed exchange rate seems to lead to the better set of outcomes, but the opposite is the case for the traded agriculture price shock cycle.

## APPENDIX A: EQUATIONS OF THE MODEL

### A.1 Introduction

In this appendix, we present a mathematical description of our Indonesian CGE model. Endogenous variables are denoted by names in capital letters. Lower case names are exogenous variables or parameters. Certain variables that can be endogenous, but which in the current version are exogenous, are shown as capital letters with a bar over them. The subscripts i and j refer to sectors, the subscript k refers to labour categories, and the subscript g refers to consumer groups.

### A.2 Prices

$$PM_i = pwm_i(1+tm_i)ER \qquad (1)$$
$$PE_i = pwe_i(1+te_i)ER \qquad (2)$$
$$P_i = (PD_i * XXD_i + PM_i * M_i)/X_i \qquad (3)$$

$$PX_i = (PD_i * XXD_i + PE_i * E_i)/XD_i \tag{4}$$
$$PV_i = PX_i(1-tx_i) - \Sigma_j aa_{ji}P_j \tag{5}$$
$$PK_i = \Sigma_j bb_{ji}P_j \tag{6}$$
$$plev = \Sigma\Omega_i PD_i \tag{7}$$

Endogenous Variables:

$PM_i$ : domestic price of imports

$PE_i$ : domestic price of exports

$P_i$ : composite good price

$PX_i$ : average price of domestic sales

$PV_i$ : value added (or net) price

$PK_i$ : price of composite capital good

$PD_i$ : domestic price of domestic output

$X_i$ : sectoral composite demand

$XD_i$ : sectoral domestic output

$XXD_i$ : domestic demand for production

$M_i$ : imports

$E_i$ : exports

Exogenous Variables

ER : exchange rate

$pwm_i$ : world price of imports

$pwe_i$ : world price of exports

$tm_i$ : tariff rate

$te_i$ : export subsidy rate

$tx_i$ : indirect tax rate

$aa_{ij}$ : input–output coefficients

$bb_{ij}$ : composite capital good coefficients

$\Omega_i$ : aggregate price index weights

plev : exogenous level of index of domestic prices

## A.3 Production, Employment, and Final Demand

$$XD_i = \alpha x_i \ast_k (L_{ik}{}^{\tau ik}) * K_i^{(1-\Sigma_j \tau_{ik})} \tag{8}$$
$$L_{ik} = (XD_i * PV_i * \tau_{ik})/(W_k * gam_{ik}) \tag{9}$$
$$LS_k = \Sigma_i L_{ik} \tag{10}$$

92

$$XD_i = \alpha t_i [\beta t_i^{\delta t_i} E_i + (1-\beta t_i)^{\delta t_i} XXD_i]^{(1/\delta t_i)} \tag{11}$$

$$X_i = \alpha c_i [\beta c_i^{-\delta c_i} M_i + (1-\delta c_i)^{-\delta c_i} XXD_i]^{(-1/\delta c_i)} \tag{12}$$

$$X_i = INT_i + C_i + G_i + Z_i + STK_i \tag{13}$$

$$INT_i = \Sigma_j aa_{ij} XD_j \tag{14}$$

$$C_i = [\Sigma_g YH_g *(1-taxh_g)*(1-savh_g)*cc_{ig}]/P_i \tag{15}$$

$$G_i = gg_i * GDTOT \tag{16}$$

$$Z_i = \Sigma_j b_{ij} DK_j \tag{17}$$

$$STK_i = inv_i * XD_i \tag{18}$$

$$DK_i = [zz_i(INVEST - \Sigma_j STK_j * P_j)]/PK_i \tag{19}$$

Endogenous Variables

$L_{ik}$ : demand for labour type k in sector i

$W_k$ : average wage of labour type k

$INT_i$ : intermediate demand by sector of origin

$C_i$ : private consumption demand by sector

$G_i$ : government consumption demand by sector

$Z_i$ : investment by sector of origin

$STK_i$ : inventory investment

$DK_i$ : investment by sector of destination


Exogenous Variables

$K_i$ : exogenous sectoral capital stock

$LS_k$ : exogenous labour supply of category k

$gam_{ik}$ : proportionality ratio of sectoral wage rate to average wage rate for labour category k

$zz_i$ : total sectoral investment allocation shares ($\Sigma_i zz_i = 1$)

$gg_i$ : government expenditure shares ($\Sigma_i gg_i = 1$)

$cc_{ig}$ : private expenditure shares ($\Sigma_i cc_{ig} = 1$)

$inv_i$ : inventory coefficients

$taxh_g$ : household income tax rates

$savh_g$ : household savings rates

$\alpha$ : shift parameters for production ($\alpha x$), CES composite goods ($\alpha c$), and CET export supply ($\alpha t$) functions

$\tau_i k$ : exponents in Cobb–Douglas production functions

$\beta$ : share parameters in CES ($\beta c$) and CET ($\beta t$) trade functions

$\delta$ : elasticities in CES ($\delta c$) and CET ($\delta t$) trade functions

The production functions are Cobb–Douglas functions of labour and capital with intermediate input requirements given by fixed input–output coefficients. Equation (9) represents the conditions that factor returns equal marginal value products for all labour inputs. With capital stocks fixed by sectors, sectoral rates of return to capital differ. For labour, the wage is assumed to adjust so that the demand for labour equals the supply, and the excess demand equation (10) is satisfied for each category of labour.

Imports and domestic goods are assumed to be imperfect substitutes. Consumers demand a composite good which is a CES aggregation of imports and domestic goods (equation (12)), with a different trade aggregation function for each sector. This specification implies that the price of imports need not equal the price of domestic goods ($PM_i$ does not equal $PD_i$) and that the domestic price system acquires some autonomy not present in standard trade models in which world prices determine domestic prices. Exports and domestic goods sold on domestic markets are imperfect substitutes as well, paralleling the treatment of imports. Export and domestic prices need not be equal, and producers maximise their revenue from dividing their sales between domestic and export markets (equation (11)).

## A.4 Foreign Trade

$$E_i = XXD_i \left[ \frac{(1-\beta t_i)\, PE_i}{\beta t_i\, PD_i} \right]^{[1/(\delta t_i - 1)]} \tag{20}$$

$$M_i = XXD_i \left[ \frac{\beta c_i\, PD_i}{(1-\beta c_i)\, PM_i} \right]^{[1/(1+\delta c_i)]} \tag{21}$$

$$\Sigma pwm_i M_i - \Sigma pwe_i E_i - rmit - pbor - gbor - FSAV = 0 \tag{22}$$

Endogenous Variables

    rmit : remittance inflows to urban capitalist households
    pbor : net foreign borrowing by private sector
    gbor : net foreign borrowing by government

## A.5 Income and Flow of Funds

$$YH_1 = \Sigma_i L_{i1} {}^* gamu_{i1} {}^* W_1 \tag{23}$$

$$YH_2 = \Sigma_i L_{i2} {}^* gamu_{i2} {}^* W_2 + \underset{j=1,2}{\Sigma} (PV_j {}^* XD_j - \Sigma_k L_{jk} {}^* gamu_{jk} {}^* W_k) \tag{24}$$

$$YH_3 = \Sigma_i L_{i3} {}^* gamu_{i3} {}^* W_3 \tag{25}$$

$$YH_4 = \Sigma_i L_{i4} {}^* gamu_{i4} W_4 + [(CORPY + pbor {}^* ER)(1 - ctax)(1 - csave)]$$
$$+ rmit \tag{26}$$

$$HHSAV = \Sigma_g YH_g (1 - taxh_g) savh_g \tag{27}$$

$$HHTAX = \Sigma_g YH_g {}^* taxh_g \tag{28}$$

$$CORPY = \underset{i=3-12}{\Sigma} (PV_i {}^* XD_i - \Sigma_k L_{ik} {}^* gamu_{ik} {}^* W_k) \tag{29}$$

$$GR = TARIFF + INDTAX + HHTAX + OILREV + gbor {}^* ER$$
$$+ (CORPY + pbor {}^* ER) {}^* ctax - EXPSUB \tag{30}$$

$$TARIFF = \Sigma_i tm_i pwm_i M_i ER \tag{31}$$

$$INDTAX = \Sigma_i tx_i P_i X_i \tag{32}$$

$$EXPSUB = \Sigma_i te_i pwe_i E_i ER \tag{33}$$

$$OILREV = oiltax {}^* (PV_{oil} {}^* XD_{oil} - \Sigma_k L_{oil,k} {}^* W_k) \tag{34}$$

$$GSAV = GR - \Sigma_i P_i G_i \tag{35}$$

$$SAVING = HHSAV + GOVSAV + FSAV {}^* ER$$
$$+ (CORPY + pbor {}^* ER) {}^* (1 - ctax) {}^* csave \tag{36}$$

$$SAVING = INVEST \quad (Walras' Law) \tag{37}$$


Endogenous Variables

$YH_1$ : income to agricultural worker households

$YH_2$ : income to agricultural owner households

$YH_3$ : income to urban worker households

$YH_4$ : income to urban owner/capitalist households

HHSAV : household savings

HHTAX : household income tax revenue

CORPY : non−agricultural corporate income

GR : government revenue

TARIFF : import tariff revenue

INDTAX : indirect (excise) taxes less subsidies

EXPSUB : export subsidies

OILREV : government revenue from oil sector

GSAV : government savings

SAVING : total savings

INVEST : total investment

Exogenous Variables

    ctax : tax rate on non–agricultural corporate income

    csave : savings rate out of non–agricultural corporate income

    oiltax : tax rate on oil sector earnings

## A.6 The Operation of Markets

There are three types of markets in the model: those for labour, output, and foreign exchange. The model assumes that these three sets of markets all "clear", which means that the excess demand equations for labour (10), output (13), and foreign exchange (22) must all equal zero at equilibrium. Indeed, the solution problem is to find a set of wages $(W_k)$, product prices $(PD_i)$ and a change in reserves (DFR) such that the three sets of excess demand equations are simultaneously satisfied.

The full equation system contains one more equation than the number of endogenous variables. As the system is a Walrasian general equilibrium system, the excess demand equations must satisfy Walras' Law; in our specification, the savings–investment identity (equation (37)) is satisfied automatically. The system can determine only relative prices; rather than choosing a single price as *numeraire*, we fix the price level (equation (6)), thereby normalising all other prices.

## APPENDIX B: DATA FOR OUR INDONESIAN MODEL

### B.1 Introduction

The primary sources of data for the Indonesian CGE model are the 1980 input–output table and the 1980 social accounting matrix (SAM) prepared by Biro Pusat Statistik (1984, 1986). The data aggregation and reconciliation occurred in a two–step process: first, a consistent data base was created containing 26 sectors and 8 labour types, and second, this data was aggregated to the 12 sectors and 4 labour types that were used in the model. The description below outlines the aggregation choices made during the process.

### B.2 Aggregating the 66 Sector Input–Output Table to 26 Sectors

Table B.1 shows the mapping scheme that was used for the aggregation. The input–output table in producer's prices was used, so that all trade and transport margins show up as intermediate demands (that is, *only* in the trade and transport rows in the input–output table), rather than as part of the purchase of each input or final good, with separate final demand columns to redistribute the margins to the trade and transport sectors. The 26 sector aggregation was chosen to permit comparability with the sectoral classification in the 1980 SAM, although some limited reconciliation at the full 170 sector level was required for full compatibility with the production sectors included in the detailed SAM.

## B.3 Labour Information from the SAM

The fully disaggregated (261x261) 1980 SAM contains 38 productive sectors and 72 labour categories. These 72 labour categories derive from 9 different types of labour, each split according to urban—rural, paid—unpaid, and male—female divisions (9x2x2x2). We have used only 9 labour types, with the exception of agricultural workers, for which the paid/unpaid distinction was maintained in order to distinguish *workers* (paid) from *proprietors* (unpaid).

Table B.1 Aggregation Scheme Used with 1980 Input—Output Table

| 26 Sector Classification | 66 Sector Classification |
|---|---|
| 1. Farm Food Crops | 1–6 |
| 2. Farm Non—Food Crops | 1–17 |
| 3. Livestock | 18–20 |
| 4. Forestry | 21,22 |
| 5. Fishery | 23 |
| 6. Coal and Petroleum | 24,25 |
| 7. Other Mining | 26 |
| 8. Food, Beverages and Tobacco | 27–34 |
| 9. Textiles and Leather | 35, 36 |
| 10. Wood and Furniture | 37 |
| 11. Paper and Printing | 38 |
| 12. Chemicals and Refining | 39–42 |
| 13. Non—Metallic Mineral | 43,44 |
| 14. Basic Metals | 45,46 |
| 15. Machinery | 47–50* |
| 16. Other Industry | 50** |
| 17. Electricity, Gas, and Water | 51 |
| 18. Construction | 52 |
| 19. Trade and Storage | 53,59 |
| 20. Restaurants and Hotels | 54 |
| 21. Rail and Road Transportation | 55,56 |
| 22. Sea & Air Transport, & Communications | 57,58,60 |
| 23. Financial Services | 61 |
| 24. Real Estate | 62 |
| 25. Public Administration | 63 |
| 26. Social and other Services | 64–66 |

   *   Includes sectors 132 to 134 from 160 sector aggregation
 **  Includes sectors 135 to 160 from 160 sector aggregation

The labour information compiled from the SAM and matched with the 26 sector input–output table included, for each labour type and sector, the level of employment (in worker equivalents) and the distribution of wages and imputed income.

### B.4 The CGE Model Data

The data used in the CGE model are obtained by aggregating the 26 sector, 9 labour category data version down to 12 sectors and 4 labour categories. The labour and sectoral aggregations are shown in Tables B.2 and B.3.

The four labour types form the basis for the four household categories used in the model. Capital income from the agricultural sectors (1 and 2) accrues to the agricultural proprietors, while capital income from the non–agricultural sectors (3 to 12) is received by white collar workers.

Table B.2 Aggregation Scheme for 1980 CGE Employment Data

| Four Labour Types | Labour Types from SAM |
| --- | --- |
| 1. Agricultural workers | Paid agricultural workers |
| 2. Agricultural proprietors | Unpaid agricultural workers |
| 3. Low wage workers | Service workers<br>Manual workers<br>Other workers and armed forces |
| 4. High wage workers | Professional workers<br>Managers<br>Clerical workers<br>Sales workers |

Table B.3 Aggregation Scheme for 1980 CGE Sectoral Data

| 12 Sector Classification | 26 Sector Classification |
|---|---|
| 1. Food Agriculture | 1. Farm Crops<br>3. Livestock |
| 2. Traded Agriculture | 2. Farm Non–Food Crops<br>4. Forestry<br>5. Fishery |
| 3. Mining | 6. Coal and Petroleum<br>7. Other Mining |
| 4. Food Industries | 8. Food, Beverages and Tobacco |
| 5. Textiles | 9. Textiles and Leather |
| 6. Wood Products | 10. Wood and Furniture<br>11. Paper and Printing |
| 7. Chemicals and Refining | 12. Chemicals and Refining |
| 8. Metal Industries | 13. Non–Metallic Mineral<br>14. Basic Metals<br>15. Machinery<br>16. Other Industry |
| 9. Utilities | 17. Electricity, Gas, and Water |
| 10. Construction | 18. Construction |
| 11. Trade and Transport | 19. Trade and Storage<br>21. Rail and Road Transportation<br>22. Sea, Air Transport, Communications |
| 12. Services | 20. Restaurants and Hotels<br>23. Financial Services<br>24. Real Estate<br>25. Public Administration<br>25. Social and Other Services |

NOTES
* This work was initiated while Behrman was in Jakarta with the Boston Institute for Developing Economics (BIDE) Development Studies Project II (DSP II). The authors thank, but do not implicate, Leroy P. Jones and Peter G. Warr for useful discussions at an early stage of this research and Jaime Marquez for helpful comments on an earlier draft of the paper. The authors themselves, and not any of the institutions with which they are affiliated, bear all responsibility for interpretations and for any errors in this paper.

1) Adams and Behrman (1982) and Behrman (1987) provide fairly recent reviews of this literature. Adams and Behrman also summarise explorations using macro econometric models for five developing countries and integrated models of the world coffee and copper markets.
2) In recent years, this class of models has been used extensively to analyse and evaluate the performance and prospects of developing nations. Much of this research has been carried out at the World Bank. For examples of CGE model applications to developing countries, see Lewis and Urata (1984) on Turkey and Robinson and Tyson (1985) on Yugoslavia. An exposition of the theory and application of these models can be found in Dervis, de Melo, and Robinson (1982); a survey of the application of CGE models to development issues is in Robinson (1988).
3) Further details on the sectoral specification and data used are presented in Appendix B.
4) A wide variety of equilibrating mechanisms have been used in applied models. For a more complete discussion of the issues and alternatives, see Dervis, de Melo and Robinson (1982).
5) In an intertemporal model in which net investment adds to existing capital stock, the investment allocation shares significantly affect the sectoral pattern of growth over time. However, in our comparative statics experiments, the capital stock is held fixed so the allocation of investment can influence the economy only indirectly as a result of the differing composition of capital goods in each sector. Since we assume that this composition is the same in all sectors, even this effect disappears, and the allocation pattern has no impact on the model results.
6) For a more complete discussion of the data used in the CGE model, see Appendix A. Long time series might be helpful for estimating structural parameters of the model, but such estimates would have to be integrated into the systematic comprehensive snapshot of the economy.
7) For clarity, in these verbal summaries we characterise what happens if there are price declines. The directions of the effects if there are price increases usually are opposite (though the magnitudes may differ).
8) This price index is the weighted sum of *composite* (that is, domestic plus imported) good prices. Since the index of *domestic* good prices is fixed at unity as the numeraire, increases in the composite good index represent an increase in purchase prices to consumers (households, government, and so on) relative to this numeraire, and thus is analogous to movements in a consumer price index relative to a wholesale price index.
9) The cost of living for each household group is the weighted sum of composite good (demand) prices, using the consumption shares in Table 8 as weights.
10) This redistribution *within* the household group is difficult to quantify further in the current model, but confirms that certain aspects of the distribution question require more detailed analysis than that attempted here.
11) Even if gains in the observed variables equal or outweigh losses over the cycle, the economy might be better off with reduced fluctuations because of distributional concerns or risk aversion.
12) In addition to adverse effects due to risk aversion and/or undesired distributional consequences.

REFERENCES

Adams, F.G. and J.R. Behrman (1982), *Commodity Exports and Economic Development*, Lexington Books, Lexington, MA.

100

Behrman, J.R. (1987), "Primary Commodity Instability and Economic Goal Attainment in Developing Economies", *World Development*, 15:5, pp.559–74.

Biro Pusat Statistik (1984), *Input–Output Table: Indonesia 1980*, two volumes, publication numbers 04420.8402 and unnumbered.

Biro Pusat Statistik (1986), *Social Accounting Matrix: Indonesia 1980*, two volumes, publication numbers 04420.8602 and 04420.8603.

Dervis, K., J. de Melo and S. Robinson (1982), *General Equilibrium Models for Development Policy*, Cambridge University Press, Cambridge.

Dick, H., S. Gupta, T. Mayer, and D. Vincent (1983), "The Short–Run Impact of Fluctuating Primary Commodity Prices on Three Developing Economies: Colombia, Ivory Coast and Kenya", *World Development*, 11:5, pp.405–16.

Gelb, A. (1985), "Are Oil Windfalls a Blessing or a Curse? Policy Exercises with an Indonesia–Like Model", World Bank, Development Research Department, Washington, DC.

Lewis, J.D. and S. Urata (1984), "Anatomy of a Balance of Payments Crisis: Application of Computable General Equilibrium Model to Turkey, 1978–80", *Economic Modeling*, 1:3, pp.281–303.

Malinvaud, E. (1977), *The Theory of Unemployment Reconsidered*, Basil Blackwell, Oxford.

Robinson, S. (1988), "Multisectoral Models of Developing Countries: A Survey" in H.B. Chenery and T.N. Srinivasan (eds.), *Handbook of Development Economics*, North–Holland, Amsterdam.

Robinson, S. and L.D. Tryson (1985), "Foreign Trade, Resource Allocation, and Structural Adjustment in Yugoslavia: 1976–80", *Journal of Comparative Economics*, 9, pp.46–70.

CHAPTER 5


# COMMODITY PRICE CONTRACTIONS, DEBT AND ECONOMIC GROWTH IN DEVELOPING ECONOMIES: THE VENEZUELAN CASE

Pedro A. Palma*, *MetroEconomica, Caracas, Venezuela*

## 1. INTRODUCTION

One of the consequences of the emergence of the Latin American foreign debt crisis in 1982 has been a growing attention to the problem of the incompatibility between internal economic growth and the honouring of external commitments by heavily indebted countries suffering the effects of a strong deterioration of their terms of trade. The latter problem, in turn, is the result of the collapse of the prices for their main export products, usually a limited gamut of primary commodities, which are particularly subject to extreme price fluctuations.

Venezuela affords a classic case to illustrate this situation. In 1987, hydrocarbon exports (crude oil, refined petroleum products, natural gas, etc.) accounted for 80% of the country's exports of goods and services and nearly 87% of its merchandise exports. This near—total dependence on a single export product makes the country dangerously vulnerable to fluctuations in world prices.

To compound the problem further, there is scarcely a commodity whose prices are more volatile than oil, reflecting a number of factors which vary in an unpredictable fashion — above all for political reasons — and are for the most part beyond the individual exporting country's control.

It is in this context that we propose to examine the options available to a heavily indebted economy such as Venezuela's, following efforts at economic adjustment over the last few years and an acceleration of the decline in the price of its main export product. Our purpose is to attempt to determine the extent to which Venezuela can reasonably expect to continue meeting its foreign debt

*L. R. Klein and J. Marquez (eds.), Economics in Theory and Practice: An Eclectic Approach, 101–127.*
© *1989 by Kluwer Academic Publishers.*

obligations and simultaneously achieve an acceptable level of internal economic activity if oil prices continue to slide.

To do so, we have used the "MODVEN VII" macroeconometric model for Venezuela[1] to simulate a variety of oil and debt service scenarios, assuming a near uniform internal economic policy. This simulation yields a number of interesting results, on which our conclusions are based.

The first part of this study consists of a brief historical review of the Venezuelan economy's performance in recent times, which we consider essential to an understanding of its current situation. Thereafter, we proceed to analyse the results of the simulations, followed by the conclusions generated by those results.

## 2. THE RECENT BEHAVIOUR OF THE VENEZUELAN ECONOMY

The Venezuelan economy has undergone deep changes over the last fifteen years. During that period, it has passed through a series of easily distinguishable and highly contrasting stages.

### 2.1 The Oil Boom (1974–1977)

This period began with the first large increase in oil prices in late 1973. Its most dramatic feature was the adoption of an ambitious development plan based on the rapid growth of the basic industries and physical infrastructure (aluminium, steel, electrification, etc.) and an improvement and expansion of public services.

In accordance with these ambitious plans, public spending grew copiously throughout the period. But due to the combination of this expansion of spending and the levelling off of revenues after 1975 as oil prices and export volume stabilised, the public sector budget fell into deficit by the end of the period.

The larger public spending had the effect of monetarising a large part of the country's oil income, as well as the inflow of funds obtained through large scale external borrowing from 1976 onwards. The latter funds were used to finance part of the public investment projects as well as the budget and current account deficits that appeared at that time.

As a result of that massive injection of funds into the economy through public spending, combined with the easy credit generated by a stimulative monetary policy, private demand grew as vigorously as public throughout the period. From 1975 to 1977, real private consumption rose at an average of 9.9%, and real gross fixed private investment grew at an annual rate of 24.6%.

Productive activity naturally responded to this expansion of demand. Production in such varied sectors as manufacturing, trade, transportation, and others enjoyed real growth rates of over 10%. Construction, for its part, reflected the extraordinary expansion of demand for non—tradeable goods by growing at a rate of more than 20%.

In spite of this, overall demand still rose much more rapidly than internal supply of goods and services; this incongruity created a growing macroeconomic disequilibrium. Under such circumstances, inflation could be kept under control only by a combination of strict price controls and subsidisation of basic consumer goods, and (more importantly) a very rapid growth of imports to complement the insufficient supply of tradeable goods. Since imports could not alleviate inflationary pressure on non—tradeables, prices for the latter expanded at rates of over 50% in certain years of the period.

As imports continued to grow while oil exports declined slightly and then stabilised, Venezuela's external accounts inevitably suffered. The current account fell from a surplus of US$ 5.760 billion in 1974 to a deficit of US$ 3.179 billion in 1977. That is why, at the end of the oil boom in 1977, the Venezuelan economy suffered from multiple disequilibria, not only in the budget and external accounts, but also in the input markets, particularly labour.

In this latter case, excess demand in relation to supply, especially of skilled and semi—skilled labour, resulted in a situation of pervasive absenteeism and high rates of personnel turnover. Labour productivity naturally declined.

## 2.2 1978–1982: Crisis and Recession

The Venezuelan economy fell into a crisis in 1978. The weakening world oil market depressed prices, thereby aggravating the existing disequilibria in spite of the fiscal and monetary discipline the authorities tried to impose in mid—1977. Those efforts could not prevent the consolidated public sector budget deficit from continuing to grow, while the current account external deficit reached a level of US$ 5.7 billion, equivalent to no less than 14% of the country's gross domestic product. Under such circumstances, widespread expectations of a devaluation of the currency came into being, and stimulated a massive flight of capital out of the country.

At this critical juncture, the Venezuelan economy was rescued by *the second oil boom of 1979–1980*, provoked by the Iranian revolution and the temporary withdrawal of that country from the world oil market. The new increase of oil prices corrected some of Venezuela's economic disequilibria, though it did not produce a new bonanza on the scale of the first oil boom. Hydrocarbon export income rose drastically, just as imports began to decline due to the completion of a number of large scale investment projects. The current account came into the black in 1979, and yielded a surplus of US$ 4.7 billion the following year.

However, in spite of the considerable growth of oil revenues and the central government's persistent efforts to control public spending, the public finances continued in deficit. According to Palma (1985), the principle cause was the continued large scale rise in spending by the decentralised public sector. The state—owned enterprises accounted for the greater part of that increased spending, as new or expanded productive plants built with the massive investments launched during the oil boom came on stream.

Spending expansion by the decentralised public sector was brought under control in 1981, but this time, central government spending rose sharply to stimulate internal economic activity, which had stagnated since 1979 in spite of growing real consolidated public spending. It was financed with the surplus funds held by the oil industry abroad, generated by its increasing export sales in the preceding two years.

Nevertheless, the stimulative effect of rising public spending in the 1979—1981 period was neutralised by a sustained contraction of private demand. Real gross fixed investment fell by an annual average of 21.6%, while real private consumption per capita declined by 2.2% on the average in the same period. Private consumption fell mainly because of the continuous decline in the purchasing power of the population, generated by higher unemployment and a contraction of real wages due to rising inflation.

The collapse of private investment reflected that contraction in consumption, the considerable increase of productive capacity created by the massive investments in plant and equipment during the oil boom years, and the increasingly attractive opportunities for investment of funds abroad as international interest rates reached very high levels.

A large portion of the resources injected into the economy by the rising public spending was transferred abroad, in spite of the disappearance of devaluation expectations after oil prices recovered in 1979. Capital flight reached massive proportions for several months in 1981, when the monetary authorities, in a deliberate attempt to stimulate capital outflow in order to keep the growing public spending from rekindling inflation, reduced local interest rates to levels below those prevailing abroad.

In August 1979, the economic authorities of the incoming administration of President Herrera Campins decided to remove the strict price controls imposed by the previous government, thereby permitting the inflationary pressures repressed by those controls to materialise. This measure reinforced the effects of an across—the—board wage increase in early 1980 and rising costs of production, both internal and external, to force prices up at the unprecedented rate of 21% that year. The impact of this inflation rate can best be appreciated by comparing it with the moderate rates prevailing during the oil boom of 1974–1977 (averaging slightly more than 8%), and an average of only 1.8% during the 1960s and early 1970s.

The distortion of relative prices created by that surge in internal prices, while the exchange rate remained frozen at Bs/US$ 4.30, led to a growing overvaluation of the bolivar, as a result of which the purchasing power parity index rose to 117 in 1981, from its base value of 100 in 1979.

This largely explains why imports continued at very high levels in spite of the general stagnation of the economy. Merchandise imports did fall somewhat in 1979, due to the conclusion of investment projects begun during the oil boom. But they began to grow again the following year, and rose at ever increasing rates in 1981 and 1982. As a result, imports of goods and services were equivalent to 32% of gross domestic product throughout this period. This is a very high level, far above those prevailing prior to the oil boom (20% on average in the 1960s and early 1970s).

However, the country could afford to import on this massive scale and to export large amounts of private capital while still conserving substantial international reserves, due to growing oil exports and large foreign borrowing. To illustrate this, at the end of 1981 Venezuela's liquid foreign assets[2] were close to US$ 17 billion.

2.3 1982–1983: Weakening of the Oil Market, Capital Flight, and Exchange Control

The situation changed in 1982, when a weakening world oil market depressed Venezuela's oil exports and it became increasingly difficult to obtain foreign loans. The inflow of foreign exchange fell, while the outflow continued to rise as imports reached a historic high and capital flight intensified, no longer due to interest rate incentives (at this time, local rates were higher than external ones), but due to growing expectations for a devaluation of the bolivar as a result of the new external disequilibrium. However, in spite of this serious deterioration of the country's external accounts, the exchange rate was maintained at Bs./US$ 4.30, and no exchange restrictions were imposed (see Rodriguez, 1987).

As a result Venezuela's foreign liquid assets suffered a severe contraction, falling from US$ 16.937 billion at the end of 1981 to US$ 8.954 billion by the end of 1982. The loss of international reserves intensified still further at the outset of 1983, until the hemorrhage was finally stopped on February 18 by the imposition of exchange controls and a system of multiple exchange rates for commercial operations; financial transactions remained free of regulation, but subject to a floating exchange rate. These measures put an end to the system of free convertibility at a fixed exchange rate in force for almost 20 years.[3]

Table 1. International Financial Assets (Billion US Dollars).

|  | 1981 | 1982* | 1982** |
|---|---|---|---|
| Central Bank of Venezuela | 8.619 | 7.084 | 10.039 |
| Venezuelan Investment Fund | 2.452 | 1.521 | 1.521 |
| Commercial Banks | 0.338 | 0.064 | 0.064 |
| Subtotal (International Reserves) | 11.409 | 8.669 | 11.624 |
| PDVSA | 5.528 | 0.285 | 0.285 |
| Total | 16.937 | 8.954 | 11.909 |

Note: Excludes PDVSA's Accounts Receivable
* Gold valued at $42.22 per Troy ounce
** Gold valued at $300.00 per Troy ounce
Source: Central Bank of Venezuela, PDVSA, MetroEconomica

Since the Central Bank automatically receives more than 90% of the foreign exchange generated by the country's exports — the State is the major exporter, of oil, aluminium, etc. — the exchange control regime has meant in practice the administration of the foreign exchange earned by the State. Policies have been adopted to limit access to those foreign resources on the part of importers and other private buyers.

The difficulties of obtaining dollars at preferential exchange rates, the large inventories of imported products accumulated in 1982 when imminent devaluation was expected to occur, and a severe recession throughout 1983, permitted imports to contract that year by no less than 52.8%.

## 2.4 1984–1988: From Adjustment to Recovery with External Crisis

It was widely believed that the low level of imports in 1983 would be unsustainable in the long run, and that imports would necessarily rise again in the years to come, due to the structural dependence of the national economy on foreign inputs. But in fact, imports recovered by 13.3% in 1984, and then stabilised in nominal terms in 1985, contracting once again in real terms.

This reflected the continuation of the economic recession provoked by the austerity policy adopted by President Lusinchi's administration in its first two years (1984–85). That policy, in turn, was a pre–condition for the restructuring of the public foreign debt, even though it was not necessary for Venezuela to reach a formal agreement with the International Monetary Fund.

However, in 1986 and 1987 imports grew only marginally, in spite of a significant real GDP growth in those years, reflecting a fiscal expansion aimed at rescuing the economy from its prolonged recession (beginning in the late seventies, and intensifying in 1983–1984).

In fact, real imports of goods and services, expressed in per capita terms and per unit of GDP, have contracted every year since 1983 except for a slight increase in 1984, and by 1987 they were below their 1973 level. This means that these real imports are smaller now than before the oil boom. (See Figure 1)

Moreover, Venezuela achieved a substantial current account surplus from 1983 to 1985, sufficient to offset the deficit in the capital account and rebuild the international reserves from the very low level to which they had fallen in early 1983. By the end of 1985, those reserves stood at US$ 15.478 billion[4], equivalent to more than 25 months of merchandise imports. More than US$ 3.854 billion had been added to the 1982 year–end reserves.

However, the situation took a drastic turn for the worse in 1986, when the collapse of world oil prices cut Venezuela's oil revenues by more than 43%, while the country made very high net foreign debt service payments (principal and interest less new loans), amounting to over 54% of its hydrocarbon exports and 41% of its total exports of goods and services.[5] As a result, international reserves contracted by US$ 3.8 billion in that year, some 25% of the total.

The country's foreign reserves continued to contract throughout 1987, though more slowly than in the previous year. This was due basically to an improvement in oil exports generated by the recovery of world prices and to a reduction in net foreign debt service payments achieved through an important increase in credit lines for imports.

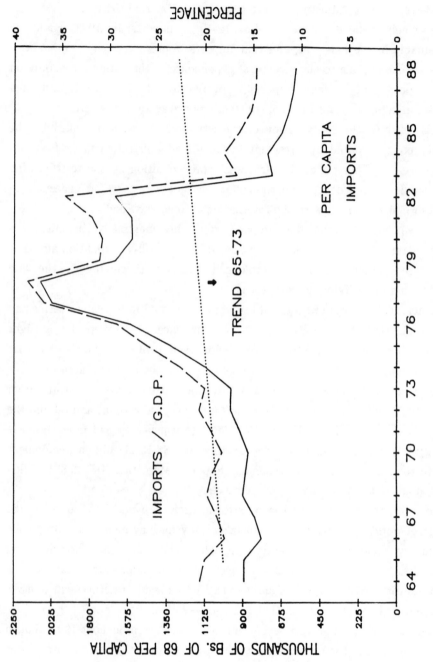

Figure 1. Per Capita Real Imports and Real Imports/Real GDP Ratio

However, the situation worsened again in the early months of 1988, when oil prices fell once again and importers found increasing difficulty in obtaining new credit lines. Liquid international reserves held by the Central Bank and the Venezuelan Investment Fund had fallen by about US$ 1.2 billion in the first third of the year. As a result, almost 63% of the country's liquid reserves, and 38% of its total international reserves, had been lost in only 28 months (January 1986 to April 1988).

Table 2. International Reserves (Billion US Dollars)

| Period | VIF Total | Central Bank Operat. | Central Bank Total | Total Central Bank + VIF Liquid | Total Central Bank + VIF Others | Total Central Bank + VIF Total |
|---|---|---|---|---|---|---|
| December 1985 | 1.748 | 8.207 | 13.746 | 9.955 | 5.539 | 15.494 |
| December 1986 | 1.837 | 4.273 | 9.858 | 6.100 | 5.585 | 11.685 |
| December 1987 | 1.385 | 3.518 | 9.376 | 4.903 | 5.858 | 10.761 |
| April 1988 | 0.693 | 3.033 | 8.939 | 3.726 | 5.906 | 9.632 |
| Variation April 88–Dec. 85: | | | | | | |
| Absolute | −1.055 | −5.174 | −4.807 | −6.229 | 0.367 | −5.862 |
| Percentage | −60.4% | −63.0% | −35.0% | −62.6% | 6.6% | −37.8% |

Note:   Liquid reserves are defined as the sum of the Central Bank's operative reserves and the VIF's reserves.
Source:   Central Bank of Venezuela and MetroEconomica

Different preferential rates have been periodically raised since exchange controls were imposed. The most drastic of those devaluations came in December, 1986, when the rate for most controlled transactions went up from Bs./US$ 7.50 to Bs./US$ 14.50. A devaluation on this scale (93%) was viewed as excessive, since correction of local currency overvaluation at that time required a much more moderate adjustment of the exchange rate.[6]

For its part, the free market rate has risen over the entire period of exchange controls, though there have been brief periods of decline and stabilisation. It has always been substantially higher than the preferential rates, at times more than double. (See Figure 2)

It will not be surprising that this situation has had an adverse impact on the economy. The level of internal prices, in particular, reflects a growing influence of the free market rate, which means that the economy has been undergoing a process of "dollarisation": more and more prices are set in terms of dollar costs at the free market exchange rate for the bolivar.[7]

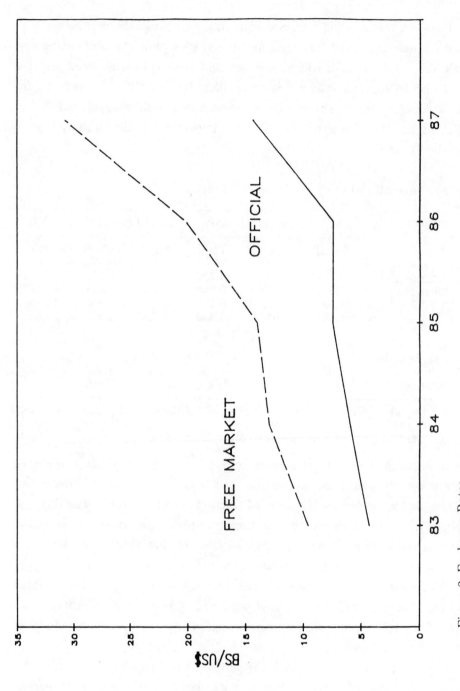

Figure 2. Exchange Rates

Inflationary pressure rose after the adoption of exchange controls, except in 1983, which saw the smallest rise in internal prices in the last fifteen years. That was due to the strict election—year price controls, politically justified by the fact that most of the products sold that year had been imported previously, at the traditional exchange rate of Bs./US$ 4.30, or produced with raw materials and inputs purchased abroad at that exchange rate. A large portion of the country's imports continued to be made with foreign exchange at the old rate even after exchange controls went into effect that year.

However, *inflation* became stronger in 1984 and thereafter, though it was moderated by a number of factors: 1) the nature of the devaluation of the controlled exchange rate for imports; 2) price controls; and 3) the weakness of internal demand — especially real private consumption — in those recession years when demand continued to fall in per capita terms due to the deterioration of the population's purchasing power.

The last two factors depressed profit margins, since the combination of price controls and falling sales volumes prevented business from passing rising production costs along to final prices. In fact, the sustained contraction of real personal disposable income since 1979 not only provoked an uninterrupted decline in real per capita consumption for more than six years (1979–1985), but also increased the price elasticity of demand.

Under those conditions, producers generally preferred to narrow their profit margins and absorb a part of their rising production costs rather than raise prices, fearing that any increased income from such a measure would be more than offset by its impact on volume.

Inflationary pressures increased somewhat in the second half of 1986 as consumption recovered in response to a fiscal expansion adopted in late 1985, and rising expectations for devaluation and inflation. The negative real interest rates stimulated credit demand in order to finance advance purchases in a widespread anti—inflationary strategy of consumers.

This rise in demand was not totally matched by growing supply. In part, this reflected a shortage of imported raw materials and inputs. The fall of oil prices generated strong expectations of future devaluation and intensified the demand for dollars at the preferential exchange rate. This led the government to strengthen its exchange controls, delaying or entirely preventing many needed import transactions. The difficulty of obtaining controlled dollars, in turn, generated growing pressure on the free market, where the exchange rate rose very rapidly.

However, the continuation of strict price controls and the persistence of a high price elasticity of demand for basic products prevented this increased inflationary pressure from fully expressing itself, with the result that the inflation figure for 1986 remained at the same level as that of the preceding two years.

*1987: A Year of Strong Inflation*

The relative price stability of the preceding years was broken in 1987, when Venezuela suffered its highest known inflation rate.[8] The 93% devaluation of the bolivar imposed in December 1986, combined with a generalised increase in production costs, wages among them, contributed to increasing prices. Additionally, an increase in private consumption created by the across–the–board wage and salary increase decreed by the government in late April 1987, a stimulative fiscal policy, and a growing demand for real estate and durable goods in response to anticipated inflation, also stimulated price hikes.

Durable goods consumption was also stimulated by the freezing of interest rates at artificially low levels bearing no relationship to the higher expected inflation. This further aggravated the problem of negative real interest rates.

The December 1986 "maxi–devaluation" led to widespread expectations of an inflation rate in the neighbourhood of 30% for 1987, since private companies were thought to be unable to continue absorbing rising production costs by narrowing their profit margins. At the same time, interest rates remained frozen at their 1985 levels, averaging 10% for deposits and 13% for loans. The contrast between these two sets of figures furnishes an idea of the magnitude of the negative real interest rates in effect at that time.

Just as the prevalence of negative real interest rates provided a powerful stimulus to speculative borrowing, they also discouraged saving. As a result, the flow of deposits into the financial institutions dried up, particularly for the mortgage banks and the savings and loan associations. The Central Bank reacted to this disequilibrium in the financial market by trying to raise interest rates to more reasonable levels, but it could not do so, due to the government's refusal to tolerate such a measure.

Government spokesmen argued that to do so would damage productive sectors of the economy, especially construction, and that more expensive credits would make it impossible for a large part of the population to acquire housing or to continue paying their existing mortgage obligations.

When it found itself unable to raise interest rates, the Central Bank tried to cope with the inflationary danger implicit in the excess demand for credit by adopting a restrictive monetary policy. It not only reduced the volume of its discounts and advances to the financial institutions, but raised the interest rate offered by its over—night financial facility in order to soak up the banks' excess reserves and thereby limiting their ability to extend credit to private customers.

These measures created a tight money environment which, in conjunction with the artificially low controlled interest rates, led to the appearance of a parallel financial market with rates much higher than the official ones.

The shortage of liquidity, together with stricter price controls, helped to moderate inflation in the opening months of 1988. It also forced many private companies to sell dollars on the free market to meet their need for bolivars, which contributed to an initial stability of the exchange rate: it remained in the neighbourhood of Bs./US$ 30.00 for several months, after having reached Bs./US$ 36.00 in September 1987.

That stability was all the more surprising in view of the precipitous decline in the country's foreign reserves and the pessimistic expectations for the oil market prevailing throughout this period.

We can conclude from the previous analysis that recent economic policy in Venezuela has been characterised by a lack of coherence and consistency, and an absence of clear goals. Economic decisions are often made in isolation, responding more to specific short term political goals, rather than to economic objectives.

## 3. IMPACTS OF DIFFERENT OIL SCENARIOS

Three alternative macroeconomic scenarios for the 1988–1991 period are simulated, reflecting the effects on the Venezuelan economy of different degrees of long term weakness in the world oil market. These estimations should not be taken as real alternative forecasts for the Venezuelan economy, but only as comparative exercises that can give information on the possible reactions of the economy under different alternatives.

The differences among these scenarios are expressed in terms of prices and physical volume of exports. The aim of this exercise is to shed light on the courses of action available to Venezuela under conditions of adversity.

Economic policy in all three scenarios does not differ substantially from the one implemented in recent years. However, we assume some efforts by the authorities to rationalise public spending in order to prevent the consolidated

Table 3. Oil Assumptions

|                                | 1988  | 1989  | 1990   | 1991   |
|--------------------------------|-------|-------|--------|--------|
| Price (US$/barrel):            |       |       |        |        |
| Base Scenario (optimistic)     | 16.1  | 16.9  | 18.2   | 19.5   |
| Intermediate Scenario          | 14.0  | 14.7  | 15.8   | 17.0   |
| Pessimistic Scenario           | 12.0  | 12.6  | 13.5   | 14.5   |
| Value of Exports (Billion US$):|       |       |        |        |
| Base Scenario                  | 8.681 | 9.385 | 10.189 | 11.336 |
| Intermediate Scenario          | 8.130 | 8.837 | 9.680  | 10.512 |
| Pessimistic Scenario           | 7.108 | 7.805 | 8.635  | 9.437  |

public sector deficit from running entirely out of control, but at the same time, trying to keep the economy from falling into a deep recession.

It is also established that Venezuela will continue to serve its public foreign debt under the terms of the current agreements, and that new foreign loans will show an upward tendency throughout the simulated period, but of moderate proportions.

### 3.1 Results of the Simulations

Naturally, a contraction in oil exports would make itself felt first and foremost in the balance of payments and public finance. It is the main cause of the deteriorating current account balance and the intensifying pressure on the country's international reserves, of which US$ 2.3 billion more would be lost under the intermediate scenario, and US$ 5.7 billion under the pessimistic scenario, than under the more favourable base scenario.

Under the less favourable scenarios, oil revenue would be severely depressed, and public sector finances would reflect that downturn in their most important revenue source. The cumulative income of the oil industry would be 5.6% lower under the intermediate scenario than under the base scenario, and the contraction would reach a full 15% under the pessimistic scenario, for the entire period simulated.

Our assumption of an attempt by the authorities to rationalise public spending without reducing it to the point of provoking a serious recession implies that the budget deficit would continue to increase. The cumulative deficit over the 1988–1991 period would equal 4.3% of cumulative gross domestic product under the base scenario, 5.5% under the intermediate scenario, and 7.5% under the pessimistic scenario. But in all three cases the deficit would shrink as a percentage of GDP.

Table 4. Balance of Payments and International Reserves (Billion US$)

|  | 1988 | 1989 | 1990 | 1991 |
|---|---|---|---|---|
| Current Account Balance: | | | | |
| Base Scenario | −0.679 | 0.773 | 1.461 | 1.983 |
| Intermediate Scenario | −1.347 | 0.141 | 1.032 | 1.369 |
| Pessimistic Scenario | −2.580 | 0.801 | 0.319 | 0.914 |
| Overall Balance of Payments: | | | | |
| Base Scenario | −1.885 | −0.839 | −0.005 | 1.253 |
| Intermediate Scenario | −2.554 | −1.470 | −0.435 | 0.639 |
| Pessimistic Scenario | −3.786 | −2.412 | −1.147 | 0.184 |
| International Reserves: | | | | |
| Base Scenario | 8.624 | 7.785 | 7.780 | 9.033 |
| Intermediate Scenario | 7.955 | 6.485 | 6.050 | 6.680 |
| Pessimistic Scenario | 6.722 | 4.311 | 3.164 | 3.348 |

Table 5. Public Deficit as Percentage of GDP

|  | 1988 | 1989 | 1990 | 1991 | Cumulative |
|---|---|---|---|---|---|
| Base Oil Scenario | 10.4 | 4.2 | 4.0 | 1.4 | 4.3 |
| Intermediate Oil Scenario | 11.4 | 5.2 | 5.0 | 3.0 | 5.5 |
| Pessimistic Oil Scenario | 11.3 | 7.2 | 6.9 | 5.0 | 7.5 |

Note: The Public Deficit is defined as the difference between the current revenues and total outlays of the Public Sector as a whole, including total public debt service payments, both internal and external.

These figures reflect the assumption of identical changes in the exchange rate for all three scenarios. But if the more adverse scenarios result in deeper devaluations, the deficit figures would be lower, since more internal revenues would be generated, either in the form of the exchange profits earned by the Central Bank or in that of higher taxes paid by the oil industry.

By the same token, if the currency were devalued in proportion to the variation in oil prices assumed by each of the scenarios, the higher relative costs of imports under the less favourable scenarios would probably provoke somewhat larger contractions of imports than herein projected.

However, real imports would not be very far from the figures yielded by these simulations, since their price and product elasticities are close to unity, as a consequence of the drastic contraction of imports since 1983 (see Section 2.4) and the gradually rising use of import substituting industrial capacity.

Curiously, at the beginning of the period, imports are higher under the intermediate and pessimistic scenarios than under the more favourable base scenario. This near J—curve effect reflects the lower relative prices of imports under the more adverse scenarios, produced by the difference between internal and external inflation rates. As a result — assuming identical exchange rates in all three scenarios — the prices of domestic products would rise faster than those of foreign goods, thereby providing a stimulus to imports.

Table 6. Merchandise Imports and Trade Balance (Billion US$)

|  | 1988 | 1989 | 1990 | 1991 |
|---|---|---|---|---|
| Merchandise Imports: | | | | |
| Base Scenario | 8.506 | 8.192 | 8.682 | 9.678 |
| Intermediate Scenario | 8.601 | 8.238 | 8.565 | 9.418 |
| Pessimistic Scenario | 8.768 | 8.102 | 8.184 | 8.752 |
| Trade Balance: | | | | |
| Base Scenario | 1.702 | 3.030 | 3.674 | 4.127 |
| Intermediate Scenario | 1.043 | 2.403 | 3.233 | 3.488 |
| Pessimistic Scenario | −0.173 | 1.448 | 2.483 | 2.966 |

However, in the later years of the period imports are slightly lower under the intermediate and pessimistic scenarios than under the base scenario, since the moderating effect of the lower levels of production is greater in absolute terms than the effect of lower relative prices.

That tendency would be further reinforced by the stricter controls on the supply of foreign exchange for imports which can be expected, in an attempt to cope with the persistent contraction of international reserves, more intense in the adverse scenarios. This could be so not only because of the fall in oil earnings, but also due to the limited availability of foreign loans that we assume, particularly in the early years of the studied period.

Throughout the period, inflation varies directly with the degree of adversity projected in each scenario: the more adverse the scenario, the higher the inflation rate. The prime cause is the greater expansion of the money supply under the more adverse scenarios, resulting in turn from the monetarisation of the larger budget deficits, which we assume would be financed for the most part by the

Central Bank.

This growing injection of funds into the economy to finance the budget deficit more than offsets the contraction of the monetary base provoked by the loss of international reserves. That is to say, the absolute effect of the monetarisation of the deficit is larger than the contraction of the monetary base as the Central Bank's international reserve holdings dwindle.

Another inflationary factor which is stronger in the more adverse scenarios is the more serious shortage of foreign exchange, which restricts imports and, consequently, internal production, thereby widening the gap between supply and demand.

Table 7. Consumer Price Variations (Percentages)

|  | 1988 | 1989 | 1990 | 1991 |
|---|---|---|---|---|
| Base Oil Scenario | 15.4 | 20.0 | 20.5 | 21.7 |
| Intermediate Oil Scenario | 18.0 | 22.4 | 22.2 | 24.1 |
| Pessimistic Oil Scenario | 22.8 | 26.7 | 25.4 | 25.7 |

Productive activity, for its part, would suffer from a combination of difficulties which are also more severe under the less favourable scenarios: on the one hand, public sector demand would be depressed by lower revenues, in spite of all efforts to keep public spending from falling too drastically; on the other, private consumption would be constrained by larger contractions of real personal disposable income provoked by higher inflation and unemployment.

This explains the differences in the non–oil GDP growth rate. After a contraction in 1989 due to the implementation of adjustment policies that we assume for the first year of the new Administration, real GDP growth becomes moderately positive in 1990 and 1991 under the base scenario, remains virtually stagnant under the intermediate scenario, and actually contracts under the pessimistic scenario. However, in this last case the real GDP contraction of the first two years (1988–1989) is severe due to the direct impact of the oil price contraction on the economy during that period.

Unemployment rises quite substantially in the more adverse scenarios, to the point where a rate of over 14.3% is projected for the last year of the period under the worst of the three scenarios. Even these figures, as serious as they are, do not reflect the whole impact of declining growth rates on the labour force, since they indicate open unemployment only among the economically active population.

Table 8. Growth of Real Non—Oil GDP and Unemployment (Percentages)

|                        | 1988  | 1989  | 1990  | 1991  |
|------------------------|-------|-------|-------|-------|
| GDP Growth Rate:       |       |       |       |       |
| Base Scenario          | 1.0   | −1.6  | 1.8   | 1.9   |
| Intermediate Scenario  | −0.8  | −2.6  | 0.5   | −0.2  |
| Pessimistic Scenario   | −4.0  | −5.7  | −1.7  | −1.4  |
| Unemployment Rate:     |       |       |       |       |
| Base Scenario          | 10.00 | 11.17 | 11.65 | 11.92 |
| Intermediate Scenario  | 10.06 | 11.49 | 12.24 | 12.78 |
| Pessimistic Scenario   | 11.19 | 12.14 | 13.38 | 14.33 |

However, they do not reveal the pervasive underemployment, formed by the group of workers who are underpaid or perform labour below the level appropriate to their education, ability, or skills. Naturally, underemployment also rises in the more adverse scenarios.

### 3.2 Options for Handling the Consequences of Lower Oil Prices

The figures shown above lead to the question of what Venezuela can do to cope with the consequences of a serious deterioration of its terms of trade provoked by falling prices on the world oil market.

One available response is the *diversification and growth of non—oil exports.* And Venezuela has considerable potential in this area, which still remains to be fully developed. However, it is dubious that the concentration of the nation's efforts on a strategy of expansion of non—oil exports is the most effective way to overcome the short term effects of a crisis created by a sharp contraction of export prices.

The crisis demands rapid and effective action, whose benefits would be felt immediately. For an economy without an export tradition (except in oil), such as Venezuela's, a broad based export strategy requires a substantial length of time to take root and then begin to yield concrete results. In the application of that strategy, exchange rate manipulation is only one of the essential components, and needs to be complemented with actions of other kinds.

It is of course necessary to adopt policies aimed at promoting "outward growth" through the development of a solid export sector, in order to reduce the country's external economic dependence and the vulnerability resulting from its reliance on highly unstable oil exports, in the medium term. But non—oil export promotion is not the way to correct the immediate effects of the oil crisis.

One alternative to that strategy is the *implementation of a more severe adjustment policy*, intended to reduce the economy's need to import. But as the results of the simulations outlined above indicate, the contraction of imports to be expected from a reduction of the level of economic activity under the more adverse scenarios is quite limited.

In fact, imports amount to a slightly larger percentage of GDP under the more adverse scenarios than under the optimistic base scenario, though the differences are only marginal. These figures support our conclusion that, following the drastic contraction of imports since 1983, there is only limited opportunity to reduce them still further (see Section 3.1).

Consequently, still other alternatives need to be explored in order to face the sudden effects of a drastic contraction of export prices. One of the most promising would seem to be a reduction of the country's net foreign debt service payments. This goal could be accomplished either through a reduction of the payments themselves, or through an offsetting inflow of new external credits, or a combination of both.

### 3.2.1 Limitation of Foreign Debt Service Payments

To examine the results of a reduction of foreign debt service payments, our three alternative scenarios were simulated once again, maintaining the oil assumptions as discussed above, but introducing a change in the external finance assumptions under which net foreign debt service payments would be limited to 20% of exports of goods and services.

As a result, net payments on the country's total foreign debts would fall by 27% under the base scenario, 30% under the intermediate scenario, and 37% under the pessimistic scenario, from the level assumed in the previous calculations. The funds thus saved could then be allocated to internal public spending under a more stimulative fiscal policy than would be viable under the conditions simulated before. With a larger injection of funds into the internal economy, growth would be more vigorous and unemployment less widespread than in the case of the previous simulations.

These new simulations yield more favourable results for the external sector of the economy. Even under the most unfavourable oil scenario, the contraction of international reserves is less pronounced; they would fall to only US$ 6.742 billion by the end of the period, equivalent to nine months of merchandise imports, in contrast to the figure of US$ 3.348 billion, equivalent to less than 5

Table 9. Average Rates of Growth and Unemployment (Percentages)

|  | Growth of Non—Oil GDP | Unemployment |
|---|---|---|
| **Scenarios Assuming Debt Service Payments Under Current Agreements:** | | |
| Base Scenario | 0.73 | 11.19 |
| Intermediate Scenario | −0.79 | 11.64 |
| Pessimistic Scenario | −3.22 | 12.76 |
| **Scenarios Assuming Debt Service Payments Equal to 20% of Exports:** | | |
| Base Scenario | 0.88 | 10.67 |
| Intermediate Scenario | −0.47 | 11.11 |
| Pessimistic Scenario | −2.67 | 11.93 |

months of merchandise imports, under the same scenario in the original set of simulations.

Most of the improvement comes in the capital account of the balance of payments, since the bulk of the reduction of debt service would take the form of postponement of principal payments.

This change of assumptions would yield higher rates of internal inflation, since the smaller contraction of the Central Bank's international reserves would allow both the monetary base and the money supply itself to grow more rapidly. However, the larger expansion of high power money might well be neutralised − and we assume it would be − by a reduction of the Central Bank's financial assistance to the banking system.

Table 10. International Reserves (Billion US$)

|  | 1988 | 1989 | 1990 | 1991 |
|---|---|---|---|---|
| **Scenario Assuming Debt Service Payments Under Current Agreements:** | | | | |
| Base Oil Scenario | 8.624 | 7.785 | 7.780 | 9.033 |
| Intermediate Oil Scenario | 7.955 | 6.485 | 6.050 | 6.680 |
| Pessimistic Oil Scenario | 6.722 | 4.311 | 3.164 | 3.348 |
| **Scenario Assuming Debt Service Payments Equal to 20% of Exports:** | | | | |
| Base Oil Scenario | 9.664 | 9.727 | 10.231 | 11.360 |
| Intermediate Oil Scenario | 9.083 | 8.603 | 8.761 | 9.391 |
| Pessimistic Oil Scenario | 8.013 | 6.770 | 6.400 | 6.742 |

Still another factor acting to limit inflation is the ability to import more due to the increased availability of foreign currency. This would not only prevent the appearance of supply bottlenecks for domestic industry, but would also discourage price increases for tradeable goods. As a result of those offsetting factors, inflation would not be markedly higher than in the original simulations.

### 3.2.2 An Alternative Treatment for the Public Foreign Debt

One of the conclusions that can be drawn from the experience of the foreign debt crisis over the last few years is that successive reschedulings of payments, as applied since 1982, cannot produce a definite solution to the problem.

The interminable negotiations merely extend the time frame, in the hope that a viable alternative, acceptable to all the parties and permitting a true solution to the problem, might emerge in the future. That is the only benefit yielded by the persistent search for another, more appropriate and functional, way to approach the debt crisis, that has been carried on over the last few years.

Among the many proposals put forward in international financial circles, one of the most interesting is the Mexican plan to purchase US$ 20 billion of its foreign debt at 50% discount, offering 20—year dollar—denominated Mexican government bonds in exchange. The face value payment of these bonds at their maturity would be guaranteed by zero—coupon bonds issued by the United States Treasury, which could be purchased by the Mexican government at a discount of about 80%.[9]

However, the first attempt to put that operation into practice was not very successful. Mexico bought only US$ 3.665 billion of its debt, at a discount of about 30%, for which it issued 20—year bonds for US$ 2.557 billion.

Among the reasons for the limited success of the Mexican plan is the inflexibility of the banking regulations, particularly those of the United States, which require creditor banks to record the amount of the discount at which they are willing to sell debts owed to them as a loss incurred at the time they announce their willingness to participate in the scheme, even if the operation is not realised.

Furthermore, the regulations require the banks to change the form of valuing their assets when they accept bonds in exchange for debts; in this case they must value the bonds at their market price. Since the Mexican bonds were likely to be heavily discounted by the market, due to the risk involved in the absence of a guarantee of interest payments, the acceptance of those bonds by the banks would imply further substantial accounting losses.

The relative failure of this interesting experiment has led to a number of suggestions for ways to make it more viable. In this context, we have made certain proposals intended, among other things, to develop a way to guarantee payment of the interest or yield of the bonds issued by debtor governments. If the bonds were fully secured, creditors would be more willing to accept them in exchange for the original debts.

In our proposal, an international financial institution such as the World Bank would play an important role: it would collect the funds for the regular payment of interest from the debtor countries which have issued the bonds, and transfer those payments to the bond holders. At the same time, it would borrow funds from industrialised countries enjoying a financial surplus (such as Japan and Germany, and certain others) to create a fund for financial assistance to the debtor countries.

That assistance could take the form of long term loans for the purchase of the zero—coupon bonds issued by the US Treasury if the debtor country in question does not have sufficient international reserves for that purpose, or that of the opening of contingent lines of credit to guarantee the payment of the interest on the debtor country's bonds. Those lines of credit would be activated if the country found itself temporarily unable to make its payments. The debtor country would serve this debt towards the international agency on the basis of a pre—established schedule of payments.

A scheme such as this would make it possible for debtor countries' debts to be bought at their market value, with a substantial discount, which would permit a reduction in their international financial obligations.

Their foreign debt service would also decline considerably, since during the next twenty years, they would pay only the interest or yield on the bonds (which in turn, would have a face value of about half the amount of the original debt), plus the cost of the financing granted by the international institution for the purchase of the zero—coupon bonds that would back the face value payment of the debtor's bonds at maturity.

In addition, the implementation of this proposal would make it much more feasible for the creditor banks to participate in a debt—for—bond swap, since the guarantee of both principal and interest payments of the bonds would raise their market value to a more reasonable level, making them more acceptable to banks and easier to market.

However, no such plan would be viable without the political support of the authorities of the industrialised countries; they would have to make their banking regulations more flexible and create conditions more conducive to participation in debt conversion schemes.[10]

### 3.2.3 Results of the Application of the Proposed Debt–Bond Conversion Plan

To analyse the possible medium term effects of the implementation of the proposal for the conversion of foreign debt to bonds on the Venezuelan economy, the three oil scenarios were simulated once again, with a public foreign debt service scheme much like the one outlined above.

The new simulation assumes that the entire Venezuelan public foreign debt held by private banks (approximately US$ 20 billion) would be purchased at a 50% discount, in exchange for 20–year bonds issued by the Venezuelan government for a total of US$ 10 billion. These bonds are assumed to yield the LIBO rate plus 1% per annum.

We also assume that the Venezuelan government would borrow a sum equivalent to 50% of the cost of the zero–coupon bonds it would have to acquire to guarantee the face value payment at maturity on its bonds from the international financial institution in question. The said zero–coupon bonds could be bought at a discount of about 80%.

That is to say, Venezuela would have to pay US$ 2.0 billion to purchase US$ 10 billion of 20–year zero–coupon bonds, of which it would contribute US$ 1.0 billion from its international reserves and borrow the rest from the international financial institutions. There would be no principal payments on that loan during the period covered by our simulation, and the interest is assumed to be at the LIBO rate.

The accumulated foreign debt service payments under this plan are even smaller than those which would be required under the scheme of limiting net payments to 20% of exports. Even in the case of the pessimistic oil scenario, which would involve the lowest debt service payments under that scheme, the payments would still be higher than under the debt–bond conversion plan. However, in our case the first year outlays under the debt–bond swap plan would be higher since we assume that 50% of the zero–coupon bond payment would be covered with international reserves.

Consequently, even under the most adverse oil scenario, the total volume of international reserves at the end of the period, in 1991, would be higher than if

Table 11. Total Net Foreign Debt Service Payments (Billion US$)

|  | 1988 | 1989 | 1990 | 1991 |
|---|---|---|---|---|
| Scenarios Assuming Debt Service Under Current Agreements | 3.729 | 3.846 | 3.612 | 3.029 |
| Scenarios Assuming Debt Service Equal to 20% of Exports | | | | |
|   Base Oil Scenario | 2.249 | 2.465 | 2.706 | 3.012 |
|   Intermediate Oil Scenario | 2.136 | 2.348 | 2.595 | 2.832 |
|   Pessimistic Oil Scenario | 1.926 | 2.130 | 2.369 | 2.595 |
| Scenarios Assuming Debt Service Under Debt—Bond Swap Plan | *2.743 | 1.786 | 1.919 | 1.829 |

\*   Includes payment of US$ 1.0 billion from international reserves for purchase of zero—coupon bonds.

net foreign debt service were limited to 20% of exports. Under the debt—bond conversion plan, Venezuela would retain US$ 7.3 billion in international reserves at the end of 1991, which is equivalent to 9.5 months of merchandise imports.

The country would therefore be in a better position to cope with further deterioration of the oil market, although its international reserve holdings would still be limited, and it would still be impossible to use them more freely to import at the level required to stimulate domestic industry without substantially increasing the country's vulnerability to future oil crises.

Table 12. International Reserves at End of 1991 Under Pessimistic Oil Scenario
(Billion US$)

|  | International Reserves | Months of Imports |
|---|---|---|
| Debt Service Under Current Agreements | 3.348 | 4.6 |
| Debt Service Equal to 20% of Exports | 6.742 | 9.0 |
| Debt Service Under Debt—Bond Conversion | 7.297 | 9.5 |

By the same token, the results for economic activity as measured by the rate of growth of non—oil real GDP are less unfavourable under the more adverse oil scenarios, since the retention of more foreign exchange would make it possible to inject more funds into the domestic economy instead of transferring them abroad. This would permit the adoption of more stimulative economic policies. Unemployment is also lower in this case than in the previous simulations.

Table 13. Average Annual Rate of Growth of Real Non–Oil GDP and Average
Unemployment Rate Under Pessimistic Oil Scenario (Percentages)

|  | Growth | Unemployment |
|---|---|---|
| Debt Service Under Current Agreement | −3.1 | 12.8 |
| Debt Service Equal to 20% of Exports | −2.7 | 11.9 |
| Debt Service Under Debt–Bond Conversion | −2.0 | 11.5 |

However, even under the most favourable schemes for debt service, rates of growth are still strongly negative in the adverse oil scenarios. This implies that the reduction of foreign debt service payments would only serve to mitigate somewhat the impact of a sustained weakness of oil prices, but would not entirely neutralise it.

Just as in the previous case, inflation is not noticeably affected by the change in the form of handling foreign debt service. The reasons are those already discussed in the context of the 20% of export limitation option (see Section 3.2.1).

## 4. CONCLUSION

This study reveals the extreme vulnerability of heavily indebted developing economies which are largely dependent on the export of a product whose price can fall drastically and remain at low levels for long periods of time, as is the case of Venezuela. These economies live under the continual threat of sudden changes in their terms of trade due to circumstances over which they have little control or influence. That is why they have to take all possible action in order to be prepared to respond to these adverse developments.

Among other things, they must be able to retain substantial international reserves, minimise their external payments, especially their foreign debt service, and gain secure access to international financing.

For these goals to be achieved, new ways of managing the developing countries' foreign debt burden need to be devised, offering more viability and acceptability for all the parties concerned. If the only concession made to a debtor country suffering the effects of a sharp fall in the prices of its export products is an extension of the maturity of its debts, the grant of a longer grace period, and lower interest spreads, its ability to cope successfully with the worsening of its terms of trade will continue to be very seriously constrained.

Even if the debtor country could reach an agreement with its foreign creditors to limit debt service net payments to a given percentage of its export earnings — 20% for example — it would still face unacceptable risks in the event of a prolonged decline in the prices of its export products.

Consequently, new arrangements for handling foreign debts need to be developed which, in addition to being acceptable to all concerned, permit a substantial and permanent reduction of external payments to the point where the debt burden and other foreign commitments become bearable. A plan to convert foreign debts into securities, such as the one outlined in this paper or another similar arrangement, could meet this need to a considerable degree.

However, the results of the simulations analysed above indicate that it will still be necessary to obtain external financing on a permanent basis, since it is only the combination of a continuing inflow of capital and a reduction of debt service payments that will allow indebted developing countries to cope with the crises provoked by the collapse of their export earnings without falling into situations of severe economic hardship.

Nevertheless, these recommendations would help these countries to handle the problem only in the short term. That is not enough. If these nations really want to reduce their vulnerability to this type of problem without suffering heavy burdens, they must implement rational and coherent economic policies aimed at achieving clear short, mid, and long term goals among which export development and diversification as well as reduction of import dependency should have the highest priority.

NOTES

* The author wants to express his gratitude to Martin Pérez for his extraordinary support in the elaboration of this paper. Also to Domingo Fontiveros and Richard Melman for their help.

1) For a detailed description of the MODVEN VII model, see Palma, P.A. and Fontiveros, D. "A Comparative Sensitivity Analysis of the Venezuelan Macroeconomic Model 'MODVEN VII'" in *Economic Modelling* vol 5, No. 4, October 1988, pp.286–346.

2) The liquid foreign assets were made up of the international reserves held by the Central Bank, the Venezuelan Investment Fund (VIF), and the commercial banks, as well as the foreign currency deposits held abroad by the Venezuelan Petroleum Corporation (PDVSA). The latter were not counted as reserves, even though they were liquid funds owned by a public agency.

The VIF was created in 1974 to administer the excess revenues from oil exports not immediately injected into the internal economy. Later, it became the chief source of financing the investments made by the state–owned corporations. PDVSA, for its part, was created as a result of the nationalisation of the oil industry in 1976, as the holding company for the state—owned oil industry.

3) In August 1982, PDVSA's financial resources kept abroad were transferred to the Central Bank, where they were registered as international reserves. Meanwhile, the gold reserves were revalued from US$ 42.22 per Troy ounce to US$ 300. This increased the reserves by US$ 2.935 billion.

4) Here the gold reserves are valued at US$ 300 per Troy ounce.

5) An agreement to restructure the public foreign debt was reached in September 1984, but was not signed until February 1986. A few weeks before signing the contracts, the government agreed with its bankers to postpone certain amortisation payments due in 1985 and 1986. For a detailed analysis of the handling of the public foreign debt problem in the 1983–1987 period, see Palma (1987).

6) According to MetroEconomica estimates, at the end of 1986, the equilibrium exchange rate for the commercial bolivar, according to the purchasing power parity and the existing capacity to import, was Bs./US$ 11.90 approximately. See Fontiveros (1987).

7) For a more detailed analysis of the effects of these exchange rate differentials, see Dornbusch (1986) and Garcia (1987).

8) According to the Central Bank, the 1987 average annual increase in the consumer price index was 28.1%. However, between December 1986 and December 1987 those prices rose by 40.3%.

9) For a more detailed explanation of this scheme, see Government of Mexico, *The United Mexican States, Collateralised Floating Rate Bonds Due 2008 (Collateralised as to Principal at Stated Maturity Only, Invitation of Bids*, January 1988.

10) For a more detailed analysis of this proposal, see Palma, P.A. (1988), "A Formula do Mexico: Uma Sugestao Venezuelana", *Gazeta Mercantil*, March 30, Sao Paulo, Brazil, p.4.

## REFERENCES

Central Bank of Venezuela (Various), *Informe Economico*, Caracas.

Dornbusch, R. (1986), "Special Exchange Rates for Capital Account Transactions", *The World Bank Economic Review*, 1, No.1.

Fontiveros, D. (1987), "The Foreign Exchange Market in Venezuela: Problems and Outlook", *MetroEconomica's Monthly Report*, VI, No.8.

Garcia, G. (1987), *El Estado y la Politica Cambiaria*, COPRE, Caracas, mimeo.

Mexican Government (1988), *The United Mexican States, Collateralised Floating Rate Bonds Due 2008 (Collateralised as to Principal at Stated Maturity Only)*, Mexico.

Palma, P.A. (1985), *1974–1983: Una Decada de Contrastes en la Economia Venezolana*, National Academy of Economic Sciences, Caracas.

Palma, P.A. (1987), *El Manejo de la Deuda Publica Externa de Venezuela: Necesidad de Urgentes Cambios*, COPRE, Caracas, mimeo.

Palma, P.A. (1988), "A Formula do Mexico: Uma Sugestao Venezuelana", *Gazeta Mercantil*, Sao Paulo, March 30.

Palma, P.A. and D. Fontiveros (1987), "A Comparative Sensitivity Analysis of the Venezuelan Macroeconomic Model 'MODVEN VII'",*Economic Modelling*, vol. 5, No. 4, October, pp.286–346.

Rodriguez, M. (1987), "Consequences of Capital Flight for Latin American Debtor Countries" in Lessard, D.R. and J. Williamson (eds.), *Capital Flight and Third World Debt*, Institute for International Economics, Washington.

CHAPTER 6


INCOME AND PRICE ELASTICITIES OF FOREIGN TRADE FLOWS:
ECONOMETRIC ESTIMATION AND ANALYSIS
OF THE US TRADE DEFICIT


Jaime Marquez, *Federal Reserve Board*


## 1. INTRODUCTION

That the rest of the world will absorb the reduction of the US trade deficit is a matter of accounting: because this deficit is the trade surplus of the rest of the world, eliminating one means eliminating the other. What is not so evident is which countries will absorb this reduction, an issue of growing interest in view of the significant re–allocation of productive factors that are likely to emerge. That the US trade deficit will improve in response to a real depreciation of the dollar is not in doubt. What is not so clear is how long it will take, an important question given the constraints that external imbalances impose on the design of macroeconomic policy.

Given the significance of these issues, it is not surprising to find an increasing interest in explaining the behaviour of the US trade deficit.[1] However, as currently developed, the literature is not well suited to addressing the issues raised here. First, existing analyses do not account for all world trade and thus cannot identify how foreign trade accounts respond to the reduction of the US trade deficit. By focusing exclusively on US multilateral trade flows, the literature implicitly assumes that policies to reduce this deficit are independent of the distribution of countries absorbing it. Second, the trade elasticities are estimated with multilateral trade flows, a feature that introduces an aggregation bias, implies that the cross price elasticities are zero, and contradicts the empirical evidence against multilateral trade equations found by Thursby and

129

*L. R. Klein and J. Marquez (eds.), Economics in Theory and Practice: An Eclectic Approach, 129–176.*
© *1989 by Kluwer Academic Publishers.*

Thursby (1984).[2] Finally, as required by the literature on the persistence of the trade deficit, the adjustment period of US net exports to a given change in exchange rates is assumed to be both fixed and known. However, to the extent that this adjustment period is a function of trade elasticity estimates, which are random variables, existing analyses rest on a very restrictive assumption.

This paper eliminates these restrictions by building and estimating an econometric trade model to explain bilateral trade flows among all trading partners in the world: Canada, Germany, Japan, the United Kingdom, the United States, other industrial countries, OPEC, non—OPEC developing countries, and the rest of the world.[3] The (non—diagonal) entries in the resulting 9x9 trade matrix are modelled as bilateral import equations and the econometric specification used to estimate the associated trade elasticities is developed in Section 2. Although the econometric estimation of trade elasticities has a history of its own, the estimation of bilateral trade elasticities has received considerably less attention, especially for bilateral trade between industrial and developing countries, and between the latter and OPEC.[4]

To relate these estimates to previous studies, the paper re—examines the asymmetries in income elasticities noted by Houthakker and Magee (1969) and tests the Marshall—Lerner condition. Finally, because of their importance for the issues raised here, the paper tests the properties of the error term, the choice of dynamic specification, and the assumed parameter constancy. Section 3 presents the econometric estimates of income and price elasticities. The analysis finds a substantial dispersion of bilateral elasticities across countries, confirms the asymmetries found by Houthakker and Magee (1969), and cannot reject the Marshall—Lerner condition.

Section 4 assembles the bilateral trade equations into a world trade model. To determine the reliability of the model as a whole, the paper uses residual based stochastic simulations and multiplier analysis. Based on the estimated model, Section 5 uses counterfactual simulations to address two key questions: which countries will absorb the US trade deficit and how sensitive is the adjustment period of net exports to alternative parameter realisations. The evidence reveals three findings of interest. First, the response of foreign trade accounts to a reduction in the US trade deficit is sensitive to the manner in which this deficit is reduced − that is, through dollar depreciation or income contraction. Differences in bilateral income and price elasticities across countries determine the type of response. Second, reliance on either foreign or domestic growth to eliminate the US external imbalance entails significant changes in income levels, both foreign and domestic. Finally, the adjustment period of the US trade deficit in response to changes in exchange rates is highly sensitive to minor perturbations of the elasticity estimates.[5]

## 2. EMPIRICAL ANALYSIS

### 2.1 Econometric Formulation

To estimate bilateral trade elasticities, the analysis relies on the imperfect–substitute model (Goldstein and Khan, 1985), in which imports of country k from country s are modelled as

$$\ln(M_{ks}/e_s P_s^*)_t = \alpha_0 + \alpha_{1ks}\ln Y_{kt}^p + \alpha_{2ks}(\ln Y_{kt} - \ln Y_{kt}^p) + \Sigma_j \alpha_{3ksj}\ln P_{ks,t-j}$$

$$+ \Sigma_j \alpha_{4ksj}\ln P_{kq,t-j} + \alpha_{5ks}\ln(M_{ks}/e_s P_s^*)_{t-1} + \delta D + u_{kst} \tag{1}$$

$M_{ks}$ = dollar value of imports of country k from country s,

$Y_k^p$ = potential income of country k,

$Y_k$ = real income of country k,

$P_{ks} = e_s P_s^*/e_k P_{yk}^*$,

$P_{kq} = [\Pi_\rho (e_\rho P_\rho^*)^{\omega_\rho}]/e_k P_{yk}^*, \quad \forall \rho \neq k, q \neq s$,

$\omega_\rho$ = fixed export share of the $\rho$th country in world exports,

$P_s^*$ = export price of country s, in domestic currency,

$P_{yk}$ = price for domestic output, in domestic currency,

$e_s$ = exchange rate (dollar/foreign),

$D$ = dummy variable for one–time events,

$u_{kst} \sim N(0, \sigma_{ks}^2), E(u_{kst} \cdot u_{ks,t-j}) = 0 \; \forall_j.$

According to (1), bilateral imports are homogeneous of degree zero in prices and imperfect substitutes both for domestic products and among themselves. The response of imports to income has two components: a secular effect, measured by the parameter $\alpha_1$, and a cyclical effect captured by the parameter $\alpha_2$.[6] The own–price elasticity is $\alpha_3$, and the effect of competing prices from third countries is captured by the cross–price elasticity $\alpha_4$. If $\alpha_4 > 0$, then $M_{ks}$ and imports from a third country are said to be substitutes; if $\alpha_4 < 0$, then these imports are complements. The choice of a logarithmic formulation is based on the results from Box–Cox tests reported in Marquez (1988). Finally, (1) also includes dummy variables to control for the effects of one–time events on imports.[7]

Equation (1) recognises that the response of imports to changes in income or prices is subject to delays that might arise from contracts and delivery lags.[8] This paper assumes that these delays follow an Almon lag:

$$\alpha_{3ksj} = \lambda_{30} + \lambda_{31}j + \lambda_{32}j^2, \quad \text{for } j=0,...,j_3 \,,$$
$$\alpha_{4ksj} = \lambda_{40} + \lambda_{41}j + \lambda_{42}j^2, \quad \text{for } j=0,...,j_4 \,.$$

The (long run) income and own–price elasticities associated with (1), $\eta_{ks}$ and $\xi_{ks}$ respectively, are constructed as[9]

$$\eta_{ks} = \alpha_{1ks}/(1-\alpha_{5ks}) \tag{2}$$

$$\xi_{ks} = \Sigma_j \alpha_{3ksj}/(1-\alpha_{5ks}) \tag{3}$$

The corresponding elasticities for multilateral imports are

$$\eta_k = \Sigma_s \phi_{ks} \eta_{ks}$$

$$\xi_k = \Sigma_s \phi_{ks} \xi_{ks}$$

where

$$\phi_{ks} = M_{ks}/\Sigma_i M_{ki} \quad \forall i, k, s; \ i \neq k \neq s$$

Finally, the residual $u_{kst}$ is assumed to be white noise and the stochastic structure associated with country k's bilateral trade equations is

$$u_k = (u_{1k} \cdots u_{nk} \quad u_{k1} \cdots u_{kn})' \sim N(\mathbf{0}, \Omega_k)$$

where

$$\Omega_k = \text{diag}(\sigma^2_{1k} \cdots \sigma^2_{nk} \quad \sigma^2_{k1} \cdots \sigma^2_{kn})$$

and n is the number of trading partners of country k, 8 in this case.

## 2.2 Hypothesis Testing

### 2.2.1 Error Properties and Choice of Dynamic Specification

The reliability of (1) depends on whether the residual exhibits serial independence, normality, and homoskedasticity. To test the first of these properties, the paper applies an F–test to the hypothesis that all the coefficients of an AR(4) for the residual are equal to zero. The hypothesis of normality is tested with the Jarque–Bera statistic (Jarque–Bera, 1980) and homoskedasticity is tested with an ARCH test (Engle, 1982).

To evaluate the validity of the Almon restrictions, the paper estimates (1) with and without the Almon restrictions and then performs an F–test. The associated F–statistic is

$$F_a = [(SSR_0 - SSR_1)/d_1]/[SSR_1/d_2] \sim F(d_1, d_2) ,$$

where

$SSR_0$ is the sum of squared residuals with the Almon lag $(H_0)$,

$SSR_1$ is the sum of squared residuals without the Almon lag $(H_1)$,

$d_1$ is the number of additional parameters under the alternative hypothesis,

$d_2$ is the number of degrees of freedom.

To determine whether the overall dynamic specification of (1) is violated by the data, the analysis compares the sum of squared residuals for both (1) and an "unrestricted" dynamic specification. The latter is constructed by eliminating the Almon restrictions and including, as additional regressors, all predetermined variables lagged one period. If these additional regressors do not contribute significantly towards the reduction of the sum of squared residuals of (1), then it is not possible to reject the choice of dynamic specification embodied in (1). The test statistic is constructed as $F_a$ above, and it is denoted $F_u$.[10]

Finally, this paper tests for the constancy in structural parameters, an important consideration in view of both the need for accurate forecasts and the volatility in prices and exchange rates. This test is also useful for determining the extent to which the hysteresis hypothesis is supported by the data.[11] To test for parameter constancy, (1) is first estimated with data through 1983Q2 and then used to forecast imports through 1985Q2. Testing for parameter constancy amounts to applying an F–test to the hypothesis that the expected forecast error is zero (Chow, 1960, p.595).[12]

## 2.2.2 Trade Elasticities

The paper tests for the presence of structural asymmetries in income elasticities – namely, $\eta_k > \eta_k^*$ and the validity of the Marshall–Lerner condition – that is, whether $\xi_k + \xi_k^* < -1$, where $\eta_k^* = \Sigma_s \phi_{sk} \eta_{sk}$ and $\xi_k^* = \Sigma_s \phi_{sk} \xi_{sk}$. Given the relevance of these two tests for evaluating the effectiveness of changes in exchange rates in correcting world external imbalances, they are applied to each country's multilateral trade flows and to world trade. Testing these hypotheses for world trade serves as a consistency check on the country estimates given that world exports and world imports have the same income and price elasticities.

Because the elasticities relevant for these tests are constructed as the ratio of normal variables (see eqs (2) and (3)), their distributions are not generally known in advance.[13] As a result, this paper generates these distributions empirically using the Monte Carlo procedure developed by Krinsky and Robb (1986).[14] To implement this procedure, this paper assumes that

$$(\hat{\alpha}_{0ks} \cdots \hat{\alpha}_{3ks}(L) \cdots \hat{\alpha}_{5ks})' = \hat{\alpha}_{ks}(L) \sim N(\alpha_{ks}, \Sigma_{ks}), \qquad (4)$$

and uses this assumption to generate a random sample of $\hat{\alpha}_{ks}$, the jth drawing of which is denoted as $\hat{\alpha}_{ks}^j$, j=1...4000. Substitution of each $\hat{\alpha}_{ks}^j$ into (2) and (3) generates random samples for the long run income and price elasticities, $(\hat{\eta}_{ks}^j)$ and $(\hat{\xi}_{ks}^j)$ respectively, from which it is possible to obtain the associated cumulative density functions, $F_{ks}^{\eta}$ and $F_{ks}^{\xi}$.[15] The paper presents the median, the scaled median absolute deviation and the 99 percent significance level for each of the empirically generated elasticity distributions.[16]

## 2.3 The Data

Data on trade flows for all countries, except data on trade flows with respect to the Rest of the World (ROW), come from the *Direction of Trade*, published by the International Monetary Fund. Bilateral imports of country k from ROW are estimated as the difference between total imports of country k and the sum of country k's imports from countries other than ROW:[17]

$$M_{kr} = M_k - \Sigma_s M_{ks} \quad \forall s \neq r, k.$$

Similarly, data for bilateral exports of country k to the ROW bloc are constructed as the difference between total exports of country k and the sum of its bilateral exports to countries other than ROW:

$$X_{kr} = X_k - \Sigma_s X_{ks} \quad \forall s \neq r, k.$$

Given data on all bilateral trade flows with respect to ROW, total exports of this bloc are $X_r = \Sigma_s \varphi_{sr} M_{sr}$, where $\varphi_{sr}$ is an adjustment factor that accounts for differences in recording practices, delivery lags, and CIF/FOB differentials. Total imports of ROW are $M_r = \Sigma_s X_{sr}$.

Real income for Canada, Germany, Japan, the United Kingdom, and the United States is defined as real GNP measured in domestic currency. For both industrial and developing countries, real income is measured as a geometric mean of industrial production for selected countries. Finally, in view of data difficulties, the paper assumes that OPEC's income equals OPEC's exports.[18]

Data on potential output for Canada, Germany, Japan, the United Kingdom, and the United States are generated using Cobb–Douglas production functions. These functions include labour (L), capital (K), oil (O), and imports (M) as inputs and the associated parameters are estimated econometrically. Potential value added $(Y_k^P)$ equals

$$Y_k^P = f(K_k^P, L_k^P, O_k, M_k) - (P_{mk}M_k/P_{yk}) \, ,$$

where $f(\cdot)$ is the predicted value of gross output, $K_k^P$ is the level of the capital stock at full capacity, $L_k^P$ is the labour force, and $(P_{mk}M_k/P_{yk})$ equals the value of imports in terms of domestic output. Data for potential output of LDCs and the bloc of industrial countries are generated as a trend of actual output.

Trade prices are measured as multilateral export unit values with 1972=1. By being both multilateral and unit values, these export prices are not ideally suited for estimating bilateral price elasticities, but data on bilateral export prices are not available. Finally, the analysis uses only four bilateral exchange rates (against the US dollar): the Canadian dollar, the DM, the pound sterling, and the yen. Data for prices of LDCs, OPEC, and the bloc of other industrial countries are denominated in US dollars.

An issue relevant to the construction of the data is the statistical discrepancy between total world imports and total world exports. These discrepancies arise for several reasons: different recording practices across countries, incomplete coverage, asymmetric valuation of imports and exports for countries with incomplete reporting, and lags in recording a given trade flow as both an export and an import because of shipment delays.[19] Figure 1 presents the behaviour of this discrepancy for 1976–1984 as a percentage of world imports. As the figure reveals, the average discrepancy fluctuates around 1 percent with a relatively large standard error. Rather than distributing this discrepancy across individual countries, this paper treats it as an exogenous variable.[20]

An examination of the evolution of the direction of trade (Table 1) reveals several features of interest. First, the share of US imports in world trade has grown from 12 percent in 1970 to 15 percent in 1984 whereas the share of US exports has declined from 12.5 percent to 10.7 percent during the same period.[21] Second, OPEC's exports represented 6 percent of world trade in 1970, but this share increased to 15 percent in 1980 as a result of the large oil price increase and the small short run price elasticity for oil consumption. By 1984, however, this share had declined to 10 percent. Third, between 1970 and 1984, Japan increased its share of the import market in all countries. Finally, the proportion of trade among developing countries, OPEC, and Centrally Planned Economies has shown a substantial increase.

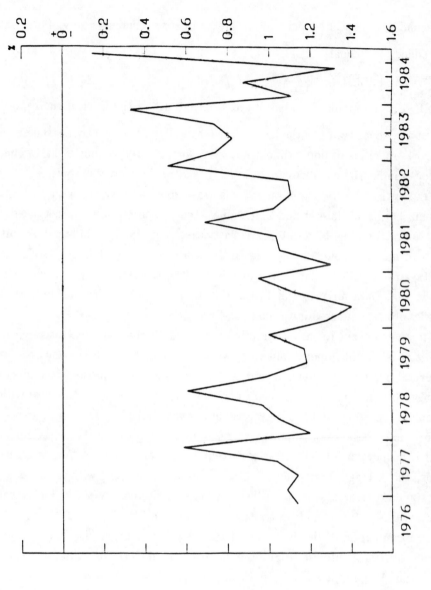

Figure 1. Discrepancy in World Trade Account (% of World Imports)

Table 1. The Structure of International Trade: Trade Matrices for Selected
Periods (percent)

Importing Country

| Exporting Country | Can | UK | Ger | Jap | US | Ind. | LDCs | OPEC | ROW | Sum |
|---|---|---|---|---|---|---|---|---|---|---|
| 1970Q4 | | | | | | | | | | |
| Canada | 0.00 | 0.44 | 0.16 | 0.25 | 3.31 | 0.41 | 0.36 | 0.06 | 0.03 | 5.02 |
| UK | 0.21 | 0.00 | 0.33 | 0.11 | 0.66 | 2.36 | 1.43 | 0.30 | 0.17 | 5.56 |
| Germany | 0.12 | 0.38 | 0.00 | 0.17 | 0.95 | 6.12 | 1.58 | 0.27 | 0.31 | 9.89 |
| Japan | 0.18 | 0.10 | 0.15 | 0.00 | 1.75 | 0.67 | 2.15 | 0.31 | 0.37 | 5.69 |
| US | 2.57 | 0.76 | 0.94 | 1.50 | 0.00 | 2.60 | 3.30 | 0.53 | 0.26 | 12.5 |
| Ind. | 0.29 | 2.37 | 4.86 | 0.72 | 1.89 | 0.00 | 3.68 | 0.78 | 9.99 | 24.6 |
| LDCs | 0.23 | 1.10 | 1.11 | 1.31 | 2.50 | 3.01 | 0.00 | 0.36 | 6.04 | 15.7 |
| OPEC | 0.13 | 0.53 | 0.53 | 0.83 | 0.43 | 1.96 | 0.84 | 0.00 | 1.06 | 6.31 |
| ROW | 0.16 | 0.28 | 0.28 | 0.27 | 0.23 | 12.2 | 1.06 | 0.32 | 0.00 | 14.8 |
| Sum | 3.88 | 5.96 | 8.36 | 5.16 | 11.7 | 29.3 | 14.4 | 2.93 | 18.2 | 100 |
| 1975Q4 | | | | | | | | | | |
| Canada | 0.00 | 0.15 | 0.07 | 0.23 | 2.38 | 0.22 | 0.23 | 0.06 | 0.34 | 3.68 |
| UK | 0.12 | 0.00 | 0.29 | 0.08 | 0.39 | 2.06 | 0.91 | 0.47 | 0.13 | 4.45 |
| Germany | 0.08 | 0.43 | 0.00 | 0.10 | 0.57 | 5.05 | 1.39 | 0.68 | 0.62 | 8.92 |
| Japan | 0.12 | 0.12 | 0.17 | 0.00 | 1.20 | 0.71 | 1.83 | 0.83 | 0.72 | 5.71 |
| US | 2.62 | 0.49 | 0.58 | 1.04 | 0.00 | 2.09 | 2.99 | 1.09 | 0.70 | 11.6 |
| Ind. | 0.24 | 2.23 | 4.23 | 0.72 | 1.34 | 0.00 | 3.59 | 1.50 | 9.95 | 23.8 |
| LDCs | 0.20 | 0.87 | 1.00 | 1.26 | 2.45 | 2.49 | 0.00 | 0.68 | 3.20 | 12.1 |
| OPEC | 0.27 | 0.63 | 0.87 | 2.08 | 1.84 | 3.41 | 2.32 | 0.00 | 1.96 | 13.4 |
| ROW | 0.16 | 0.17 | 0.33 | 0.23 | 0.29 | 11.6 | 2.97 | 0.56 | 0.00 | 16.3 |
| Sum | 3.81 | 5.09 | 7.54 | 5.74 | 10.5 | 27.6 | 16.2 | 5.87 | 17.6 | 100 |
| 1980Q4 | | | | | | | | | | |
| Canada | 0.00 | 0.13 | 0.08 | 0.19 | 1.92 | 0.23 | 0.26 | 0.08 | 0.23 | 3.12 |
| UK | 0.07 | 0.00 | 0.54 | 0.12 | 0.44 | 2.37 | 0.87 | 0.49 | 0.10 | 5.00 |
| Germany | 0.05 | 0.52 | 0.00 | 0.10 | 0.46 | 4.68 | 1.23 | 0.54 | 0.38 | 7.96 |
| Japan | 0.13 | 0.16 | 0.27 | 0.00 | 1.40 | 0.76 | 2.12 | 0.84 | 0.51 | 6.20 |
| US | 2.02 | 0.54 | 0.56 | 1.04 | 0.00 | 1.84 | 3.25 | 0.77 | 0.43 | 10.4 |
| Ind. | 0.17 | 2.22 | 4.01 | 0.61 | 1.21 | 0.00 | 3.47 | 1.68 | 8.99 | 22.4 |
| LDCs | 0.16 | 0.62 | 0.98 | 1.29 | 2.69 | 2.77 | 0.00 | 0.77 | 4.25 | 13.5 |
| OPEC | 0.20 | 0.41 | 0.87 | 2.53 | 2.28 | 3.58 | 2.73 | 0.00 | 2.73 | 15.3 |
| ROW | 0.14 | 0.14 | 0.35 | 0.20 | 0.35 | 11.1 | 3.12 | 0.60 | 0.00 | 16.0 |
| Sum | 2.94 | 4.74 | 7.66 | 6.08 | 10.8 | 27.3 | 17.1 | 5.77 | 17.6 | 100 |
| 1984Q4 | | | | | | | | | | |
| Canada | 0.00 | 0.10 | 0.06 | 0.22 | 3.10 | 0.19 | 0.29 | 0.06 | 0.27 | 4.29 |
| UK | 0.09 | 0.00 | 0.54 | 0.09 | 0.69 | 2.04 | 0.65 | 0.34 | 0.09 | 4.53 |
| Germany | 0.08 | 0.65 | 0.00 | 0.13 | 0.78 | 4.44 | 1.09 | 0.42 | 0.32 | 7.90 |
| Japan | 0.21 | 0.21 | 0.30 | 0.00 | 2.62 | 0.83 | 2.43 | 0.70 | 0.45 | 7.76 |
| US | 2.55 | 0.60 | 0.49 | 1.20 | 0.00 | 1.78 | 2.99 | 0.63 | 0.49 | 10.7 |
| Ind. | 0.24 | 2.20 | 3.62 | 0.72 | 1.90 | 0.00 | 3.14 | 1.42 | 8.40 | 21.7 |
| LDCs | 0.27 | 0.67 | 0.92 | 1.53 | 4.04 | 2.81 | 0.00 | 0.93 | 5.30 | 16.5 |
| OPEC | 0.07 | 0.15 | 0.35 | 1.91 | 1.06 | 1.83 | 2.19 | 0.00 | 2.32 | 9.89 |
| ROW | 0.16 | 0.14 | 0.39 | 0.21 | 0.73 | 9.82 | 4.39 | 0.92 | 0.00 | 16.7 |
| Sum | 3.67 | 4.72 | 6.67 | 6.01 | 14.9 | 23.7 | 17.2 | 5.42 | 17.6 | 100 |

Entries are bilateral imports as a share of world imports, expressed in percent; for a given period, the sum of shares across countries might not add up to 100% because of rounding. Source: *Direction of Trade*, International Monetary Fund.

138

## 3. ESTIMATION RESULTS

### 3.1 Trade Elasticities

This paper applies ordinary least squares to estimate the parameters associated with (1).[22] The estimation sample is based on quarterly data for 1973Q1 – 1985Q2 for imports of non–OPEC countries and 1973Q1 – 1984Q4 for imports of OPEC. Marquez (1988) presents all of the estimated equations along with several descriptive statistics.

The evidence on secular income elasticities (Table 2) offers several features of interest. First, bilateral income elasticities exhibit a large range of variation, a dispersion that weakens the case for aggregate import demand equations. Second, countries fall into one of two categories depending on whether their secular income elasticity is below or above one. The "low" income elasticity countries are Japan and LDCs; the "high" income elasticity countries are Canada, Germany, the United Kingdom, the United States, and other industrial countries; the income elasticities for OPEC's bilateral imports are near unity. Third, the income elasticity for multilateral imports ranges from 0.3 for Japan to 3.1 for the United Kingdom; multilateral exports have an income elasticity ranging between –0.1 for OPEC to 2.3 for LDCs.[23] The negative income elasticity for multilateral exports of OPEC might be the result of a reduction in oil dependence by non–OPEC countries or a bias in favour of non–OPEC oil suppliers.[24] Finally, based on the 99 percent confidence interval, the evidence suggests that 44 of the 56 elasticity estimates are statistically significant.

One of the questions more commonly analysed in the trade literature is whether imports and exports have different income elasticities. These elasticity differentials can be used to determine whether a *ceteris paribus* world wide expansion deteriorates the US trade account. To that end, the paper applies the one–tail test

$$H_0: \eta_k^* - \eta_k \geq 0 \quad \text{versus} \quad H_1: \eta_k^* - \eta_k < 0 .$$

Thus if $\hat{\eta}_k^* - \hat{\eta}_k < -1.65 [\text{vâr}(\hat{\eta}_k) + \text{vâr}(\hat{\eta}_k^*)]^{\frac{1}{2}}$, then reject the null hypothesis.[25]

The last row of Table 2 presents the elasticity differential between exports and imports for each country and for the world. Based on the results, the income elasticity for US imports is significantly greater than the income elasticity for US exports – a result first noted by Houthakker and Magee (1969).[26] The results also indicate that, for the world as whole, the income elasticity of world imports is not significantly different from the income elasticity for world exports, an equality not imposed in estimation.

The pattern of cyclical income elasticities (Table 3) is very similar to that exhibited by secular elasticity estimates. There are, however, some important differences worth noting. First, based on the 99 percent confidence interval, half of the elasticity estimates are not statistically significant, whereas 78 percent of the secular elasticity estimates are statistically significant. Second, the cyclical elasticity for multilateral exports of OPEC is 1.75, which is considerably larger than the corresponding secular elasticity estimate. Third, the cyclical elasticity for imports from LDCs are smaller than their secular counterparts, a finding of interest for studying the outlook for LDC debtors. Finally, with the exception of Germany and OPEC, the elasticity differential between imports and exports is smaller than that exhibited by secular elasticities. Note also that world exports and world imports do not have statistically different cyclical elasticities.

The results for the own–price elasticity (Table 4) indicate all of these elasticities are negative, but also that many of them are not statistically significant (27 out of 56) at the 1 percent significance level. The own–price elasticities for multilateral imports, $\xi_k$, are twice as large as their standard errors and range from −0.5 for the United Kingdom to −1.1 for OPEC. The own–price elasticities for exports, $\xi_k^*$, are also highly significant and range from −0.4 for the United Kingdom to −1.0 for the United States.

The magnitude of the multilateral own–price elasticities is of interest because they determine the stability of the trading system. Specifically, the response of trade to changes in prices is said to be stable if it satisfies the Marshall–Lerner condition: $\xi_k + \xi_k^* < -1$. This condition is tested with a one–tail test:

$$H_0: \xi_k + \xi_k^* \geq -1 \text{ against } H_1: \xi_k + \xi_k^* < -1 \,.$$

If $\xi_k + \xi_k^* < -1 - 1.65[\hat{var}(\xi_k) + \hat{var}(\xi_k^*)]^{\frac{1}{2}}$, then reject the null hypothesis.[27] The last row of Table 4 computes the value for this condition and, based on the evidence, it is not possible to reject the Marshall–Lerner condition for any of the countries here. Furthermore, the entry in the lower right hand corner represents the difference in the price elasticities for world imports and world exports, and as the evidence suggests, it is not possible to reject the hypothesis that world exports and world imports have the same price elasticity.

Finally, Table 5 presents the estimated cross–price elasticities. As the table reveals, the econometric estimation of these elasticities proved extremely difficult and some of them are constrained to zero. According to these results, US exports to Germany, the United Kingdom, other OECD countries, and developing

Table 2. Secular Elasticities

| Exporting Country | Importing Country | | | | | | | | |
|---|---|---|---|---|---|---|---|---|---|
| | Can | Ger | Jap | UK | US | Ind | LDCs | OPEC | $n_k^*$ |
| Canada | — | 2.73 | 0.35 | 0.14 | 1.87 | 3.43 | 0.35 | 0.92 | 1.69 |
| Std. Error | | (0.9) | (0.1) | (1.6) | (0.3) | (0.8) | (0.2) | (0.4) | (0.2) |
| 99% Band: l | | 0.5 | 0.1 | -13.4 | 1.3 | 1.5 | -0.1 | -0.2 | |
| u | | 5.1 | 0.7 | 15.7 | 2.5 | 5.6 | 0.8 | 2.0 | |
| Germany | 2.16 | — | 0.56 | 5.61 | 2.90 | 1.80 | 0.30 | 1.55 | 1.86 |
| Std. Error | (0.5) | | (0.3) | (1.7) | (0.7) | (0.3) | (0.1) | (0.5) | (0.2) |
| 99% Band: l | 0.9 | | -0.1 | 1.7 | 1.3 | 1.1 | 0.1 | 0.2 | |
| u | 3.5 | | 1.2 | 10.9 | 4.7 | 2.6 | 0.6 | 3.1 | |
| Japan | 3.13 | 3.89 | — | 4.83 | 3.56 | 2.17 | 0.60 | 0.65 | 1.98 |
| Std. Error | (0.8) | (1.1) | | (1.6) | (1.0) | (1.8) | (0.2) | (0.3) | (0.4) |
| 99% Band: l | 1.0 | 1.5 | | 0.8 | 1.2 | -2.3 | 0.6 | 0.0 | |
| u | 5.2 | 6.7 | | 9.0 | 6.3 | 7.2 | 1.2 | 1.4 | |
| UK | 0.0$^r$ | 4.61 | 0.82 | — | 2.67 | 2.66 | 0.08 | 1.14 | 2.10 |
| Std. Error | | (0.2) | (0.5) | | (0.7) | (0.6) | (0.1) | (0.4) | (0.3) |
| 99% Band: l | | 4.1 | -0.4 | | 0.8 | 1.2 | -0.1 | 0.1 | |
| u | | 5.1 | 2.1 | | 4.6 | 4.1 | 0.3 | 2.3 | |
| US | 2.01 | 1.95 | 0.79 | 4.11 | — | 2.32 | 0.54 | 0.96 | 1.52 |
| Std. Error | (0.3) | (0.3) | (0.3) | (1.3) | | (0.6) | (0.2) | (0.3) | (0.2) |
| 99% Band: l | 1.3 | 1.2 | -0.1 | 0.8 | | 0.7 | -0.1 | 0.2 | |
| u | 2.9 | 2.7 | 1.7 | 7.4 | | 3.9 | 1.3 | 1.8 | |
| Industrial | 1.29 | 2.15 | -0.04 | 3.43 | 2.51 | — | 0.47 | 1.06 | 1.75 |
| Std. Error | (0.6) | (0.5) | (0.3) | (1.0) | (0.5) | | (0.2) | (0.4) | (0.2) |
| 99% Band: l | 0.3 | 1.0 | -0.8 | 1.2 | 1.4 | | 0.1 | 0.1 | |
| u | 2.9 | 3.6 | 0.7 | 6.0 | 3.7 | | 0.9 | 2.1 | |

| | | | | | | | | | |
|---|---|---|---|---|---|---|---|---|---|
| LDCs | 2.83 | 2.29 | 1.22 | 1.45 | 3.04 | 2.61 | — | 0.53 | 2.26 |
| Std. Error | (0.7) | (0.4) | (0.4) | (0.6) | (1.0) | (0.4) | | (0.2) | (0.3) |
| 99% Band: l | 1.3 | 1.3 | 0.4 | 0.1 | 0.9 | 1.6 | | 0.2 | |
| u | 4.6 | 3.4 | 2.3 | 3.3 | 7.0 | 3.7 | | 1.2 | |
| OPEC | $0.0^r$ | $0.0^r$ | -0.42 | $0.0^r$ | $0.0^r$ | -0.18 | 0.10 | — | -0.14 |
| Std. Error | | | (0.5) | | | (0.5) | (0.2) | | (0.2) |
| 99% Band: l | | | -14.7 | | | -1.8 | -0.3 | | |
| u | | | 11.2 | | | 1.3 | 0.5 | | |
| $\eta_k$ $ | 1.89 | 2.15 | 0.34 | 3.09 | 2.27 | 2.01 | 0.39 | 1.07 | |
| | (0.2) | (0.3) | (0.2) | (0.5) | (0.3) | (0.2) | (0.1) | (0.2) | |
| $\eta_k^* - \eta_k$ ¥ | -0.20 | -0.29 | 1.64 | -0.98 | -0.75 | -0.25 | 1.87 | -1.21 | 0.0007 |
| | (0.3) | (0.37) | (0.44) | (0.62) | (0.35) | (0.33) | (0.34) | (0.28) | (0.41) |

f) For a given bilateral trade flow, the first entry represents the median of the distribution of $\hat{\eta}_{ks}$. The second entry represents the scaled median absolute deviation: median $[\hat{\eta}_{ks}^j$ - median $(\hat{\eta}_{ks}^j)]/0.6745$, where $\hat{\eta}_{ks}^j$ is the long run elasticity associated with the jth drawing, $j = 1, ..., 4000$. The third and fourth entries are the bounds for the 99% confidence band. The lower bound is given by $\hat{\eta}_l$ where $F_{ks}^l = 0.005$; the upper bound is given by $\hat{\eta}_u$ where $1-F_{ks}^u = 0.005$.

$) The multilateral income elasticity, $\eta_k$, is defined as $\eta_k = \Sigma_s \phi_{ks} \eta_{ks}$, and its variance is computed as $var(\hat{\eta}_k) = \Sigma_s \phi_{ks}^2 \sigma_{ks}^2$, where $\phi_{ks}$ = mean $[M_{ks}/\Sigma_i M_{ki}]$, $\sigma_{ks}^2$ = square of the scaled median absolute deviation of the elasticity for imports of country k from country s.

¥) The rightmost entry gives the difference between income elasticities for world imports and world exports.

r) The coefficient is restricted to zero in estimation.

Table 3. Cyclical Income Elasticities[f]

| Exporting Country | Importing Country | | | | | | | | $\eta^*_k$ |
|---|---|---|---|---|---|---|---|---|---|
| | Can | Ger | Jap | UK | US | Ind | LDCs | OPEC | |
| Canada | — | 2.73 | 1.73 | 1.52 | 2.72 | 1.76 | -0.25 | 0.09 | 2.25 |
| Std. Error | | (1.4) | (0.9) | (0.8) | (0.8) | (0.4) | (0.4) | (0.4) | (0.6) |
| 99% Band: l | | -0.9 | -0.6 | -0.5 | 0.7 | 0.7 | -1.3 | 0.0 | |
| u | | 6.3 | 4.1 | 3.6 | 4.8 | 2.8 | 0.8 | 0.2 | |
| Germany | 2.93 | — | 1.89 | 1.33 | 2.75 | 0.95 | 0.32 | 0.08 | 0.97 |
| Std. Error | (0.8) | | (0.8) | (0.6) | (0.8) | (0.2) | (0.1) | (0.03) | (0.2) |
| 99% Band: l | 0.9 | | -0.2 | -0.2 | 0.7 | 0.4 | 0.1 | 0.0 | |
| u | 5.0 | | 4.0 | 2.9 | 4.8 | 1.5 | 0.6 | 0.2 | |
| Japan | 1.44 | 1.01 | — | -0.19 | 1.17 | 0.40 | 0.01 | 0.05 | 0.47 |
| Std. Error | (0.9) | (0.8) | | (0.7) | (0.6) | (0.3) | (0.1) | (0.02) | (0.2) |
| 99% Band: l | -0.9 | -1.0 | | -2.0 | -0.4 | -0.4 | -0.3 | 0.0 | |
| u | 3.8 | 3.1 | | 1.6 | 2.7 | 1.2 | 0.3 | 0.1 | |
| UK | 1.75 | 2.91 | 2.39 | — | 1.60 | 1.05 | 0.20 | 0.06 | 1.05 |
| Std. Error | (0.7) | (0.6) | (1.6) | | (0.7) | (0.3) | (0.1) | (0.02) | (0.2) |
| 99% Band: l | -0.1 | 1.4 | -1.7 | | -0.2 | 0.3 | -0.1 | 0.0 | |
| u | 3.6 | 4.5 | 6.5 | | 3.4 | 1.8 | 0.5 | 0.1 | |
| US | 2.50 | 2.15 | 0.97 | 0.99 | — | 0.98 | 0.11 | 0.05 | 1.00 |
| Std. Error | (0.5) | (0.6) | (0.7) | (0.7) | | (0.3) | (0.2) | (0.02) | (0.2) |
| 99% Band: l | 1.2 | 0.6 | -0.8 | -0.8 | | 0.2 | -0.4 | 0.0 | |
| u | 3.8 | 3.7 | 2.8 | 2.8 | | 1.8 | 0.6 | 0.1 | |
| Industrial | 1.78 | 1.78 | 1.11 | 1.12 | 1.48 | — | 0.24 | 0.06 | 1.04 |
| Std. Error | (0.6) | (0.4) | (0.7) | (0.4) | (0.5) | | (0.1) | (0.02) | (0.2) |
| 99% Band: l | 0.2 | 0.7 | -0.7 | 0.1 | 0.2 | | 0.0 | 0.0 | |
| u | 3.3 | 2.8 | 2.9 | 2.2 | 2.8 | | 0.5 | 0.1 | |

142

|  | | | | | | | | | |
|---|---|---|---|---|---|---|---|---|---|
| LDCs | 1.95 | 1.74 | 0.53 | 1.54 | 0.09 | 1.27 | --- | 0.47 | 0.84 |
| Std. Error | (0.7) | (0.5) | (0.6) | (0.7) | (0.4) | (0.2) | | (0.1) | (0.2) |
| 99% Band: l | 0.1 | 0.5 | -1.0 | -0.3 | -0.9 | 0.8 | | 0.2 | |
| u | 3.8 | 3.0 | 2.1 | 3.5 | 1.1 | 1.8 | | 0.7 | |
| OPEC | 1.11 | 2.99 | 0.02 | 7.07 | 2.26 | 1.31 | 0.44 | --- | 1.75 |
| Std. Error | (0.7) | (1.2) | (1.0) | (1.5) | (1.5) | (0.3) | (0.2) | | (0.4) |
| 99% Band: l | -0.7 | -0.1 | -2.6 | 3.2 | -1.6 | 0.5 | -0.1 | | |
| u | 2.9 | 6.1 | 2.6 | 10.9 | 6.1 | 2.1 | 1.0 | | |
| $n_k$ $ | 2.24 | 1.97 | 0.62 | 1.69 | 1.54 | 1.21 | 0.21 | 0.14 | |
| | (0.4) | (0.3) | (0.4) | (0.3) | (0.3) | (0.1) | (0.1) | (0.02) | |
| $n_k^* - n_k$ * | -0.02 | -1.00 | -0.15 | -0.64 | -0.54 | -0.16 | 0.63 | 1.61 | 0.01 |
| | (0.68) | (0.32) | (0.46) | (0.33) | (0.37) | (0.20) | (0.19) | (0.45) | (0.38) |

f For notes see Table 2.

144

Table 4. Price Elasticities$^f$

Importing Country

| Exporting Country | Can | Ger | Jap | UK | US | Ind | LDCs | OPEC | $\xi^*_k$ |
|---|---|---|---|---|---|---|---|---|---|
| Canada | — | -0.67 | -0.36 | -1.62 | -0.80 | -0.91 | -0.95 | -1.03 | -0.83 |
| Std. Error | | (0.5) | (0.2) | (1.2) | (0.3) | (0.4) | (0.6) | (0.5) | (0.2) |
| 99% Band: l | | -2.2 | -1.3 | -25.0 | -1.6 | -2.0 | -4.3 | -3.9 | |
| 99% Band: u | | 0.6 | 0.0 | 19.4 | 0.0 | -1.2 | 0.3 | -0.1 | |
| Germany | -0.84 | — | -1.31 | -0.49 | -1.70 | -0.26 | -1.42 | -1.19 | -0.65 |
| Std. Error | (0.3) | | (0.6) | (0.3) | (0.8) | (0.2) | (0.5) | (0.5) | (0.2) |
| 99% Band: l | -2.2 | | -5.6 | 1.7 | -4.2 | -0.8 | -4.3 | -2.9 | |
| 99% Band: u | -0.3 | | -0.1 | 10.9 | 2.5 | 0.1 | -0.6 | -0.3 | |
| Japan | -1.28 | -1.51 | — | -0.29 | -1.13 | -0.78 | -0.78 | -0.91 | -0.92 |
| Std. Error | (0.6) | (0.6) | | (0.4) | (0.6) | (0.8) | (0.4) | (0.3) | (0.2) |
| 99% Band: l | -4.7 | -3.3 | | -3.1 | -6.4 | -6.9 | -2.2 | -2.1 | |
| 99% Band: u | -0.2 | -0.4 | | 1.3 | 0.2 | 2.0 | 0.1 | -0.3 | |
| UK | -0.46 | -0.11 | -0.74 | — | -0.34 | -0.55 | -0.15 | -0.81 | -0.44 |
| Std. Error | (0.2) | (0.2) | (0.6) | | (0.4) | (0.3) | (0.1) | (0.4) | (0.2) |
| 99% Band: l | -1.4 | -0.6 | -3.5 | | -3.4 | -1.5 | -0.6 | -2.3 | |
| 99% Band: u | 0.0 | 0.4 | 0.6 | | 1.0 | 0.1 | 0.2 | 0.2 | |
| US | -0.99 | -0.89 | -0.72 | -0.88 | — | -0.72 | -1.45 | -0.52 | -0.99 |
| Std. Error | (0.3) | (0.3) | (0.4) | (0.6) | | (0.4) | (1.2) | (0.3) | (0.4) |
| 99% Band: l | -2.4 | -1.8 | -2.9 | -10.7 | | -2.9 | -34.7 | -1.6 | |
| 99% Band: u | -0.3 | -0.3 | -0.3 | -0.9 | | 0.0 | 15.2 | 0.1 | |
| Industrial | -1.73 | -0.73 | -2.84 | -0.13 | -1.17 | — | -0.67 | -1.17 | -0.83 |
| Std. Error | (1.3) | (0.2) | (1.1) | (0.2) | (0.4) | | (0.3) | (0.5) | (0.1) |
| 99% Band: l | -5.6 | -1.6 | -7.5 | -0.7 | -2.7 | | -2.6 | -2.9 | |
| 99% Band: u | 1.5 | -0.3 | -1.0 | 0.3 | -0.4 | | 0.0 | -0.4 | |

| | | | | | | | | |
|---|---|---|---|---|---|---|---|---|
| LDCs | -1.17 | -0.16 | -1.22 | -0.17 | -0.45 | -0.60 | --- | -1.33 | -0.63 |
| Std. Error | (0.4) | (0.2) | (0.5) | (0.2) | (0.3) | (0.2) | | (0.4) | (0.1) |
| 99% Band: l | -2.9 | -0.7 | -2.8 | -0.8 | -4.8 | -1.4 | | -2.7 | |
| u | -0.4 | 0.3 | -0.2 | 0.3 | -0.5 | -0.3 | | -0.6 | |
| OPEC | -0.52 | -0.25 | -0.24 | -1.94 | -1.29 | -0.19 | -0.11 | --- | -0.55 |
| Std. Error | (0.8) | (0.2) | (0.2) | (0.2) | (0.8) | (0.1) | (0.1) | | (0.2) |
| 99% Band: l | -16.0 | -0.8 | -6.8 | -2.5 | -9.9 | -0.6 | -0.5 | | |
| u | 15.0 | 0.3 | 10.7 | -1.4 | -1.3 | 0.1 | 0.2 | | |
| | -0.95 | -0.60 | -0.93 | -0.48 | -0.92 | -0.49 | -0.81 | -1.14 | |
| | (0.3) | (0.1) | (0.2) | (0.1) | (0.2) | (0.1) | (0.3) | (0.2) | |
| | -1.78 | -1.25 | -1.86 | -0.91 | -1.91 | -1.32 | -1.44 | -1.69 | -0.02 |
| | (0.33) | (0.21) | (0.33) | (0.20) | (0.43) | (0.18) | (0.32) | (0.28) | (0.31) |

f) For a given bilateral trade flow, the first entry represents the median of the distribution of $\hat{\xi}_{ks}$. The second entry represents the scaled median absolute deviation: median$[\hat{\xi}^j_{ks} - $median$(\hat{\xi}^j_{ks})]/0.6745$, where $\hat{\xi}^j_{ks}$ is the long-run elasticity associated with the jth drawing, $j = 1, \ldots, 4000$. The third and fourth entries are bounds for the 99% confidence band. The lower bound is given by $\hat{\xi}_1$ where $F^{\hat{\xi}_1}_{ks} = 0.005$; the upper bound is given by $\hat{\xi}_u$ where $1 - F^{\hat{\xi}_u}_{ks} = 0.005$.

$) The multilateral own-price elasticity is defined as $\xi_k = \Sigma_k \phi_{ks} \xi_{ks}$, and its variance is constructed as $\text{var}(\hat{\xi}_k) = \Sigma_s \phi^2_{ks} \sigma^2_{ks}$, where $\phi_{ks} = \text{mean}[M_{ks}/\Sigma_i M_{ki}]$, $\sigma^2_{ks}$ = square of the scaled median absolute deviation of the elasticity for imports of country k from country s.

¥) The rightmost entry gives the difference between own-price elasticities for world imports and world exports.

146

Table 5. Cross-Price Elasticities^f

Importing Country

| Exporting Country | Can | Ger | Jap | UK | US | Ind | LDCs | OPEC |
|---|---|---|---|---|---|---|---|---|
| Canada | — | 0.00 | 0.00 | 1.30 | 0.00 | -1.74 | 0.00 | 0.00 |
| Std. Error | | | | (1.2) | | (1.2) | | |
| 99% Band: l | | | | -2.3 | | -6.7 | | |
| u | | | | 7.1 | | 1.2 | | |
| Germany | 0.00 | — | 0.00 | 0.00 | 0.77 | 0.15 | 0.42 | 0.00 |
| Std. Error | | | | | (0.8) | (0.2) | (0.4) | |
| 99% Band: l | | | | | -1.2 | -0.3 | -0.9 | |
| u | | | | | 3.1 | 0.6 | 1.6 | |
| Japan | 0.00 | 0.77 | — | 0.00 | -0.08 | 2.67 | 0.00 | 0.00 |
| Std. Error | | (0.4) | | | (0.5) | (3.6) | | |
| 99% Band: l | | -0.2 | | | -1.9 | -51.1 | | |
| u | | 1.9 | | | 1.2 | 48.7 | | |
| UK | 0.00 | 0.00 | 0.00 | — | 0.00 | -0.73 | 0.00 | 0.00 |
| Std. Error | | | | | | (0.6) | | |
| 99% Band: l | | | | | | -6.7 | | |
| u | | | | | | 1.0 | | |
| US | 0.00 | 0.58 | 0.00 | 1.01 | — | 0.29 | 0.39 | 0.00 |
| Std. Error | | (0.3) | | (0.6) | | (0.9) | (1.1) | |
| 99% Band: l | | -0.2 | | -0.4 | | -2.3 | -2.6 | |
| u | | 1.4 | | 2.6 | | 3.1 | 3.7 | |
| Industrial | 0.95 | 0.12 | 2.30 | 0.00 | 0.00 | — | 0.41 | 0.00 |
| Std. Error | (1.5) | (0.1) | (0.8) | | | | (0.5) | |
| 99% Band: l | -3.3 | -0.2 | 1.0 | | | | -0.9 | |
| u | 6.3 | 0.5 | 4.6 | | | | 1.9 | |

| | | | | | | | | |
|---|---|---|---|---|---|---|---|---|
| LDCs | 0.00 | -0.41 | 0.81 | 0.00 | 0.00 | 0.00 | 0.00 | 0.00 |
| Std. Error | | (0.2) | (0.5) | | | | | |
| 99% Band: l | | -1.1 | 0.0 | | | | — | |
| u | | 0.0 | 2.5 | | | | | |
| OPEC | 0.00 | 0.00 | 0.00 | 0.00 | 0.00 | 0.00 | 0.00 | — |
| Std. Error | | | | | | | | |
| 99% Band: l | | | | | | | 0.00 | |
| u | | | | | | | | |

f For notes see Table 4

Table 6. Coefficient Estimate for Lagged Dependent Variables (T-Statistic)

Importing Country

| Exporting Country | Can | Ger | Jap | UK | US | Ind | LDCs | OPEC |
|---|---|---|---|---|---|---|---|---|
| Canada | — | 0.48 (4.0) | 0.34 (2.5) | 0.68 (5.3) | $0.00^r$ | 0.53 (5.6) | 0.41 (3.0) | 0.52 (4.4) |
| Germany | 0.54 (5.4) | — | 0.65 (7.1) | 0.59 (5.3) | 0.33 (2.2) | 0.31 (3.2) | 0.69 (9.3) | 0.74 (13.3) |
| Japan | 0.60 (6.2) | 0.51 (5.4) | — | 0.60 (5.0) | 0.55 (4.8) | 0.72 (7.5) | 0.63 (6.3) | 0.63 (10.3) |
| UK | 0.45 (3.7) | $0.00^r$ | 0.62 (5.3) | — | 0.58 5.1 | 0.42 (3.5) | 0.34 (2.4) | 0.73 (14.8) |
| US | 0.13 (1.0) | 0.25 (2.9) | 0.75 (9.0) | 0.50 (4.6) | — | 0.52 (4.8) | 0.83 (13.2) | 0.74 (13.1) |
| Industrial | 0.54 (4.6) | 0.09 (0.6) | 0.53 (5.4) | 0.56 (4.8) | 0.29 (2.4) | — | 0.61 (5.8) | 0.73 13.2 |
| LDCs | 0.42 (3.4) | 0.14 (1.2) | 0.56 (5.7) | 0.35 (2.6) | 0.52 (3.8) | 0.21 (1.8) | — | $0.00^r$ |
| OPEC | 0.82 (10.3) | 0.60 (5.3) | 0.61 (7.1) | $0.00^r$ | 0.63 (6.2) | 0.53 (7.1) | 0.53 (5.1) | — |

r Parameter constrained to zero in estimation.

countries will increase if third country prices increase. Similarly, US imports from both Japan and Germany will increase if third country prices increase. Finally, an increase in third country prices lowers exports of LDCs to Germany and raises LDCs exports to Japan.

### 3.2 Test Results for Parameter Reliability

To evaluate the reliability of these estimates, Tables 7–9 present test results for the assumptions of normality, serial independence, and homoskedasticity in the error term. The results from the Jarque–Bera test (Table 7) indicate that the data do not violate the normality assumption for any of the 56 bilateral trade equations considered here. Based on the evidence of the F–tests for serial correlation (Table 8), it is not possible to reject the assumption of serial independence for the residuals in 54 out of 56 cases. Finally, the results from the ARCH–test (Table 9) indicate that it is not possible to reject the assumption of homoskedastic errors for any of the 56 trade equations.

To examine further the reliability of the estimates, the paper tests for the choice of dynamic specification and for parameter constancy. On the basis of F–tests, it is not possible to reject the restrictions associated with the Almon distributed lag (Table 10) for the equations in which they were used (30 in total). Furthermore, F–tests comparing the dynamic specification of (1) against an unrestricted dynamic specification (Table 11) reveal that including additional lagged variables and eliminating the Almon restrictions does not provide a significant increase in the explanatory power of (1) − that is, the data do not reject the dynamic specification associated with (1) for any of the 56 cases considered here. Finally, the results associated with the Chow test (Table 12) indicate that it is not possible to reject the hypothesis of parameter constancy in 53 out of 56 trade equations.[28]

## 4. MODEL VALIDATION

To study the dynamic response of trade to changes in prices and income, this section assembles the estimated equations into a world trade model in which each country's trade account, denominated in current dollars, is explained as the difference between multilateral exports and multilateral imports. Country k's multilateral imports are determined by the sum of 8 bilateral imports, 7 of which are explained with 7 import demand equations. The eighth bilateral trade flow is with respect to Centrally Planned Economies and is taken as exogenous.

Table 7. Significance Levels for Testing Normality in the Residuals: Jarque-Bera Statistic

Importing Country

| Exporting Country | Can | Ger | Jap | UK | US | Ind | LDCs | OPEC |
|---|---|---|---|---|---|---|---|---|
| Canada | — | 0.66 | 0.48 | 0.86 | 0.12 | 0.18 | 0.15 | 0.76 |
| Germany | 0.31 | — | 0.67 | 0.47 | 0.18 | 0.73 | 0.61 | 0.26 |
| Japan | 0.21 | 0.21 | — | 0.05 | 0.24 | 0.82 | 0.20 | 0.49 |
| UK | 0.42 | 0.71 | 0.72 | — | 0.62 | 0.54 | 0.16 | 0.91 |
| US | 0.35 | 0.50 | 0.62 | 0.77 | — | 0.56 | 0.57 | 0.26 |
| Industrial | 0.31 | 0.35 | 0.31 | 0.77 | 0.40 | — | 0.08 | 0.39 |
| LDCs | 0.07 | 0.08 | 0.69 | 0.87 | 0.08 | 0.11 | — | 0.81 |
| OPEC | 0.22 | 0.35 | 0.29 | 0.10 | 0.26 | 0.49 | 0.31 | — |

The Jarque-Bera statistic is constructed as

$$JB = T[\mu_3^2/(6\mu_2^3) + (1/24)(\mu_4/\mu_2^2 - 3)^2] \sim \chi^2(2),$$

where $\mu_j$ is the jth central moment of the distribution of the estimated residuals.

Entries in the table represent $Pr(\chi^2(2) < JB)$.

Table 8. Significance Level for Testing Serial Correlation in the Residuals:
(Degrees of freedom)

Importing Country

| Exporting Country | Can | Ger | Jap | UK | US | Ind | LDCs | OPEC |
|---|---|---|---|---|---|---|---|---|
| Canada | — | 0.12 (4,42) | 0.40 (4,41) | 0.09 (4,42) | 0.00 (4,42) | 0.57 (4,42) | 0.50 (4,42) | 0.44 (4,35) |
| Germany | 0.29 (4,42) | — | 0.95 (4,41) | 0.01 (4,42) | 0.78 (4,42) | 0.34 (4,42) | 0.65 (4,42) | 0.12 (4,35) |
| Japan | 0.50 (4,42) | 0.30 (4,42) | — | 0.83 (4,42) | 0.96 (4,42) | 0.46 (4,42) | 0.00 (4,42) | 0.96 (4,35) |
| UK | 0.54 (4,42) | 0.33 (4,42) | 0.72 (4,41) | — | 0.57 (4,42) | 0.50 (4,42) | 0.66 (4,42) | 0.98 (4,35) |
| US | 0.30 (4,42) | 0.15 (4,42) | 0.63 (4,41) | 0.49 (4,42) | — | 0.30 (4,42) | 0.60 (4,42) | 0.55 (4,35) |
| Industrial | 0.75 (4,42) | 0.13 (4,42) | 0.41 (4,41) | 0.07 (4,42) | 0.49 (4,42) | — | 0.73 (4,42) | 0.80 (4,35) |
| LDCs | 0.92 (4,42) | 0.85 (4,42) | 0.80 (4,41) | 0.71 (4,42) | 0.31 (4,42) | 0.60 (4,42) | — | 0.09 (4,35) |
| OPEC | 0.81 (4,40) | 0.61 (4,42) | 0.33 (4,37) | 0.26 (4,32) | 0.20 (4,33) | 0.79 (4,42) | 0.92 (4,40) | — |

The test for serial correlation is based on $\hat{u}_t = \Sigma_j \phi_j \hat{u}_{t-j}$ for $j = 1, \ldots, 4$, where $\hat{u}_t$ is the regression residual. The null hypothesis of no serial correlation is $H_0$: $\phi_1 = \ldots = \phi_4 = 0$, which is tested with F* = $((SSR_o - SSR_1)/4)/(SSR_1 d_2)) \sim F(4, d_2)$, where $SSR_o$ and $SSR_1$ are the sum of squared residuals under the null and the alternative hypothesis, respectively; $d_2$ is the number of degrees of freedom. Entries in the table represent $Pr(F(4, d_2) < F*)$.

Table 9. Significance Levels for Testing Homoskedasticity in the Residuals: (ARCH-Statistic)

Importing Country

| Exporting Country | Can | Ger | Jap | UK | US | Ind | LDCs | OPEC |
|---|---|---|---|---|---|---|---|---|
| Canada | — | 0.34 | 0.02 | 0.14 | 0.19 | 0.82 | 0.85 | 0.31 |
| Germany | 0.76 | — | 0.07 | 0.53 | 0.26 | 0.27 | 0.39 | 0.60 |
| Japan | 0.75 | 0.79 | — | 0.95 | 0.64 | 0.18 | 0.80 | 0.31 |
| UK | 0.78 | 0.29 | 0.78 | — | 0.45 | 0.46 | 0.84 | 0.53 |
| US | 0.87 | 0.50 | 0.74 | 0.23 | — | 0.44 | 0.43 | 0.09 |
| Industrial | 0.81 | 0.65 | 0.42 | 0.23 | 0.93 | — | 0.92 | 0.20 |
| LDCs | 0.59 | 0.92 | 0.41 | 0.13 | 0.58 | 0.89 | — | 0.40 |
| OPEC | 0.66 | 0.65 | 0.14 | 0.90 | 0.32 | 0.51 | 0.69 | — |

The test for homoskedasticity is based on $\hat{u}_t^2 = \gamma_o + \gamma_1 \hat{u}_{t-1}^2$ where $\hat{u}$ is the regression residual. Under the null hypothesis of homoskedastic residuals, $\gamma_1 = 0$ which is tested with a t-test. The entries in the table show $Pr(|t_{T-K}| < t^*)$ where $t^* = \hat{\gamma}_1 / [\sqrt{var(\hat{\gamma}_1)}]$

Table 10. Significance Level for Testing Almon Restrictions (degrees of freedom)

Importing Country

| Exporting Country | Can | Ger | Jap | UK | US | Ind | LDCs | OPEC |
|---|---|---|---|---|---|---|---|---|
| Canada | — | 0.90 (1,39) | 0.06 (4,37) | 0.69 (8,31) | 0.33 (1,39) | — | — | 0.56 (6,30) |
| Germany | — | — | 0.69 (4,37) | 0.68 (5,37) | 0.93 (6,29) | — | — | 0.30 (6,30) |
| Japan | — | — | — | 0.66 (5,37) | — | — | — | 0.37 (6,30) |
| UK | — | — | — | — | — | — | 0.01 (3,39) | 0.72 (6,29) |
| US | 0.78 (9,31) | — | 0.76 (4,37) | 0.49 (10,31) | — | — | — | 0.86 (6,30) |
| Industrial | 0.56 (4,35) | — | — | 0.14 (5,37) | 0.58 (6,34) | — | — | 0.10 (6,30) |
| LDCs | — | — | 0.44 (8,32) | 0.52 (5,37) | 0.61 (6,35) | — | — | — |
| OPEC | 0.02 (3,38) | 0.82 (2,38) | 0.93 (6,29) | 0.63 (16,18) | 0.43 (16,18) | 0.81 (3,7) | — | — |

The test for Almon restrictions is based on $F_a = (SSR_o - SSR_1)/d_1 / (SSR_1/d_2)) \sim F'(d_1, d_2)$, where $SSR_o$ is the sum of squared residuals using the Almon restrictions, $SSR_1$ is the sum of squared residuals without the Almon rstrictions, and $d_1$ is the total number of Almon restrictions. Entries in the table respresent $Pr(F(d_1, d_2) < F_a)$.

Table 11. Significance Levels for Testing Dynamic Specification (degrees of freedom)

Importing Country

| Exporting Country | Can | Ger | Jap | UK | US | Ind | LDCs | OPEC |
|---|---|---|---|---|---|---|---|---|
| Canada | — | 0.51 (5,35) | 0.26 (8,33) | 0.40 (13,26) | 0.82 (4,36) | 0.89 (4,37) | 0.83 (4,37) | 0.27 (9,27) |
| Germany | 0.03 (4,38) | — | 0.58 (8,33) | 0.32 (9,33) | 0.89 (11,24) | 0.92 (5,35) | 0.22 (4,37) | 0.26 (9,27) |
| Japan | 0.14 (4,38) | 0.42 (6,34) | — | 0.81 (9,33) | 0.80 (5,34) | 0.52 (4,37) | 0.21 (4,37) | 0.56 (9,27) |
| UK | 0.30 (6,37) | 0.34 (5,26) | 0.86 (4,37) | — | 0.16 (4,32) | 0.75 (4,37) | 0.66 (5,37) | 0.85 (10,25) |
| US | 0.89 (13,27) | 0.87 (6,34) | 0.55 (8,33) | 0.72 (15,26) | — | 0.73 (4,37) | 0.63 (4,37) | 0.91 (9,27) |
| Industrial | 0.74 (9,30) | 0.64 (6,34) | 0.78 (5,35) | 0.15 (9,33) | 0.76 (10,30) | — | 0.83 (3,39) | 0.69 (9,27) |
| LDCs | 0.64 (4,38) | 0.82 (6,34) | 0.89 (13,27) | 0.23 (9,33) | 0.68 (10,32) | 0.59 (3,39) | — | 0.64 (2,26) |
| OPEC | 0.86 (6,35) | 0.94 (5,35) | 0.90 (9,26) | 0.69 (19,15) | 0.33 (19,15) | 0.87 (7,33) | 0.13 (4,35) | — |

The null hypothesis is represented by equation (1). The alternative hypothesis is constructed by including, as regressors, both the dependent and predetermined variables lagged one period. The test for dynamic specification is based on an F-test: $F_u = (SSR_o - SSR_1)/d_1/(SSR_1/d_2)$, where $SSR_o$ is the sum of squared residuals under the null hypothesis, $SSR_1$ is the sum of squared residuals under the alternative hypothesis, $d_1$ is the number of additional parameters, and $d_2$ is the number of degrees of freedom. Entries in the table represent $Pr(F(d_1, d_2) \geq F_u)$.

Table 22. Significance Levels for Testing Parameter Constancy (Chow Test)
(degrees of freedom)

Importing Country

| Exporting Country | Can | Ger | Jap | UK | US | Ind | LDCs | OPEC |
|---|---|---|---|---|---|---|---|---|
| Canada | — | 0.25 (8,32) | 0.69 (8,33) | 0.56 (8,31) | 0.75 (8,32) | 0.72 (8,33) | 0.15 (8,33) | 0.35 (8,28) |
| Germany | 0.47 (8,34) | — | 0.23 (8,33) | 0.00 (8,34) | 0.90 (8,27) | 0.64 (8,32) | 0.19 (8,33) | 0.64 (8,28) |
| Japan | 0.74 (8,34) | 0.43 (8,32) | — | 0.37 (8,34) | 0.85 (8,31) | 0.42 (8,33) | 0.16 (8,33) | 0.81 (8,28) |
| UK | 0.88 (4,39) | 0.83 (8,23) | 0.63 (8,33) | — | 0.38 (8,28) | 0.45 (8,33) | 0.11 (8,34) | 0.97 (8,27) |
| US | 0.88 (8,32) | 0.20 (8,32) | 0.15 (8,33) | 0.09 (8,33) | — | 0.70 (8,33) | 0.91 (8,33) | 0.91 (8,28) |
| Industrial | 0.92 (8,31) | 0.77 (8,32) | 0.34 (8,32) | 0.00 (8,34) | 0.99 (8,32) | — | 0.21 (8,34) | 0.70 (8,28) |
| LDCs | 0.75 (8,34) | 0.30 (8,32) | 0.09 (8,32) | 0.42 (8,34) | 0.80 (8,34) | 0.41 (8,34) | — | 0.72 (8,21) |
| OPEC | 0.40 (8,33) | 0.92 (8,32) | 0.83 (8,27) | 0.19 (8,26) | 0.96 (8,26) | 0.93 (8,32) | 0.55 (8,31) | — |

To test for parameter constancy, all equations are first estimated with data ending in 1983 and then used to forecast trade volumes through 1985Q2. Under the null hypothesis of parameter constancy, the expected forecast error is zero. The test-statistic used is

$$F_c = \{ [\sum_j \hat{u}_j^2 / T_2] - \sum_k \hat{u}_k^2] / [\sum_k \hat{u}_k^2 / (T_1 - K)] \sim F(T_2, T_1 - K)$$

where $\hat{u}_j$ is the estimated residual for $j = 1, T_1 + T_2$; $\hat{u}_k$ is the forecast residual for $k = 1, T_1$; $T_1$ is the number of observations in the estimation period, $T_2$ is the number of observations in the forecast period; $K$ is the number of regressors. Entries in the table represent $Pr(F(T_2, T_1 - K) \leq F_c)$.

In principle, multilateral exports of country k equal the sum of bilateral imports of other countries from country k. In practice, however, differences in recording practices across countries, shipment delays, and CIF/FOB differentials introduce a discrepancy between the value of exports of country k to country s and the value of imports of country s from country k. This discrepancy is the more serious the higher the frequency of observation. To take into account these measurement problems, the model includes estimated bridge equations that link $X_{ks}$ to $M_{sk}$:

$$\ln X_{ks} = \beta_{0ks} + \beta_{1ks}\ln M_{sk} + \text{error term} , \tag{5}$$

where $M_{sk}$ is determined endogenously as in (1). In the absence of systematic measurement errors, one would expect that $\beta_0 = 0$ and $\beta_1 = 1.$[29]

Given equations (1) and (5), the trade account of country k is

$$\begin{cases} X_{kst} = \exp(\beta_{0ks} + \beta_{1ks}\ln M_{skt} + \text{error term}), \\ M_{kst} = M_{ks}(Y_{kt}, p_{kt}, \hat{\alpha}_{ks}(L), \hat{u}_{kst}) , \\ NX_{kt} = \Sigma_s X_{kst} - \Sigma_s M_{kst} = NX_k(y_t, p_{kt}, \hat{u}_{kt}, \hat{\alpha}_k(L)), \forall s \neq k \end{cases} \tag{6}$$

where
$$y_t' = (Y_{1t} \cdots Y_{nt}) ,$$
$$p_{kt}' = (P_{1kt} \cdots P_{kst} \cdots P_{knt}) ,$$
$$\hat{\alpha}_k(L) = \text{vec}(\hat{\alpha}_{1k}(L) \cdots \hat{\alpha}_{nk}(L)\ \hat{\alpha}_{k1}(L) \cdots \hat{\alpha}_{kn}(L))' ,$$

where L is the lag operator and $\hat{\alpha}_{ks}(L)$ is defined by equation (4). To ensure equality between world exports and world imports, the trade account of the bloc of other OECD countries (k=i) is determined as

$$X_{it} = M_{it} + \Sigma_k M_{kt} - \Sigma_k X_{kt}, \quad \forall k \neq i \tag{7}$$

where

$$M_{it} = \Sigma_s M_{ist} = \Sigma_s M_{ist}(Y_{it}, p_{it}, \hat{\alpha}_{is}(L), \hat{u}_{ist}), \quad \forall s \neq i .$$

Although (7) guarantees that a reduction in the US trade deficit is absorbed by the rest of the world, it does not determine the extent to which a given country absorbs this deficit reduction.

## 4.1 Historical Tracking

Traditionally, econometric models are evaluated by deterministic methods — that is, model predictions are compared against actual values under the assumption that the error terms take their means — namely, zero. However, when applied to nonlinear models, deterministic methods lead to biased model predictions because the expectation of a function of a random variable is not, in general, equal to the function of the expectation of that variable. In other words, because $M_{kst}$ is a nonlinear function of $u_{kst}$, it follows that

$$E[M_{kst}(Y_{kt}, P_{kt}, \hat{\alpha}_{ks}(L), \hat{u}_{kst})] \neq M_{kst}[Y_{kt}, P_{kt}, \hat{\alpha}_{ks}(L), E(\hat{u}_{kst})] \, ,$$

the latter being the deterministic prediction. Biased model predictions produce, in turn, biased measures of model performance.

To avoid these biases, the paper relies on residual–based stochastic simulations as developed by Brown and Mariano (1984). Implementing their approach requires simulating the model over the historical period for alternative values of the residuals. These alternative values are generated following McCarthy's method (McCarthy, 1972) — that is,

$$u^*_{kst} = T^{-\frac{1}{2}} \hat{u}_{kst} \varphi_t, \; \varphi \sim N(0,1) \quad \forall k,s,t \, .$$

Under the assumption that both $E(\varphi_{t-j} \hat{u}_{kst-j})=0 \; \forall_j$ and $E(u^*_{pqt} u^*_{kst})=E(u^*_{pqt})$ $E(u^*_{kst})=0 \; \forall p,q,t$, it is possible to show (McCarthy, 1972) that $u^*_k \sim N(0, \Omega_k)$, which is the distribution of the original disturbances (see equation (1)). One advantage of residual based stochastic simulations is that the number of drawings is equal to the sample size used in parameter estimation, which in this case equals 50.[30]

Based on these 50 stochastic simulations, the paper computes the (in–sample) Mean Absolute Percentage Error (MAPE) as

$$MAPE_t = (\Sigma_t |M_{kst} - (\Sigma_\tau \hat{M}_{kst\tau}/50)|/M_{kst})/36,$$
$$t=1976Q1-1984Q4, \; \tau=1,\ldots,50,$$

where $\hat{M}_{kst\tau}$ is the simulated value of $M_{kst}$ for the $\tau$th drawing. According to Table 13, the model exhibits relatively small errors in dynamic simulations with a MAPE ranging from 0.8 percent for total imports of other OECD countries to 3.5 percent for total imports of OPEC. For the United States, total exports have a MAPE of 2.8 percent and total imports have a MAPE of 2.5 percent. With respect to the trade account, the model exhibits a Mean Absolute Error (MAE) ranging from $7.9 billion for the United States to $2.1 billion for Canada. Note that multilateral trade flows exhibit lower MAPEs than the associated bilateral trade flows, a result that suggests that overpredictions in some trade flows are offset by underpredictions in other flows.

As an additional criterion for model evaluation, the analysis examines a regression of actual on mean predicted values:

Table 13. Model Validation: Measures of Performance in Stochastic Simulations (1976-1984)

| Exporting Country | | Importing Country | | | | | | | | Total Export |
|---|---|---|---|---|---|---|---|---|---|---|
| | | Can | Ger | Jap | UK | US | Ind | LDCs | OPEC | |
| Canada | MAPE[a] | — | 9.5 | 5.9 | 8.5 | 4.4 | 6.2 | 6.8 | 11.9 | 3.2 |
| | F-Test* | — | 0.63 | 0.99 | 0.41 | 0.44 | 0.10 | 0.02 | 0.01 | 0.02 |
| Germany | MAPE | 8.7 | — | 4.9 | 4.6 | 4.7 | 1.9 | 3.1 | 9.5 | 1.6 |
| | F-Test | 0.01 | — | 0.34 | 0.62 | 0.56 | 0.15 | 0.21 | 0.02 | 0.09 |
| Japan | MAPE | 9.2 | 4.7 | — | 6.2 | 5.6 | 9.5 | 4.2 | 6.2 | 3.1 |
| | F-Test | 0.01 | 0.85 | — | 0.22 | 0.43 | 0.06 | 0.92 | 0.38 | 0.98 |
| UK | MAPE | 9.7 | 3.9 | 14.6 | — | 6.3 | 4.3 | 3.6 | 4.3 | 2.9 |
| | F-Test | 0.82 | 0.61 | 0.06 | — | 0.01 | 0.62 | 0.06 | 0.31 | 0.94 |
| US | MAPE | 3.0 | 4.6 | 5.0 | 6.3 | — | 4.4 | 8.4 | 8.3 | 2.8 |
| | F-Test | 0.12 | 0.87 | 0.22 | 0.95 | — | 0.09 | 0.00 | 0.43 | 0.00 |
| Ind. | MAPE | 5.4 | 1.7 | 4.7 | 3.8 | 4.1 | — | 3.1 | 5.1 | 1.3 |
| | F-Test | 0.01 | 0.23 | 0.95 | 0.11 | 0.19 | — | 0.03 | 0.06 | 0.71 |
| LDCs | MAPE | 7.2 | 2.6 | 3.6 | 6.4 | 3.5 | 2.3 | — | 7.0 | 1.0 |
| | F-Test | 0.00 | 0.53 | 0.07 | 0.20 | 0.35 | 0.85 | — | 0.61 | 0.53 |
| OPEC | MAPE | 18.7 | 6.6 | 4.3 | 17.5 | 9.6 | 4.8 | 5.9 | — | 2.6 |
| | F-Test | 0.00 | 0.16 | 0.10 | 0.00 | 0.16 | 0.13 | 0.02 | — | 0.06 |
| Total Imports | MAPE | 3.0 | 1.5 | 2.8 | 3.5 | 2.5 | 0.8 | 2.1 | 3.5 | |
| | F-Test | 0.04 | 0.52 | 0.09 | 0.18 | 0.82 | 0.29 | 0.02 | 0.04 | |
| Trade Balance | MAE[b] | 2.1 | 3.0 | 3.1 | 3.7 | 7.9 | 5.7 | 7.6 | 4.7 | |
| | F-Test | 0.03 | 0.07 | 0.15 | 0.19 | 0.54 | 0.00 | 0.14 | 0.66 | |

a) Mean Absolute Percentage Error for 1976Q1-1984Q4 using the mean of simulated values from 50 stochastic simulations.

*) F-test for $H_o$: a=0 and b=1 in the regression $Y_{it} = a + b\tilde{Y}_{it}$ where $Y_{it}$ is the actual value of the ith variable and $\tilde{Y}_{it}$ is the mean associated with 50 stochastic simulations. The entry represents Prob($F(2,34)$>F-value).

b) Mean absolute error, expressed in US $ billion.

$$M_{kst} = \varphi_0 + \varphi_1(\Sigma_{\tau}\hat{M}_{kst\tau}/50) + v_{kst}, \quad v_{kst} \sim N(0, \sigma_v^2) .$$

If model predictions do not deviate systematically from actual values, then it must be true that *both* $\varphi_0=0$ and $\varphi_1=1$, a joint hypothesis tested with an F– statistic distributed as $F(2,34)$. Based on the significance levels associated with $H_0: \varphi_0=0$ and $\varphi_1=1$ (Table 13), there are 13 (out of 56) bilateral trade equations for which it is not possible to accept the above null hypothesis. Equations failing this test include multilateral imports of Canada, LDCs and OPEC; multilateral exports of Canada and the United States; and the trade balances of Canada and the bloc of other OECD countries.

## 4.2 Multiplier Analysis

To evaluate the properties of the model as a whole, the analysis examines the response of trade accounts to changes in exogenous variables:

Case 1: A 1 percent decline in the annual growth rate for the United States;

Case 2: A 1 percent increase in the annual growth rate of foreign countries;

Case 3: A 50 percent depreciation of the US dollar;

Case 4: Cases 1–3 combined.

These simulations use historical data over 1980Q1–1984Q4 as the baseline and the results are shown in Table 14. Note that, by construction, they guarantee that the sum of trade account responses across countries adds up to zero.

A reduction in the US growth rate of 1 percent produces, after five years, an improvement in the US trade account of $31 billion.[31] This improvement stems from a reduction in US imports that translates into a deterioration of the trade accounts for the remaining countries. The countries absorbing the bulk of the improvement in the US trade deficit are Canada (28%), Japan (25%), and the bloc of other industrial countries (15%). The results also indicate that LDCs experience a small reduction in their trade account given the small cyclical income elasticity for US imports from LDCs (see Table 3).

An expansion in foreign economic activity (Case 2) raises US exports and reduces the US trade deficit by $21 billion after five years.[32] The effect of this foreign expansion on foreign trade accounts depends on the magnitude of the income elasticity for exports relative to the magnitude of the income elasticity for imports. For OPEC and LDCs, the cyclical income elasticity for their exports is greater than the income elasticity for their imports, and therefore, their trade accounts improve in response to an expansion in non–US countries. For the remaining countries, the cyclical income elasticity for imports is greater than the

Table 14. Response of Trade Accounts to Exogenous Changes in Income and
Prices (Deviations from Baseline, billions of US$)

| | 80Q4 | 81Q4 | Years 82Q4 | 83Q4 | 84Q4 |
|---|---|---|---|---|---|
| **Case 1: Slower US Growth**[a] | | | | | |
| Canada | −1.25 | −2.64 | −3.76 | −6.42 | −8.88 |
| United Kingdom | −0.35 | −0.91 | −1.64 | −1.87 | −2.65 |
| Germany | −0.44 | −1.21 | −1.58 | −2.58 | −3.66 |
| Japan | −0.68 | −1.99 | −2.58 | −4.94 | −7.75 |
| Industrial | −0.89 | −2.04 | −2.76 | −3.16 | −4.58 |
| LDCs | −0.13 | −0.35 | −0.49 | −0.79 | −1.00 |
| OPEC | −1.54 | −2.45 | −1.91 | −3.04 | −2.85 |
| United States | 5.28 | 11.60 | 14.71 | 22.80 | 31.35 |
| **Case 2: Faster Foreign Growth**[b] | | | | | |
| Canada | −1.68 | −3.99 | −5.18 | −9.18 | −12.86 |
| United Kingdom | −1.19 | −2.64 | −3.43 | −4.72 | −6.70 |
| Germany | −2.32 | −3.53 | −4.79 | −5.97 | −6.70 |
| Japan | −1.32 | −3.24 | −4.49 | −7.00 | −9.04 |
| Industrial | −0.80 | −1.23 | −1.89 | 0.18 | −0.39 |
| LDCs | 1.06 | 1.82 | 2.41 | 4.03 | 5.61 |
| OPEC | 3.44 | 6.00 | 7.59 | 7.79 | 8.47 |
| United States | 2.81 | 6.81 | 9.79 | 14.87 | 20.57 |
| **Case 3: 50% Dollar Depreciation**[c] | | | | | |
| Canada | −2.67 | −6.07 | −13.96 | −21.97 | −23.56 |
| United Kingdom | 2.97 | −4.17 | −1.43 | −4.27 | −6.22 |
| Germany | 11.43 | 6.13 | 5.40 | 1.31 | 6.18 |
| Japan | −4.36 | −7.83 | −8.77 | −8.56 | −5.97 |
| Industrial | −20.12 | −16.43 | −21.99 | −14.71 | −20.14 |
| LDCs | −56.35 | −75.63 | −67.12 | −63.02 | −68.51 |
| OPEC | 76.72 | 53.48 | 40.85 | 33.22 | 29.36 |
| United States | −7.63 | 50.53 | 67.02 | 78.00 | 88.86 |
| **Case 4: Cases 1–3 Combined** | | | | | |
| Canada | −6.08 | −14.12 | −25.75 | −42.69 | −52.40 |
| United Kingdom | 0.85 | −9.10 | −8.60 | −13.64 | −19.51 |
| Germany | 7.09 | −0.38 | −3.32 | −10.12 | −5.83 |
| Japan | −6.74 | −13.94 | −17.08 | −22.29 | −24.92 |
| Industrial | −22.60 | −21.10 | −27.71 | −17.63 | −25.35 |
| LDCs | −54.90 | −73.40 | −64.26 | −58.20 | −61.78 |
| OPEC | 79.68 | 59.51 | 50.44 | 42.34 | 39.78 |
| United States | 2.70 | 72.53 | 96.29 | 122.24 | 150.02 |

Notes:   a) US growth is reduced by 1 percent per year
b) Foreign growth rate increases by 1 percent per year
c) Dollar depreciates 50 percent against all currencies

cyclical income elasticity for exports, and therefore, their trade accounts deteriorate.

A 50 percent sustained real depreciation of the dollar against all currencies is effective in improving the US trade account.[33] There is a short lived J—curve, and the US trade account improves by $89 billion after five years. The results also indicate that Canada, the bloc of other OECD countries, and LDCs show deteriorations in their trade accounts, with LDCs, experiencing a deterioration of $69 billion in their trade account. There are several reasons for this result. First, the dollar depreciation induces a revaluation of the dollar value of LDCs' baseline trade deficit. Second, the depreciation of the US dollar relative to LDCs' currency increases US real net exports to developing countries, which reinforces the deterioration induced by the revaluation effects. Finally, the dollar depreciation has a depressing effect on third markets for LDC exports — that is, the export gains arising from complementarity are more than offset by the export losses arising from the substitution effects.[34]

To the extent that the events discussed in cases 1–3 can take place at the same time, it is of interest to determine their effects when operating simultaneously. The results reveal that after five years, the US trade account improves by $150 billion. Because international imbalances add up to zero in this model, the improvement in the US trade account implies a deterioration in foreign trade accounts and the countries experiencing the largest deteriorations are Canada ($52 billion) and the LDCs ($62 billion).[35]

## 5. MODEL APPLICATIONS

### 5.1 The Absorption of the US Trade Deficit

To study how foreign trade accounts respond to the elimination of the US trade deficit, the paper endogenises the level of real income in the United States and exogenises the US trade deficit, which is then set to zero both at once and permanently.[36] The resulting pattern of foreign balances depends on both the associated change in US real income and the assumed level of foreign income. For example, if the United States adjusts the deficit on its own, then foreign economies experience a deterioration of their external accounts because of the contraction in US demand for their products. By expanding their economic activity, foreign economies also experience a deterioration of their trade accounts, but in the process they both reduce the degree of adjustment that is needed by the United States and avoid the contraction in their own income that would arise if the United States were the only country adjusting. To examine the role of foreign income, the analysis considers two cases: no foreign income response (Case 1) and a foreign income response (Case 2). These simulations are performed over 1980Q1–1984Q4 and, by construction, they guarantee that the improvement in the US trade account is equal to the historical trade deficit.

The results for Case 1 (Table 15) exhibit several features of interest. First, reliance on US income alone to eliminate the US trade deficit requires a 15 percent fall in US real GNP after five years. Even this sizeable reduction in income is unrealistic because it assumes that prices, exchange rates, and real income in other countries remain unchanged in the face of a contraction in US real income — that is, these are partial equilibrium results. To the extent that income in the United States does not adjust to such a level, the model predicts that the process of eliminating the US trade deficit will require a combination of further dollar depreciation, further expansion abroad, higher foreign prices, and lower US prices.[37] Second, the model indicates that the countries absorbing most of the reduction in the US trade deficit are Japan (29%), Canada (24%), the bloc of other OECD countries (15%), and Germany (11%).

The case of foreign income response (Case 2) is modelled as an increase of 1 percent per year in the growth rate of all non–US countries while US real income adjusts in order to support a zero trade deficit. Based on the simulation results, this foreign expansion raises the level of US real income consistent with balanced trade by 4.5 percent after five years. Intuitively, a foreign expansion raises US exports and improves the trade account. To avoid a surplus, US imports have to increase which implies an increase in US real income. Note that, because income elasticities differ across countries, the trade account effects of faster foreign growth are not the same for all non–US countries: the trade account improves for some countries but deteriorates for others. On balance, however, the non–US balances must weaken. Finally, the foreign expansion alters the degree to which different countries would absorb the reduction in the US trade deficit. Specifically, the deterioration in the combined trade accounts of Japan, Germany, Canada, and other OECD countries would account for 89 percent of the improvement in the US trade account, compared with 79 percent in the absence of a foreign expansion.[38]

Table 15. Trade Account Effects of Lowering the US Trade Deficit to Zero
(Deviations from Baseline, billions of US$)

| | 80Q4 | 81Q4 | Years 82Q4 | 83Q4 | 84Q4 |
|---|---|---|---|---|---|
| **Case 1: Foreign Income Unchanged** | | | | | |
| Trade Account Responses | | | | | |
| Canada | −3.76 | −8.64 | −11.05 | −24.78 | −26.18 |
| United Kingdom | −2.27 | −3.71 | −5.54 | −6.98 | −9.61 |
| Germany | −2.17 | −4.75 | −5.24 | −9.43 | −12.07 |
| Japan | −4.20 | −8.15 | −9.01 | −19.97 | −30.82 |
| Industrial | −4.96 | −8.22 | −9.46 | −12.44 | −16.43 |
| LDCs | −0.82 | −1.45 | −1.78 | −3.47 | −4.50 |
| OPEC | −8.08 | −7.87 | −5.35 | −10.07 | −8.52 |
| United States | 26.26 | 42.78 | 47.44 | 87.14 | 108.11 |
| US real GNP[a] (% deviation) | −3.01 | −6.76 | −9.21 | −17.14 | −15.90 |
| **Case 2: Higher Foreign Income** | | | | | |
| Trade Account Responses | | | | | |
| Canada | −4.73 | −10.96 | −13.48 | −29.40 | −32.45 |
| United Kingdom | −3.28 | −5.83 | −7.94 | −10.57 | −14.84 |
| Germany | −4.26 | −7.60 | −9.07 | −13.95 | −15.75 |
| Japan | −5.15 | −10.15 | −11.71 | −23.40 | −34.41 |
| Industrial | −5.28 | −8.24 | −9.51 | −10.10 | −13.66 |
| LDCs | 0.53 | 0.61 | 1.01 | 1.26 | 2.08 |
| OPEC | −3.90 | −0.62 | 3.27 | −0.99 | 0.92 |
| United States | 26.26 | 42.78 | 47.44 | 87.14 | 108.11 |
| US real GNP[a] (% deviation) | −2.42 | −5.37 | −6.76 | −13.50 | −11.39 |

Note: a) Entries for US real GNP represent percentage deviation from baseline.

## 5.2 Quantifying the Uncertainty in the J—Curve

To quantify the uncertainty surrounding the response of net exports to changes in exchange rates, the analysis defines the J—curve as

$$\hat{J}_{kt} = NX_k(y_t, \lambda p_{kt}, \hat{u}_{kt}, \hat{\alpha}_k(L)) - NX_k(y_t, p_{kt}, \hat{u}_{kt}, \hat{\alpha}_k(L)) \qquad (8)$$
$$= J_{kt}(\hat{\alpha}_k(L), \hat{u}_{kt}, \lambda) ,$$

where $\lambda$ is the shock to exchange rates, and the dynamic nature of the J—curve is embedded in the lag distribution of the parameter estimates, $\hat{\alpha}_k(L)$. Inspection of (8) reveals that the uncertainty associated with the J—curve stems from parameter uncertainty, $\hat{\alpha}_k(L)$, and model uncertainty, $\hat{u}_k$.

Uncertainty in the response of net exports to changes in exchange rates translates into uncertainty about the length of time required to restore external balance. Specifically, let $T_k^*$ be the number of periods that it takes for the J—curve to cross the "zero" line — that is, $J_{k,T_k^*} = 0$. For a fixed $T_k^*$, as assumed in the literature, the notion of deficit persistence is formally expressed as $J_{kt} < J_{k,T_k^*} = 0$ for some $t > T_k^*$. Unfortunately, only the estimate of $T_k^*$, $\hat{T}_k^*$, is known and is given by (8) as $\hat{T}_k^* = T_k(\lambda, \hat{\alpha}_k(L), \hat{u}_{kt})$. Therefore, the adjustment period is a random variable and a comparison between $\hat{T}_k^*$ and $t$ is not informative for determining whether the deficit is persistent because $t \gtrless \hat{T}_k^*$ depending on the realisations of $\hat{\alpha}_k$ and $\hat{u}_{kt}$.[39]

From a policy standpoint, however, the question is not whether $\hat{T}_k^*$ is literally fixed, but how sensitive it is to alternative realisations of elasticity estimates and residuals. If the crossing date were to exhibit a large range of variation in response to these alternative realisations, then this evidence would indicate that the data do not permit identifying the adjustment date with any precision and, therefore, that it is not possible to establish whether the US trade deficit is persistent.

One difficulty in addressing this issue is that $\hat{J}_k$ is a nonlinear function, which complicates the derivation of analytical expressions for its moments. To bypass this difficulty, the paper performs Monte Carlo simulations that permit estimating the relative importance of parameter uncertainty and model uncertainty in accounting for the overall uncertainty of $\hat{J}_k$. Specifically, to evaluate the uncertainty associated with the residuals, this paper applies a 50 percent exchange rate shock ($\lambda=1.5$) while simultaneously drawing random values for the residuals from their joint density function.[40] The values of $u_{kst}$ are drawn following the discussion in section 4; there are 50 drawings for each residual in the model and for each period from 1980Q1 to 1984Q4. The value of $\hat{J}_{kt}$ associated with the $\tau$th drawing of the residuals is

$$\hat{J}_{kt\tau} = J_k(\lambda, \hat{\alpha}_k(L), \hat{u}_{kt\tau}) = \hat{J}_{kt\tau}(\lambda), \tag{9}$$

and the associated mean and 95 percent confidence interval, for each period, are

$$\left\{ \begin{array}{l} \hat{J}_{kt}^e(\lambda) = [\Sigma_\tau \hat{J}_{kt\tau}(\lambda)]/50 , \\ \{\hat{J}_{kt}^e(\lambda) - 2\sqrt{\hat{var}[\hat{J}_{kt\tau}(\lambda)]}, \ \hat{J}_{kt}^e(\lambda) + 2\sqrt{\hat{var}[\hat{J}_{kt\tau}(\lambda)]} \} \end{array} \right\}, \tag{10}$$

respectively. Figure 2 plots the time series for both the mean and the 95 percent confidence interval for the J–curve of the United States. For comparison purposes, the figure also shows the deterministic J–curve, that is, $\hat{J}_{kt}^d = J_k(\lambda, \hat{\alpha}_k(L), 0)$.

The evidence reveals several features of interest. First, the initial deterioration of nominal net exports ranges from \$30 billion to \$90 billion, at annual rates. After one year, nominal net exports improve and the range of uncertainty declines considerably, but it does not vanish and generally involves several billion dollars. Second, despite this uncertainty in the initial response, model uncertainty does not induce a large dispersion of crossing dates, which range between four and five quarters. In other words, $\hat{T}_{us}^*$ is robust to alternative realisations of model residuals. Finally, there are important differences between the deterministic J–curve and the mean of the stochastic J–curve, a difference due to the presence of nonlinearities.

To quantify the uncertainty associated with $\hat{\alpha}_k$, the paper applies an exchange rate shock while drawing alternative values for the parameter estimates from their distribution. Specifically, let $\hat{J}_{kt\epsilon}$ be the value of $\hat{J}_{kt}$ associated with the $\epsilon$th drawing of $\hat{\alpha}_k$, $\hat{\alpha}_{k\epsilon}$, where $\hat{\alpha}_{k\epsilon}(L) = (1+\Psi)\hat{\alpha}_k(L)$, with $\Psi=0.1, 0.2, -0.1$, and $-0.2$. All of these elasticity shocks are within one standard deviation of the point estimates of these elasticities (see Table 4). Figure 3 shows the effects of these parameter changes for the J–curve of the United States.[41] Based on the

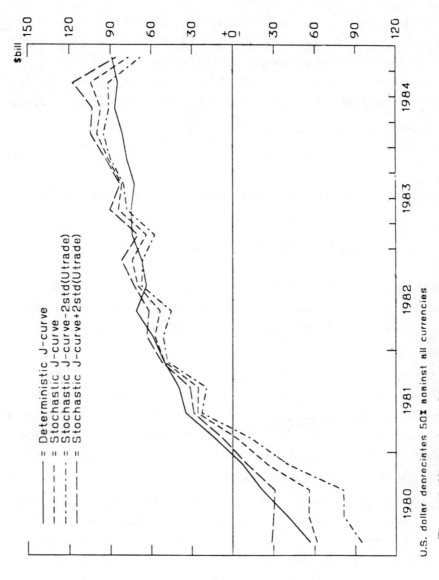

U.S. dollar depreciates 50% against all currencies

Figure 2. Uncertainty of Exchange Rate Effects
Response of Nominal US Merchandise Trade Account

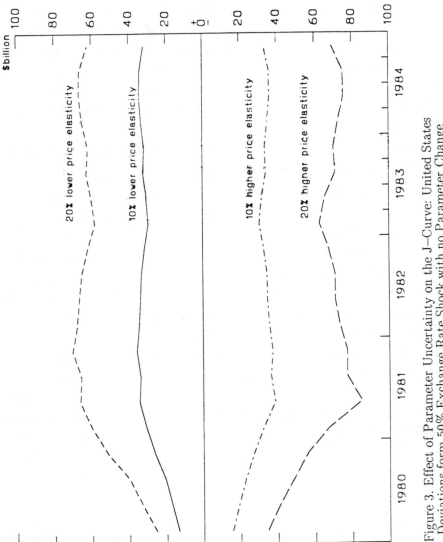

Figure 3. Effect of Parameter Uncertainty on the J-Curve: United States Deviations form 50% Exchange Rate Shock with no Parameter Change

evidence, a 20 percent reduction in the own–price elasticity (an increase in the associated absolute value) could increase the effect of a 50 percent depreciation by as much as $60 billion, at an annual rate. A 20 percent increase in the own–price elasticities, on the other hand, dampens the improvement of the depreciation by approximately $60 billion, at an annual rate. This symmetry of the J–curve to parameter changes is also present for a 10 percent change in parameters.

Associated with these parameter changes there is a dispersion of crossing dates, $\hat{T}^*_{us}$. To estimate this dispersion, Figure 4 presents the J–curves associated with each of these parameter changes. The evidence reveals two features. First, the adjustment period of net exports is subject to a wide range of variation with crossing dates varying from 1 to 12 quarters depending on the parameter shock.[42] Second, the response of the crossing date to the change in the own–price elasticity is not symmetrical. Relative to the case of no parameter change, a 20 percent reduction in the (actual) price elasticity shortens the adjustment period by 2 quarters whereas a 20 percent increase lengthens it by 8 quarters. To the extent that an appreciation of the dollar displaces domestic production, there is a reduction in the own–price elasticity for imports and exports which, based on these results, lengthens the adjustment period associated with a dollar depreciation.

As it stands, the evidence suggests that the crossing date is more sensitive to parameter uncertainty than to model uncertainty and that the assumption of a fixed crossing date, as required by the literature on deficit persistence, is not supported by the data.

## 6. CONCLUSIONS

This paper builds, estimates, and simulates a world trade model to study how the pattern of external imbalances responds to changes in income and prices. The econometric estimation of the associated income and price elasticities reveals a substantial dispersion of bilateral elasticities, confirms the findings of Houthakker and Magee (1969), and cannot reject the Marshall–Lerner condition.

Based on simulations of this model, the analysis finds that reliance on a foreign expansion to eliminate a trade deficit of the size recorded by the United States in the mid 1980s requires extremely implausible increases in foreign growth rates. Similarly, eliminating this deficit through US growth alone would entail substantial losses in income. Finally, and in line with earlier studies, the

169

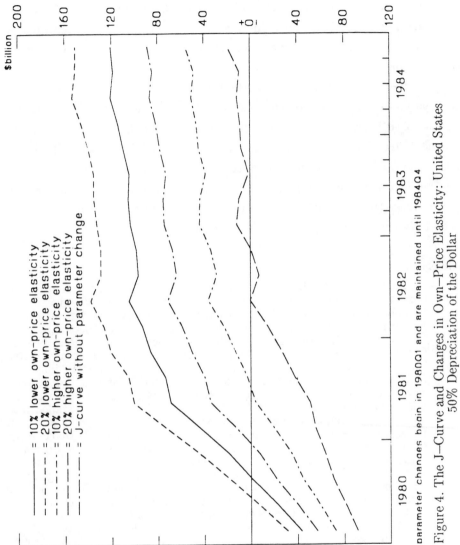

Figure 4. The J–Curve and Changes in Own–Price Elasticity: United States
50% Depreciation of the Dollar

paper finds that changes in relative prices have played the central role in the development of external imbalances during the 1980s. As a result, it seems that a depreciation of the dollar must play a major role in the process of eliminating US external imbalances.

The paper also quantifies the uncertainty associated with the response of US net exports to exchange–rate changes. The findings indicate that the initial response of US net exports is subject to a wide margin of variation ranging between $30 billion and $90 billion, at an annual rate. In addition, the paper finds that small changes in own–price elasticities induce a large range of variation in the adjustment period of US net exports to a given exchange rate shock. Uncertainty about the adjustment period translates, in turn, into uncertainty about the persistence of the US trade deficit.

## NOTES

\* I want to thank Ralph Tryon for his comments and encouragement in this project. I have also benefited from the comments of Russell Cooper, Frank Diebold, Jonathan Eaton, Hali Edison, Sebastian Edwards, Neil Ericsson, Richard Haas, William Helkie, David Howard, Joe Gagnon, David Gordon, Peter Hooper, Maureen Kilkenny, Edward Leamer, Ross Levine, Cathy Mann, Paul Masson, Marc Noland, Adrian Pagan, and Peter Tinsley. I am also grateful to Carolyn Litynski and Michael Mabry for their excellent research assistance and to Linda Matthews for typing several drafts of this paper. The empirical tests are performed with the GIVE computer software developed by David Hendry and installed into TROLL by Ralph Tryon. Earlier versions of this paper have been presented in seminars at the Federal Reserve Board, the US Department of Agriculture, the 1987 and 1988 meetings of the Society for Economic Dynamics and Control, and the 1987 Summer School in Dynamic Organisation, Dublin, Ireland. I am responsible for any remaining errors. This paper represents the views of the author and should not be interpreted as reflecting the views of the Board of Governors of the Federal Reserve System or other members of its staff.
1) See Krugman and Baldwin (1987), Bryant and Holtham (1987), Helkie and Hooper (1987), Feldstein (1986), Hooper and Mann (1987), Eichengreen (1987), Cline (1988), Marris (1987), Hooper (1988).
2) Exceptions include Bergsten and Cline (1985) and Haynes, Hutchison, and Mikesell (1986). These studies focus on US–Japan trade without considering other US bilateral trade flows. Houthakker and Magee (1969) are among the first to study the behaviour of bilateral trade for the United States. This paper extends their analysis by considering all countries.
3) This selection of country disaggregation is designed to match that of the FRB Multicountry Model (MCM).
4) See Goldstein and Khan (1985) and Magee (1975) for surveys of the literature. Other models estimating bilateral trade flows are Houthakker and Magee (1969), Hickman and Lau (1973), Armington (1969), and Edison et.al. (1987).
5) Existing Computable General Equilibrium models (Whalley 1985, Fretz et.al. 1986, Deardorff and Stern 1986, Srinivasan and Whalley 1986, and

Schwartz and Krissoff 1987) are not well suited to address the questions raised in this paper. First, they introduce a real–financial dichotomy that negates the role of changes in nominal exchange rates in affecting the structure of trade. Second, they lack dynamic considerations and thus leave unspecified both the period required for adjustment and the properties of the associated adjustment path. Finally, parameter values are not estimated but drawn from literature surveys, which precludes statistical inferences. This paper also relaxes some of the assumptions embodied in existing econometric trade models. For example, the World Trade Model of the International Monetary Fund uses multilateral trade flows for industrial countries disaggregated across commodities but it pays little attention to trade vis–a–vis developing countries (see Spencer 1984, Deppler and Ripley 1978). The World Model of Project Link explains bilateral trade flows across commodities and with developing countries, but it assumes constant trade shares.

6) Haynes and Stone (1983) obtain a frequency decomposition for US data and estimate income elasticities for each frequency. Their method is not applied here because it would require generating a series of trade matrices – one for each frequency, which is an overwhelming task given the size of the trade matrix used in this analysis (9x9).

7) In addition to being bilateral, equation (1) is not included in the list of models that Thursby and Thursby (1984) examine. In their notation, equation (1) is
$Q_t = f(Y_t, Y_t/YT_t,$ Almon on $P_1$ and $P_2$, Dummies for one–time events, $Q_{t-1})$.

8) Equation (1) also assumes that the length of these lags is fixed; Gagnon (1987) and Husted and Kollintzas (1984) develop models that allow the speed of adjustment to change.

9) The cross–price elasticity is constructed as $\zeta_{ks} = \Sigma_j \alpha_{4ksj}/(1-\alpha_{5ks})$.

10) It is evident that the selection of a dynamic specification entails a certain amount of data mining, a process that requires an increase in the size of the significance level for significance tests. As a result, this paper uses the 99 percent significance level.

11) According to the hysteresis hypothesis, exchange rate changes produce asymmetric changes in the speed of response of trade flows. Losses in export markets, import penetration, and displacement of domestic production account for a slow adjustment in response to a depreciation (see Krugman and Baldwin, 1987). Krugman and Baldwin (1987) test hysteresis with dummy variables, which is formally equivalent to the Chow test performed here.

12) Marquez (1988) presents sequential Chow tests for the one–period ahead forecast errors.

13) The conditions (Greenberg and Webster, 1983) that permit deriving the exact density function of this ratio are not met in this paper.

14) It is possible to re–parameterise (1) in order to estimate directly both the long run elasticity and its associated standard error. However, this procedure gives only asymptotic results. The advantage of the Monte Carlo approach is that it avoids reliance on asymptotic properties.

15) The reliability of this procedure depends on the assumption that (2) and (3) are continuous functions, an assumption that is violated if $\alpha_5=1$.

Based on the evidence presented below (Table 6), the continuity assumption is not violated by the data.

16) The critical values associated with the 99 percent confidence interval are

derived to ensure that the cumulative density at the tails of the distribution is the same for both critical values. An alternative procedure would be to derive these critical values to ensure that they have equal density.

17) One implication of the residual nature of the ROW sector is that bilateral trade between ROW and another country *bloc* (e.g., OPEC) includes intra—trade of the latter country bloc. For example, exports of OPEC to ROW include exports of OPEC to OPEC; similarly, imports of OPEC from ROW include imports of OPEC from OPEC. Although treating ROW as a residual biases the estimates of its trade flows vis—a—vis other country *blocs*, this bias is the same for exports and imports and thus cancels out in the computation of trade accounts.

18) As a result, the model determines OPEC's income endogenously. The countries included in the aggregate of developing countries (fixed weights in parentheses) are South Korea (32%), Mexico (36%), and Taiwan (32%). The countries included in the bloc of other OECD countries are Austria (5%), Belgium (15%), France (26%), Italy (18%), the Netherlands (17%), Norway (4%), Sweden (8%), and Switzerland (7%).

19) See International Monetary Fund (1987), pp.v–vi. Note that, despite treating the ROW sector as a residual category, world exports are not equal to world imports in this analysis because it is not assumed that $X_{sk}=M_{ks}$. In other words, there are two trade matrices: one for exports and one for imports, which for the reasons mentioned in the text, account for the discrepancy in world trade figures.

20) To the extent that the analysis focuses on trade responses, this exogeneity assumption ensures that the adding—up constraint holds because *changes* in world exports are still identical to *changes* in world imports.

21) Exports of the United States do not include exports of products made by US multinationals operating in foreign countries.

22) To simplify the analysis, this paper treats trade flows with respect to the rest—of—the—world (region r) as exogenous; as a result, there are 56 import demand equations ($9^2-9-2*8$). Estimation with both OLS and 2SLS gives similar parameter estimates. This finding would arise if the demand—supply system were recursive because in this case FIML and OLS give the same parameter estimates. To explore this possibility, the analysis estimates an import supply equation and finds (Marquez 1988) that the data do not violate the conditions needed to support a recursive system in 45 out of 56 cases. For the remaining 11 cases, reliance on ordinary least squares could introduce a simultaneity bias. Whether this bias actually exists depends on whether the residuals are correlated with all predetermined variables or with a subset of them (see Johnston, 1984, p.202, problem 5–13). Finally, Marquez (1988) presents Brown—Durbin—Evans results to test for parameter constancy in the processes determining the exogenous variables. Based on the notion of super exogeneity (Engle, Hendry, and Richard, 1983), the results support taking income and prices as exogenous for estimation for the majority of the equations.

23) The estimates of Warner and Kreinin (1983) range from 0.2 for the United Kingdom to 2.95 for the United States; those of Thursby and Thursby (1984) vary between 1.1 for the United Kingdom to 1.7 for the United States. The secular income elasticity for LDC multilateral exports is smaller than the cyclical estimate of Cline (1984).

24) Note that some of the secular elasticities for imports from OPEC are constrained to zero. These constraints are needed in view of the collinearity between the real price of oil and potential GNP observed in

the data. A change in the real price of oil affects the imports from OPEC through two channels: the substitution effect and the effect on potential output. Unfortunately, the estimation results do not permit identifying the separate influences of these two channels.

25) This test assumes that both $\hat{\eta}_k$ and $\hat{\eta}_k^*$ converge in distribution to independent normal variables.

26) Although this result implies that the US trade account would deteriorate as a result of a world expansion, the actual path for the trade account depends on the paths of both relative prices and relative incomes, not just the latter. Consequently, it does not seem valid to argue against the possibility of a differential in trade elasticities on the basis of assumed income paths without specifying the paths for prices.

27) This test assumes that the own–price elasticities converge in distribution to independent normal variables.

28) The equations failing the Chow test are US imports from both other industrial countries and OPEC, as well as UK imports from OPEC.

29) The model, which is shown in Marquez (1988) includes only twenty equations such as (5). Of these, $\beta_0=0$ in seven equations and $\beta_1=1$ in eleven equations.

30) For the purpose of generating random numbers, the seed for the normal distribution of $\varphi$ is indexed by the replication number — that is, there are 50 seeds, one for each replication. Fair (1986) reviews alternative procedures for evaluating model performance with stochastic simulations.

31) This shock is applied to the growth rate of actual US GNP; US potential output remains on its baseline path.

32) The income shock is applied to actual foreign GNP, leaving potential foreign GNP on its baseline path; US real income also remains on its baseline path.

33) The analysis assumes that the "pass–through" coefficient is equal to one. Under the assumption that the prices of LDCs, OPEC, and other industrial countries remain constant in their currencies, P(fx), a dollar depreciation raises their prices denominated in dollars, P($), because P($)=P(fx) e($/fx), where e($/fx) is the bilateral dollar exchange rate, which by assumption is increasing in value.

34) LDC exports have a cross–price elasticity of −0.41 with respect to Germany but 0.81 with respect to Japan (see Table 5).

35) If the model were linear, then the trade account responses from case 4 would exactly equal the sum of the trade account responses for cases 1–3. For the United States, the sum of these responses is $141 billion whereas the response in case 4 is $150 billion. The comparisons for other countries reveal small, but not negligible, differences between the sum of the trade account responses and the response of case 4. Based on these results, it is possible to conclude that the model is nonlinear.

36) Although the assumption of an immediate return to external balance is extreme, it is adopted here because it avoids the ambiguities associated with selecting any other target path for the trade account. The framework could also be used to determine the change in the exchange rate required to eliminate the trade deficit, but it is not presented here because of space considerations.

37) This paper does not address the question of what combination of dollar depreciation and growth adjustment would be most effective or desirable for reducing the US trade deficit.

38) A technical note describing the analytical solution associated with these

simulations is available on request. Also, it is possible to examine the effects of a change in the distribution of world income with the level of world income fixed. These simulation results are also available on request.

39) Note that $E(\hat{T}_k^*) \neq T_k[\lambda, E(\hat{\alpha}_k(L)), E(\hat{u}_{kt})]$ because $\hat{T}_k^*$ is a nonlinear function of its arguments.

40) For this purpose, it is important to note that the estimator of the variance of the residuals is statistically independent from the estimator of $\alpha$; this independence justifies shocking both the residuals and the parameter estimates.

41) The baseline for these comparisons is the J—curve for a 50 percent depreciation without parameter changes — that is, Figure 3 shows $J_{kt}(\lambda, \Psi) - J_{kt}(\lambda, \Psi=0)$. This method allows for uncertainty about both initial and terminal conditions.

42) This dispersion of crossing dates assumes that prices and income are exogenous. Allowance for endogenous responses of income and prices to the dollar depreciation is likely to exacerbate the associated uncertainty. Note that the probability that all of the US own—price elasticities change *simultaneously* by a given magnitude might be small. There is ongoing research to relax this limitation via stochastic simulations.

## REFERENCES

Armington, P. (1969), "Adjustment of Trade Balances: Some Experiments with a Model of Trade among many Countries", IMF Staff Papers, 27, pp.488—526.

Bergsten, F. and W. Cline (1985), "The US—Japan Economic Problem", Policy Analysis in International Economics, No.13, Institute for International Economics, Washington, D.C.

Brown, B. and R. Mariano (1984), "Residual—Based Procedures for Prediction and Estimation in a Nonlinear Simultaneous Model", *Econometrica*, 52, pp.321—43.

Bryant, R. and G. Holtham (1987), "The US External Deficit: Diagnosis, Prognosis, and Cure", Brookings Discussion Papers No.55, The Brookings Institution, Washington, D.C.

Chow, G. (1960), "Tests of Equality between Sets of Coefficients in Two Linear Regressions", *Econometrica*, 28, pp.591—605.

Cline, W. (1984), *International Debt*, MIT Press, Cambridge.

Cline, W. (1988), "Medium—Term Prospects for the US External Current Account", Institute for International Economics, mimeo.

Deardorff, A. and R. Stern (1986), "The Structure and Sample Results of the Michigan Computational Model of World Production and Trade", in Srinivasan, T. and J. Whalley (eds.), *General Equilibrium Trade Policy and Modeling*, MIT Press, Cambridge.

Deppler, M. and D. Ripley (1978), "The World Trade Model: Merchandise Trade", IMF Staff Papers, 25, pp.147—206.

Edison, H., J. Marquez, and R. Tryon (1986), "The Structure and Properties of the FRB MultiCountry Model", International Finance Discussion Paper, No. 293, Federal Reserve Board, Washington, D.C.

Eichengreen, B. (1987), "Trade Deficits in the Long Run", Paper presented at the conference "The US Trade Deficit — Causes, Consequences, and Cures", Federal Reserve Bank of St. Louis, October 23—24, 1987.

Engle, R. (1982), "Autoregressive Conditional Heteroskedasticity with Estimates of the Variance of United Kingdom Inflation", *Econometrica*, 50, 997–1008.

Engle, R., D. Hendry, and J. Richard (1983), "Exogeneity", *Econometrica*, 51, 227–304.

Fair, R. (1986), "Evaluating the Predictive Accuracy of Models" in Z. Griliches and M. Intriligator (eds.), *Handbook of Econometrics*, vol. 3, North–Holland, Amsterdam.

Feldstein, M. (1986), "Correcting World Trade Imbalances", mimeo.

Fretz, D., T. Srinivasan, and J. Whalley (1986), "Introduction", in T. Srinivasan and J. Whalley (eds.), *General Equilibrium Trade Policy Modeling*, MIT Press, Cambridge.

Gagnon, J. (1987), Adjustment Costs and International Trade Dynamic, Ph.D. dissertation, Stanford University.

Goldstein, M. and M. Khan (1985), "Income and Price Elasticities in Foreign Trade" in R. Jones and P. Kenen (eds.) *Handbook of International Trade*, vol. 2, North–Holland, Amsterdam.

Greenberg, E. and C. Webster (1983), *Advanced Econometrics: A Bridge to the Literature*, Wiley, New York.

Haynes, S. and J. Stone (1983), "Secular and Cyclical Responses of US Trade to Income: An Evaluation of Traditional Models", *Review of Economics and Statistics*, 65, pp.87–95.

Haynes, S., M. Hutchinson, and R. Mikesell (1986), "Japanese Financial Policies and the US Trade Deficit", Essays in International Finance, No. 162, Princeton University.

Helkie, W. and P. Hooper (1987), "The US External Deficit in the 1980s: An Empirical Analysis", International Finance Discussion Papers, No. 304, Federal Reserve Board, Washington, D.C.

Hickman, B. and L. Lau (1973), "Elasticities of Substitution and Export Demand in a World Trade Model", *European Economic Review*, 4, pp.347–80.

Hooper, P. and C. Mann (1987), "The US External Deficit: Its Causes and Persistence", International Finance Discussion Papers, No. 316, Federal Reserve Board, Washington, D.C.

Hooper, P. (1988), "The Dollar, External Imbalances, and the US Economy", *Journal of Economic and Monetary Affairs*, 2, pp.30–53.

Houthakker, H. and S. Magee (1969), "Income and Price Elasticities in World Trade", *Review of Economics and Statistics*, 51, pp.111–25.

Husted, S. and T. Kollintzas (1984), "Import Demand with Rational Expectations: Estimates for Bauxite, Cocoa, Coffee, and Petroleum", *Review of Economics and Statistics*, 66, pp.608–18.

International Monetary Fund (1987), *Direction of Trade*, International Monetary Fund, Washington, D.C.

Jarque, C. and A. Bera (1980), "Efficient Tests for Normality, Homoskedasticity, and Serial Independence of Regression Residuals", *Economic Letters*, 6, pp.255–59.

Johnston, J. (1984), *Econometric Methods*, Third Edition, McGraw–Hill, New York.

Khan, M. and K. Ross (1977), "The Functional Form of the Aggregate Import Equation", *Journal of International Economics*, 7, pp.149–60.

Krinsky, I. and L. Robb (1986), "On Approximating the Statistical Properties of Elasticities", *Review of Economics and Statistics*, 68, pp.715–19.

Krugman, P. and R. Baldwin (1987), "The Persistence of the US Trade Deficit", Brookings Papers on Economic Activity, 1, pp.1–56.

McCarthy, M. (1972), "Some Notes on the Generation of Pseudo–Structural Errors for Use in Stochastic Simulation Studies" in B. Hickman (ed.), *Econometric Methods of Cyclical Behavior*, Columbia University Press,

New York.

Magee, S. (1975), "Prices, Income, and Foreign Trade" in P. Kenen (ed.), *International Trade and Finance: Frontiers for Research*, Cambridge University Press, Cambridge.

Marquez, J. (1988), "Income and Price Elasticities of Foreign Trade Flows: Econometric Estimation and Analysis of the US Trade Deficit", *International Finance Discussion Papers*, No. 324, Federal Reserve Board, Washington, D.C.

Marris, S. (1987), "Deficits and the Dollar: The World Economy at Risk", Policy Analyses in International Economics, No. 14, Institute for International Economics, Washington, D.C.

Spencer, G. (1984), "The World Trade Model: Revised Estimates", IMF Staff Papers, 31, pp.469–98.

Schwartz, N. and B. Krissoff (1987), "How Strategies to Reduce US Bilateral Trade Deficits in Manufactures Affect US Agricultural Exports", US Department of Agriculture, Economic Research Service.

Srinivasan, T. and J. Whalley (1986) (eds.), *General Equilibrium Trade Policy Modeling*, MIT Press, Cambridge.

Thursby, J. and M. Thursby (1984), "How Reliable are Simple, Single Equation Specifications of Import Demand?", *Review of Economics and Statistics*, 66, pp.120–28.

Warner, D. and M. Kreinin (1983), "Determinants of International Trade Flows", *Review of Economics and Statistics*, 65, pp.96–104.

Whalley, J. (1985), *Trade Liberalisation Among Major World Trading Areas*, MIT Press, Cambridge.

PART III

**INDUSTRIAL ORGANISATION AND GOVERNMENT POLICY**

CHAPTER 7

PREVIOUS CARTEL EXPERIENCE: ANY LESSONS FOR OPEC?

James M. Griffin*, *Texas A&M University*

## 1. INTRODUCTION

The remarkable success of the OPEC cartel over the last fifteen years has challenged the widely held view among economists that cartels are inherently unstable and short lived. Econometric tests of alternative models of OPEC behaviour point clearly to the conclusion that OPEC is a cartel and owes its success to the willingness of the bulk of its 13 members to voluntarily restrict crude oil production.[1] While OPEC appears to have similar structural characteristics as other cartels, its performance has confounded some of the leading economic experts. For example, in Milton Friedman's now infamous article in Newsweek on March 4, 1974, he predicted that the cartel would soon collapse.[2] Morris Adelman in his 1972 article in *Foreign Policy* is even more explicit:[3]

> "Every cartel has in time been destroyed by one then some members chiselling and cheating; without the instrument of the multinational companies and the cooperation of the consuming countries, OPEC would be an ordinary cartel."

History has since shown that OPEC made what Adelman considered the fatal mistake of replacing the multinational oil companies as the marketers of OPEC crude; nevertheless, even though there have been numerous reports of various members cheating on output quotas,[4] the OPEC cartel has not to date met the fate of "every cartel".

Since Jerry Adams has been known to quip that "A vigorous assertion is no substitution for a proof" it is benefitting that the primary focus of this paper is the empirical basis for the proposition that "cartels are inherently unstable and short lived". While OPEC appears to offer a convincing counterexample to the

179

*L. R. Klein and J. Marquez (eds.), Economics in Theory and Practice: An Eclectic Approach, 179–206.*
© *1989 by Kluwer Academic Publishers.*

universality of this proposition, the proposition may still contain considerable predictive power. By examining the history of other cartels, we may be able to isolate those characteristics shared by weak, short lived cartels from those exhibited by the more virile varieties. Additionally, we examine the implications of these findings for the future evolution of the OPEC cartel. Section 2 surveys the existing cartel literature, examining whether in fact cartels are unstable and short lived. Section 3 proposes a simple methodology for relating cartel characteristics to the monopoly power of a cartel. Section 4 presents the empirical results based on a sample of 54 cartels. Section 4 also examines the causes of cartel disintegration. Section 5 recapitulates the major findings and considers the implications of these findings for the future stability and success of OPEC.

## 2. A REVIEW OF CARTEL LITERATURE

Cartels have enjoyed a venerable history, dating back to ancient Babylonia, Greece, and Rome. In the *Wealth of Nations*, Adam Smith (1937) notes that "people of the same trade seldom meet together, even for merriment and diversion, but the conversation ends in a conspiracy against the public, or in some contrivance to raise prices."[5] Even though loose agreements to fix prices have existed for years, the term "cartel" is a relatively new term coined in Germany in 1879 to describe elaborate institutions designed to fix prices and divide markets.[6] In the United States, collusive behaviour among competitors has been illegal since the Sherman Antitrust Act of 1890. Nevertheless, there are numerous instances in which collusive agreements have been uncovered and prosecuted. Probably, the most famous of these was the electrical equipment conspiracy of the 1950s, involving General Electric, Westinghouse, and 27 other manufacturers.[7] In Europe, prior to World War II, cartels operated openly with no public stigma. In fact, legal systems operated to enforce contractual agreements among cartel members. In such a climate, it is understandable that cartels would flourish. Indeed, export cartels were formed involving basically every major commodity in which European producers were major participants. Fritz Voigt reports thousands of cartels active in Germany over the period 1873 to 1933.[8] So strong was the cartel movement that in 1918, the Webb–Pomerance Act allowed US companies involved in international trade to participate in cartels, providing the goods affected were not subsequently sold in the US.[9]

While postwar economic reforms in Europe have made cartels illegal in West

Germany and the United Kingdom, cartels remain legal in Japan. Caves and Uekusa note in 1972 the existence of 9 authorised depression cartels, 10 rationalisation cartels, 175 export cartels, 2 import cartels, and 604 small business cartels.[10] It is not possible to compare the frequency of cartels in areas and time periods in which cartels are illegal with the frequency of cartel occurrence in other areas and time periods in which cartels are legal. The great frequency with which cartels appear in a legalised environment versus the "apparent" relative infrequency with which such arrangements are uncovered in environments banning cartels does suggest that the legal system is itself an important determinant of cartel behaviour. The costs of maintaining and enforcing cartel agreements are increased significantly when such arrangements are illegal. In the United States, the Sherman Antitrust Act explicitly forbids price fixing. Discovery of clandestine meetings results in civil and criminal penalties.

Consequently, in examining the proposition that cartels are inherently unstable and short lived, one must first stipulate the legal environment within which cartels are assumed to operate. Given our interest in OPEC, it seems most appropriate to focus on cartels which exist in a legal environment in which cartels face no legal restrictions. Therefore, the pre—World War II data for European cartels will be particularly useful. In addition, we consider more recent cartels involving countries which do not explicitly forbid cartelisation. For example, the United Nations Conference on Trade and Development (UNCTAD) encourages various commodity agreements aimed at restricting supply and raising prices of various commodities and raw materials produced by developing countries.

A close look at the available European cartel literature suggests that in areas in which cartels are legalised, it is by no means clear that cartels were doomed to failure. Several extensive reviews of cartels were published in the mid 1940s, reviewing the European cartel experience. In *International Cartels*, Ervin Hexner provides a careful discussion of cartel attributes and a list of over 100 products involved in cartelisation efforts. Hexner had this to say[11]:

> "Those who assume that the pursuit of self—interest by the free entrepreneur results necessarily in competition will find after reconsideration based on economic facts that self—interest, more often than not, may lead to non—competition and even to combinations."

In another major work in 1946, Stocking and Watkins' *Cartels in Action* examines the case histories of the following eight international cartels: sugar, rubber, nitrogen, iron and steel, aluminium, magnesium, electric lamps, and chemicals.[12] This work illustrates the great heterogeneity among cartels. The cartels differed greatly in market structure, the importance of patent barriers, and the role of government involvement. For example, the sugar and rubber cartels depended on state sponsorship in allocating and policing export quotas. In the nitrogen and iron and steel cartels, private producers promoted the cartels but received public support. In contrast, the aluminium, magnesium, and electric lamps cartels were primarily private business arrangements. The history of these eight cartels suggests that each cartel is a unique institution and that broad generalisations are not particularly useful. For example, the success of cartels ranged from the numerous, short lived, and relatively ineffectual sugar cartels to the prosperous aluminium cartel, which was suspended only by the advent of World War II.

In a more recent survey, Frederic Scherer would also appear to reject the notion that cartels are inherently unstable and short lived[13]:

"... we cannot conclude that explicit collusion is necessarily ineffective or unsuccessful. ... an agreement successful for even a short period may yield monopoly profits sufficient to make the effort worth while."

Scherer's comments are interesting in several respects. First, according to Scherer, cartels can be relatively successful in charging supra–competitive prices even if in some instances they may be short lived. Second, Scherer elaborated his statement and used OPEC as his counterexample of a successful cartel. Thus even though Scherer would not appear to support the proposition as a universal conclusion, his remarks implicitly would suggest that as an empirical proposition, it may have considerable predictive power.

Several sources suggest that as an empirical proposition, a randomly selected cartel tends to be unstable and short lived. Fritz Voigt surveyed over 1000 German cartels and found that a combination of chiselling, bickering among insiders, and new entry from outside caused most price fixing agreements to break down.[14] Paul Eckbo surveyed 51 cartels over the last 80 years and found that the average life expectancy of the 51 cartels was 4.3 years. Eckbo also categorised the 51 cartels into those which he termed "effective" versus those considered "ineffective". By his definition, an effective cartel is one that is believed to charge a price roughly twice the competitive price. Given the absence of good cost data, Eckbo's categorisation is subject to considerable subjectivity. Of the 51 cartels, Eckbo labelled a surprisingly high number of 19 cartels as "effective", whereas 32 were termed "ineffective". Curiously, both "effective" and "ineffective" cartels were found to be relatively short lived. The 19 "effective" cartels had a life expectancy of 6.6 years, whereas the "ineffective" cartels lasted only for an average of 2.9 years. Eckbo warns that markets which have been successfully cartelised in the past are likely to experience future efforts to reestablish cartels.[15]

While the preceding literature does offer some predictive support for the proposition that cartels are inherently unstable and short lived, the literature is not particularly suited for inter—cartel comparisons. The account of each cartel is an individual case history. There are no readily available measures of the success of a cartel other than the time period it was in effect. Nor, are there published measures of the profitability of a cartel. Consequently, it is not obvious how one would identify highly profitable, short lived cartels from lower profitability, longer lived varieties. Furthermore, there are few quantitative measures of the attributes of cartels, which might determine its performance. The discussions are primarily qualitative. Data on costs and price elasticities of market demand and competitive fringe supply are rare. Other important variables are essentially qualitative in nature. For example, patent protection may appear to play a vital role in the success of one cartel and yet another cartel may benefit from government policing of export quotas. The appearance is that of isolated case histories, where the threads of commonality are not visible. Section 3 has the ambitious task of pulling these threads together and specifying the structural determinants of cartel performance.

## 3. A METHODOLOGY FOR IDENTIFYING DETERMINANTS OF MARKET POWER

The purpose of this section is to identify the determinants of the market power of a cartel and to specify empirical tests which would link these factors with this measure of cartel performance. Initially, we isolate those factors external to the cartel performance. Next, we examine two internal factors affecting the cohesion of a cartel. Finally, both internal and external factors affecting market power are combined to describe a model capable of empirical rejection.

### 3.1 External Factors Affecting Cartel Performance

Initially, it is instructive to view a cartel as a monolithic institution and consider what external factors limit the power of the cartel to charge a price in excess of the competitive level. Consider first the simple case of a monolithic cartel selling in a market in which fringe producers behave competitively. Assuming the cartel's marginal cost of production is C per unit of output, the cartel's profit function ($\pi$) is given as follows:

$$\pi = PQ_1(P) - CQ_1 \tag{1}$$

where P is the price, $Q_1(P)$ is the cartel's output, and $CQ_1$ are total costs. The cartel's demand schedule ($Q_1(P)$) is related as follows to the market demand schedule ($Q(P)$) and the supply schedule from the competitive fringe producers ($Q_f(P)$).

$$Q_1(P) = Q(P) - Q_f(P) \tag{2}$$

Substituting equation (2) into (1), the profit maximising result is:

$$\frac{d\pi}{dP} = \left[\frac{dQ}{dP} - \frac{dQ_f}{dP}\right] P + Q_1(P) - C \left[\frac{dQ}{dP} - \frac{dQ_f}{dP}\right] = 0 \tag{3}$$

Rearranging equation (3), we obtain:

$$\frac{P-C}{P} = \frac{1}{-\dfrac{Q}{Q_1}\dfrac{dQ}{dP}\dfrac{P}{Q} + \dfrac{Q_f}{Q_1}\dfrac{dQ_f}{dP}\dfrac{P}{Q_f}} \tag{4}$$

Recognising that $\dfrac{dQ}{dP}\dfrac{P}{Q}$ and $\dfrac{dQ_f}{dP}\dfrac{P}{Q_f}$ are merely the price elasticities of market demand and competitive fringe supply, ($E_d$, $E_f$), equation (4) can be simplified as follows:

$$\frac{P-C}{P} = \frac{1}{-E_1} = \frac{1}{-\dfrac{Q}{Q_1} E_d + \dfrac{Q_f}{Q_1} E_f} \tag{5}$$

Equation (5) restates the well known result that the Lerner index $\left[\frac{P-C}{P}\right]$ of monopoly power equals the inverse of the elasticity of demand facing the cartel ($E_1$): In turn, the elasticity of demand facing the cartel ($E_1$) depends on the sum of the output weighted elasticities of market demand ($E_d$) and supply from the competitive fringe ($E_f$).

In effect, economic theory exactly identifies the factors external to a cartel which determine the market power of the cartel. The Lerner index (L) is a natural measure of at least one cartel performance indicator, i.e., it measures the ability to charge a price in excess of unit cost.[16]

$$L = \frac{P-C}{P} \tag{6}$$

Under competition, prices equilibrate with marginal costs and the Lerner index is zero. At the other extreme, the Lerner index takes on a value of unity for the special case of a successful cartel producing a costless commodity. Furthermore, the Lerner index varies inversely with the price elasticity of total market demand and the elasticity of supply from fringe producers, weighted by their relative market shares. Clearly, the greater in absolute value is the demand and fringe supply elasticities, *ceteris paribus*, the greater substitution possibilities consumers face, the lower the Lerner index and the lower is monopoly power. Also note that the lower the share of the market controlled by the cartel, the lower is the Lerner index. In sum, equation (5) identifies the following three external factors as critical: (a) the price elasticity of market demand; (b) the supply elasticity of the competitive fringe; and (c) the share of total output controlled by the cartel.

### 3.2 Internal Factors Influencing Cartel Cohesion

The previous section treated the cartel as a monolithic institution in which all cartel members own shares in a hypothetical firm called "Cartel Incorporated" and exert no influence over their own production. Since the shares owned by any cartel member are predetermined, there are no internal conflicts as each shareholder desires the same objective of maximising Cartel Inc.'s total profits. The joint profit maximising solution readily obtains.

In reality, cartels seldom operate as a single enterprise with complete autonomy. Instead, cartel members generally maintain control over their output. Economic interests among the participants can diverge greatly for a number of reasons. Due to cost differences, discount rates, reserve levels, and market shares, each firm may desire a different market price and output. For example, contrasted to the joint profit maximising solution, cartel members with small market shares will have sharp incentives to cheat by only slightly lowering price and greatly increasing output. Particularly, if small producers have readily expandable capacity, the temptation to cheat may be overwhelming.

Economic theory is much less explicit in identifying factors influencing internal cartel cohesion. When the output decision is jointly dependent on the production responses of other cartel members, the ability to predict the output of any one cartel member is not subject to a general solution. Game theory suggests that a number of equilibria may exist under alternative behavioural assumptions, but, there is no unanimity on behavioural assumptions.[17]

Accordingly, efforts to identify and relate measures of internal cohesion to the Lerner index are necessarily *ad hoc*. Fortunately, we do have the benefit of previous empirical research, which from trial–and–error has demonstrated a considerable degree of explanatory power. Specifically, collusive behaviour has been frequently linked to two factors. First, historical studies suggest that the form of cartel organisation differs dramatically and can heavily influence its success. Furthermore, the relative size of firms in the cartel can also influence the likelihood of cheating. For example, with a cartel membership of a few firms each with large market shares, collusion is more likely to be sustained than in a cartel consisting of many producers with relatively low market shares. Accordingly, we adopt the commonly used Herfindahl index of market concentration (HERF) as a measure of the concentration of economic power among cartel members. Note that usually the Herfindahl index is measured based on a firm's share of the total market; here we take the cartel member's market share of the cartel's output, rather than the total market.[18] Thus the Herfindahl index approximately measures the concentration of economic power *within* the cartel.

In addition to a concentration measure, which reflects interfirm size differences, the form of the cartel organisation can also independently affect cartel cohesion. Cartel organisations are unique, yet they can be roughly classified according to the strength of the organisation *per se*. In the European Steel cartel, each producer was allotted a quota. Firms exceeding quotas were fined while those producing below quotas received subsidies.[19] In the Rubber cartel, the British government issued export quotas, which were closely policed. Similarly, when the Dutch colonies joined in the second cartel (1934–1941), the Dutch, likewise, policed exports.[20] In other instances, the electric lamp cartel cross licensed its patents among the cartel members, giving cartel members a patent barrier to protect them against entry by non–cartel members,[21] and so deter rivalry in the R&D among cartel members. At the other extreme are cartels with little means of controlling the production of cartel members, except for their voluntary compliance. For example, OPEC has one of the more fragile cartel structures; while the cartel fixes quotas, it is difficult to police compliance and there are no penalties for quota violations. In this latter situation, the only glue holding together the quota agreement is the knowledge that if cheating exceeds some unspecified level, the cartel may fall apart and prices and profits will plummet.

Even though cartel organisation is thought to be terribly important, it is not a published series. Indeed, one can argue that it is not quantifiable. Our approach is to construct a subjective index, which on a scale of 1 to 10 ranks cartel organisations according to the direct and indirect policing powers of the cartel organisation index (ORG). Accordingly, equation (5), which pertains to a monolithic cartel, must be modified to allow for the differences in cartel organisation (ORG) and intra–cartel concentration (HERF). Modifying equation (5) and incorporating equation (6), we obtain:

$$L = \frac{\varphi(\text{HERF}, \text{ORG})}{-E_1} \tag{7}$$

where

$$E_1 = \frac{Q}{Q_1} E_d - \frac{Q_f}{Q_1} E_f \tag{8}$$

### 3.3 Specification of the Empirical Relationship Determining the Lerner Index

The preceding sections identify five factors which should determine the monopoly power of a cartel, as measured by the Lerner index. While economic theory is useful in identifying the appropriate determinants of monopoly power, it remains an empirical issue as to exactly how influential these variables are. Our objective is to test the empirical importance of these variables and thereby examine the validity of generalisations concerning cartel stability and viability. First, we examine the determinants of the Lerner index as discussed previously since this is a measure of the monopoly power exercised by a cartel. Second, we perform a post–mortem, categorising the causes of cartel deaths based on the available literature. By examining both the causes of the economic strength of a cartel and the causes of its demise, we are able to better predict and understand the viability of cartels.

From the preceding theoretical discussion of the determination of the Lerner index, we postulate the following log–linear relationship based on equation (7):

$$\ln L_i = \alpha + \beta \ln(-E_{1_i}) + \gamma \ln \text{HERF}_i + \delta \ln \text{ORG}_i + \epsilon_i \tag{9}$$

where the Lerner index (L) depends on the Herfindahl concentration index (HERF), the cartel's organisation structure (ORG), and the elasticity of demand facing the cartel ($E_1$). The latter is calculated in equation (8) and depends in turn on the cartel's market share and elasticities of total market demand and supply from the competitive fringe.

Because of the numerous missing estimates for the elasticities of demand and competitive fringe and the possibility of measurement error in those for which estimates are available, we employ an alternative specification that does not rely on these elasticity estimates. Note from equation (8) that *ceteris paribus*, the elasticity of cartel demand varies inversely with the market share controlled by the cartel (MS). Accordingly, we replace the elasticity of demand ($E_1$) in equation (9) with the cartel's market share (MS) as follows:

$$\ln L_i = \alpha + \beta \ln MS_i + \gamma \ln HERF_i + \delta \ln ORG_i + \epsilon_i \tag{10}$$

## 3.4 Data Construction and Measurement Issues

In order to estimate the coefficients in equation (9) and (10), it is necessary to compile cross sectional data across various cartels. A sample of 54 important international cartels was selected for which most of the relevant data were available. Table 1 reports the cartels selected, the years they were active, and the average Lerner index for the period. Several observations about Table 1 are of importance. First, the sample includes both non—renewable and renewable resource products. Sugar, coffee, tea, cocoa, wheat, and rubber are renewable products while the remainder involve non—renewable resources. Second, as the first column indicates, many products have experienced multiple efforts at cartelisation, confirming Eckbo's point that new cartels are likely to grow from the ashes of old cartels. Sugar, copper, aluminium, mercury, and sulphur offer strong classic examples. Third, with the exception of the first copper cartel (1888—1890), all of the cartels occurred in this century. Fourth, while the life of each cartel varies widely, the average life expectancy is 7.3 years. This is a longer period than the 4 to 6 years average computed by Eckbo. Nevertheless, it does substantiate the conclusion that life expectancy is rather short. Fifth, the Lerner indexes of monopoly power vary widely from —.12 for the first wheat cartel (1933—1934) to .80 for the rubber cartel of 1923—28. This pattern indicates that the success of cartels varies quite widely. Even though the average Lerner index is .31, suggesting that on average, cartels do result in significant monopoly profits, an estimate of .31 is not likely to be an accurate predictor of the Lerner index for any one specific cartel. Finally, this wide variation in cartel life and the Lerner index affords us a rich data set by which to explain the determinants of cartel performance.

Previous studies of cartel performance such as Eckbo's have made no attempt to measure the Lerner index. Whereas price data exist for the period over which the cartel was active, cost estimates are extremely scarce. Cost data are often tightly guarded secrets of the producers and, when available, are not generally available on an annual basis. To overcome these difficulties, all of the

Table 1. Cartels and Their Performance Attributes

| Cartel | Years Active | Life (years) | Lerner Index |
|---|---|---|---|
| Sugar I | 1926–1928 | 2 | .10 |
| Sugar II | 1931–1935 | 4 | .13 |
| Sugar III | 1937–1939 | 2 | .06 |
| Sugar IV | 1959–1961 | 2 | .01 |
| Sugar V | 1968–1973 | 5 | .12 |
| Sugar VI | 1974–1977 | 3 | .28 |
| Sugar VII | 1978–1981 | 3 | .13 |
| Coffee I | 1905–1923 | 18 | .34 |
| Coffee II | 1963–1973 | 10 | .15 |
| Coffee III | 1976–1981 | 5 | .47 |
| Tea I | 1933–1943 | 10 | .26 |
| Tea II | 1950–1955 | 5 | .24 |
| Cocoa I | 1973–1979 | 6 | .59 |
| Wheat I | 1933–1934 | 1 | −.12 |
| Wheat II | 1942–1971 | 29 | .11 |
| Rubber I | 1923–1928 | 5 | .80 |
| Rubber II | 1934–1944 | 10 | .66 |
| Steel I | 1926–1929 | 3 | .12 |
| Steel II | 1933–1938 | 5 | .28 |
| Copper I | 1888–1890 | 2 | .34 |
| Copper II | 1918–1922 | 4 | −.01 |
| Copper III | 1926–1932 | 6 | −.04 |
| Copper IV | 1935–1939 | 4 | −.06 |
| Copper V | 1968– | 19 | .20 |
| Lead I | 1921–1933 | 14 | .17 |
| Zinc I | 1928–1929 | 2 | .27 |
| Zinc II | 1931–1935 | 4 | .13 |
| Bauxite I | 1974–1984 | 10 | .15 |
| Tin I | 1921–1924 | 3 | .18 |
| Tin II | 1929–1931 | 2 | .13 |
| Tin III | 1931–1946 | 15 | .24 |
| Tin IV | 1956–1981 | 26 | .32 |
| Aluminium I | 1901–1908 | 7 | .67 |
| Aluminium II | 1912–1914 | 2 | .40 |
| Aluminium III | 1926–1931 | 5 | .31 |
| Aluminium IV | 1931–1939 | 8 | .34 |
| Mercury I | 1928–1950 | 22 | .52 |
| Mercury II | 1954–1970 | 16 | .73 |
| Mercury III | 1975–1982 | 7 | .30 |
| Sulphur I | 1907–1910 | 3 | .53 |
| Sulphur II | 1922–1932 | 10 | .24 |
| Sulphur III | 1934–1939 | 5 | .45 |
| Sulphur IV | 1947–1958 | 11 | .28 |
| Uranium I | 1972–1975 | 3 | .50 |
| Platinum I | 1919–1927 | 8 | .43 |
| Platinum II | 1931–1933 | 2 | .10 |
| Phosphate I | 1933–1937 | 4 | .42 |
| Potash I | 1927–1939 | 12 | .36 |
| Coke | 1937–1939 | 2 | .46 |
| Nitrogen I | 1919–1930 | 11 | .50 |

| Nitrogen II | 1931–1932 | 2 | .30 |
| Nitrogen III | 1932–1939 | 7 | .22 |
| Magnesium I | 1927–1939 | 12 | .38 |
| Magnesium II | 1934–1937 | 3 | .25 |
| Average | | 7.3 years | .31 |

price data were deflated by the US wholesale price deflator in order to measure prices in real terms. When cost data were unavailable, the trends–in–peak procedures for measuring the Wharton index of capacity utilisation[22] was adapted to measuring the long run costs (C in equation (6)) in the Lerner index computation. The idea is that by connecting the points of the lowest real prices over time, the resulting lines approximate long run costs. The assumption is that when prices fall sharply, the cartel has collapsed and prices approximate long run marginal costs. Once given the trend lines formed by connecting these minimum price "lows", long run costs are approximated and the Lerner index for any year can be estimated. In turn, the average Lerner index shown in Table 1 is found by averaging the Lerner index for each year the cartel is active.

There are a number of objections to such an approach which deserve mention. First, it is not obvious that the valleys in price truly reflect long run costs. Even when prices fall sharply indicating cartel weakness, latent monopoly power may still be present and the price may still lie well above long run costs. Alternatively, minimum prices may reflect a period during which prices have fallen all the way to short run marginal costs, which may lie below long run marginal costs. Yet another objection is that the prices expressed in real US dollars may not directly translate into producer costs in the exporting countries, due to changes over time in exchange rates. All of these factors clearly suggest that the Lerner indexes in Table 1 are subject to measurement error. To the extent that these errors are random across cartels, measurement error in the dependent variable does not necessarily result in biased estimators.

Table 2 reports the data for the hypothesised determinants of monopoly power. Specifically, these variables include the Herfindahl intercartel measure of concentration (HERF), cartel organisation structure (ORG), and the price elasticity of demand facing the cartel ($E_1$). In turn, the elasticity of demand facing the cartel which is defined in equation (8), depends on the price elasticities of market demand ($E_d$) and of fringe supply ($E_f$), and the market share weights ($Q_1/Q$). The Herfindahl measure of intracartel concentration was available from market share data and is calculated in a straightforward fashion. The organisation index (ORG) is a subjective measure assigned after reading the available descriptions of the effectiveness of the cartel structure. The calculation of the price elasticity of demand facing the cartel depends critically on the price elasticities of market demand $(E_d)$ and competitive fringe supply $(E_f)$. Independent elasticity estimates are extremely difficult to obtain. One must search through the available published literature for such elasticities. Fortunately, the work of Walter Labys in tabulating elasticity estimates and identifying commodity market models helped to partially alleviate this onerous burden. Note that for 7 of the 54 cartels, estimates for both the price elasticity of market demand and competitive fringe supply were unavailable. For another 13 of the 54 cartels, there were no estimates of the fringe supply elasticity. Thus complete data were available for only 34 of the 54 cartels. Even for these 34 cartels, the measurement of the supply elasticity from the competitive fringe must be viewed with scepticism. Aggregate supply elasticities from markets partially controlled by cartels are not meaningful, yet econometric models predicated on competitive behaviour routinely compute them. Alternatively, supply elasticities from competitive fringe suppliers is the appropriate measure. The available estimates do not always make this distinction. Furthermore, the differing methodologies used in estimating the remaining elasticities may result in considerable measurement bias. Precisely for these reasons, the alternative model set forth in equation (10) is presented.

Table 2. Cartel Characteristics

| Cartel | HERF | ORG | $E_1$ | $E_d$ | $E_f$ | MS |
|---|---|---|---|---|---|---|
| Sugar I | 10,000 | 7 | −2.08 | −.21 | .2 | 18 |
| Sugar II | 2,613 | 3 | −.83 | −.21 | .2 | 40 |
| Sugar III | 1,627 | 6 | −.36 | −.21 | .2 | 70 |
| Sugar IV | 1,313 | 5 | −.83 | −.21 | .2 | 40 |
| Sugar V | 850 | 5 | −.62 | −.21 | .2 | 50 |
| Sugar VI | 1,195 | 5 | −.85 | −.21 | .2 | 39 |
| Sugar VII | 942 | 5 | −.60 | −.21 | .2 | 51 |
| Coffee I | 10,000 | 7 | −1.13 | −.17 | 1.00 | 55 |
| Coffee II | 1,642 | 5 | −.34 | −.17 | 1.00 | 87 |
| Coffee III | 1,201 | 5 | −.30 | −.17 | 1.00 | 90 |
| Tea I | 4,569 | 4 | −.67 | −.39 | .73 | 80 |
| Tea II | 4,181 | 5 | −.67 | −.39 | .73 | 80 |
| Cocoa I | 1,587 | 5 | −.47 | −.41 | .34 | 93 |
| Wheat I | 2,297 | 4 | −1.13 | −.20 | .20 | 30 |
| Wheat II | 3,466 | 5 | −.98 | −.20 | .20 | 34 |
| Rubber I | 6,082 | 7 | −1.65 | −.77 | .40 | 57 |
| Rubber II | 3,408 | 8 | −.94 | −.77 | .40 | 87 |

| | | | | | |
|---|---|---|---|---|---|
| Steel I | 2,538 | 8 | NA | −.85 | NA | 33 |
| Steel II | 2,787 | 8 | NA | −.85 | NA | 40 |
| Copper I | 6,953 | 9 | −1.54 | −.90 | 1.67 | 80 |
| Copper II | 3,542 | 5 | −3.80 | −.90 | 1.67 | 47 |
| Copper III | 1,787 | 3 | −2.76 | −.90 | 1.67 | 58 |
| Copper IV | 1,609 | 7 | −3.68 | −.90 | 1.67 | 48 |
| Copper V | 2,966 | 5 | −6.62 | −.90 | 1.67 | 31 |
| Lead I | 1,664 | 3 | NA | NA | NA | 61 |
| Zinc I | 2,011 | 3 | NA | −.165 | NA | 47 |
| Zinc II | 1,163 | 6 | NA | −.165 | NA | 66 |
| Bauxite I | 2,689 | 2 | −1.93 | −1.3 | .40 | 73 |
| Tin I | 3,773 | 7 | −2.81 | −1.26 | 1.07 | 60 |
| Tin II | 7,169 | 3 | −4.35 | −1.26 | 1.07 | 43 |
| Tin III | 2,611 | 5 | −1.70 | −1.26 | 1.07 | 84 |
| Tin IV | 2,612 | 8 | −1.55 | −1.26 | 1.07 | 89 |
| Aluminium I | 3,263 | 8 | −2.04 | −.98 | 1.5 | 70 |
| Aluminium II | 2,506 | 6 | −3.36 | −.98 | 1.5 | 51 |
| Aluminium III | 2,795 | 7 | −5.39 | −.98 | 1.5 | 36 |
| Aluminium IV | 2,874 | 9 | −3.36 | −.98 | 1.5 | 51 |
| Mercury I | 5,000 | 9 | −.95 | −.42 | .53 | 64 |
| Mercury II | 2,000 | 9 | −1.54 | −.42 | .53 | 46 |
| Mercury III | 3,789 | 6 | −1.91 | −.42 | .53 | 39 |
| Sulphur I | 5,578 | 6 | NA | −.38 | NA | 90 |
| Sulphur II | 6,250 | 8 | NA | −.38 | NA | 95 |
| Sulphur III | 6,250 | 7 | NA | −.38 | NA | 76 |
| Sulphur IV | 8,042 | 7 | NA | −.38 | NA | 55 |
| Uranium I | 3,702 | 9 | NA | NA | NA | 45 |
| Platinum I | 3,482 | 4 | NA | NA | NA | 90 |
| Platinum II | 3,482 | 6 | NA | NA | NA | 95 |
| Phosphate I | 3,994 | 5 | NA | −.79 | NA | 90 |
| Potash I | 5,878 | 5 | NA | −.46 | NA | 89 |
| Coke I | 3,203 | 8 | NA | NA | NA | 45 |
| Nitrogen I | 10,000 | 8 | NA | −1.42 | NA | 28 |
| Nitrogen II | 10,000 | 8 | NA | −1.42 | NA | 9 |
| Nitrogen III | 3,970 | 8 | NA | −1.42 | NA | 80 |
| Magnesium I | 10,000 | 10 | NA | NA | NA | 100 |
| Magnesium II | 7,450 | 8 | NA | NA | NA | 95 |

NA = Not Available

## 4. EMPIRICAL RESULTS

### 4.1 Determinants of the Lerner Index

Given the data in Tables 1 and 2, it would appear to be a straightforward exercise to estimate equation (9) by ordinary least squares. Four estimates of the Lerner index in Table 1 violate the theoretical lower bound of zero on the Lerner index. Furthermore, it is impossible to measure the logarithm of a negative number. Our solution is simply to omit those four observations for which non−positive Lerner indexes are observed in equation (9). This reduces the sample from 34 to 30 cartels for the model using $E_1$ and reduces the model in equation (10) from 54 to 50 observations.

Table 3 reports the regression results obtained under both models. Equations (3.1) to (3.4) of Table 3 are based on equation (9) whereas equations (3.5) to (3.8) utilise the market share variable in equation (10).

Before turning to equation (3.4), we examine the effect of entering each of the three explanatory variables in equation (9) using the restricted data set of 30 cartels. From equation (1), organisation is shown to be positively related to cartel performance. Moreover, the coefficient of 1.10 implies that a 10 percent increase in the organisation index results in an 11 percent increase in the Lerner index. Equation (3.2) examines the relationship between the Lerner index and the Herfindahl index. With a t–statistics of 1.74, the variable is significant for a one–tailed t test at a 5 percent level. The coefficient estimate of .41 indicates that tight knit cartels consisting of a few large producers produce higher monopoly profits. The effect of the elasticity of demand on the Lerner index in equation (3.3) of Table 3 is shown to be statistically insignificant and of the wrong sign. The inclusion of all three variables in equation (3.4) of Table 3 is disappointing. Only cartel organisation is statistically significant. The Herfindahl index has the correct sign but fails to reach statistical significance. Particularly disappointing is the fact that the elasticity of demand facing the cartel ($E_1$) shows no evidence of confirming theoretical postulates. The most likely reason for this latter result is that the elasticity estimates are subject to large measurement errors. The estimates come from a large variety of studies of varying quality. In some instances, it is unclear whether the supply elasticity estimates pertain only to the competitive fringe. Furthermore, over very long time periods elasticities may change due to technological advances so that elasticity estimated based on data over the last 25 years may be uncharacteristic for a cartel in the 1930s.

If the principal cause for the insignificance of the elasticity variable is error in the elasticity estimates, then equation (10) based on replacing the elasticity of cartel demand with the cartel's share of total market demand should result in a positive, statistically significant relationship. The greater the cartel's market share, the more inelastic is its demand schedule, *ceteris paribus*. Equations (3.5) to (3.8) of Table 3 utilise the expanded cartel data set of 50 observations. Equations (3.5), (3.6), and (3.7) suggest that individual organisation, intracartel concentration, and cartel market share individually have the correct sign and at least approach marginal significance. Equation (3.8) shows that all three variables when combined, maintain reasonably close values and are all

Table 3. Determinants of the Lerner Index

| Equation | Organisation (ln ORG) | Herfindahl Index (ln HERF) | Elasticity of cartel Demand (ln-$E_1$) | Cartel Market Share (ln MS) | Constant | $R^{-2}$ | s.e. |
|---|---|---|---|---|---|---|---|
| Results Using Equation (9) with 30 Cartel Data Set: | | | | | | | |
| (3.1) | 1.10 (2.48) | | | | -3.37 (4.27) | .151 | .796 |
| (3.2) | | .413 (1.74) | | | -4.747 (2.49) | .065 | .835 |
| (3.3) | | | .159 (.80) | | -1.484 (8.93) | -.013 | .870 |
| (3.4) | .948 (2.04) | .276 (1.03) | .007 (.03) | | -5.317 (2.56) | .132 | .805 |
| Results using Equation (10) with 50 Cartel Data Set: | | | | | | | |
| (3.5) | .75 (2.52) | | | | -2.72 (5.00) | .098 | .704 |
| (3.6) | | .412 (2.72) | | | -4.73 (3.82) | .115 | .697 |
| (3.7) | | | | .31 (1.41) | -2.62 (2.94) | .020 | .734 |
| (3.8) | .54 (1.77) | .34 (2.14) | | .40 (2.02) | -6.73 (4.42) | .197 | .664 |

statistically significant at the 5 percent level for a one–tailed t test. The coefficient estimates imply fairly large effects of each of the variables. The elasticity of .54 for cartel organisation with respect to the Lerner index reinforces the finding that cartel organisation can play an important role. Moreover, the coefficient of .34 for intra–cartel concentration (the Herfindahl index) in the presence of the cartel organisation variable indicates the importance of a few dominant producers. Finally, the coefficient of .40 for the cartel's market share implies that cartels controlling a large share of the market are able to obtain appreciably larger monopoly profits.

For those searching for a magical equation by which to predict the monopoly power of the cartel, these results are disappointing. While the three explanatory variables have the correct signs and are statistically significant, the adjusted coefficient of determination of .197 and the standard error of .664 indicate equation (3.8) falls short of this goal. There are several explanations for the low explanatory power of the equation. First, because of the assumptions necessary to measure the Lerner index, the dependent variable no doubt contains random measurement error, reducing the explanatory power of the equation. But probably of greater importance is that each cartel's monopoly power has been influenced by individual, cartel–specific effects, such as market conditions unique to that period, the personality attributes of key cartel organisers, and so forth. Obviously, by extending the list of explanatory variables the power of the equation could by improved; nevertheless, the overall explanation is likely to remain low since individual cross sectional relationships often leave large amounts of variation unexplained.

## 4.2 Causes of the Death of Cartels

The preceding section utilises the Lerner index to measure the health of a cartel while it is active; it says nothing about the causes of its death. This section attempts to categorise the causes of death as reported in the various historical accounts of the 54 cartels. The analysis is necessarily subjective and non–quantitative in nature, but nevertheless quite illuminating.

The conventional reasons given for the demise of all cartels is Adelman's explanation — cheating and chiselling. In effect, cartel members find themselves no longer able to agree on the division of the monopoly rents available to the cartel. But the real question is why were the members unable to agree on a division of the monopoly rents. Had the monopoly rents shrunk to such small proportions that collusive behaviour resulted in lower profits for the cartel members than profits at the competitive equilibrium? Or alternatively, had the monopoly rents remained sufficiently large to yield profits for collusive behaviour, but opportunistic behaviour by cartel members had lead to chiselling and cheating and ultimately to the disintegration of the cartel? This distinction leads to the taxonomy of cartel disintegration shown in Figure 1, which posits that cartel disintegration can occur for structural, behavioural, and other reasons.

The symptoms of a structural cause for cartel disintegration is that the market share or economic pie remaining for the cartel is so small that collusion is unprofitable for the cartel as a whole.[24] Structural reasons in turn can be broken down between technological changes or conventional substitution responses — the effects of high prices either on the demand side via substitution against other commodities or supply side expansion. The invention of synthetic rubber is a prime example of technological change radically altering the supply of rubber. In many instances, technological advances appear induced by the cartel's high price. To Joseph Schumpeter, technological advances were the sure and steady source that would render all cartels powerless in the long run.[25] While less glamorous, conventional substitution responses on both the demand side and the fringe supply work inexorably to reduce the cartel's output and limit its monopoly power. In fact, the long run substitution responses can be so strong as to completely vitiate the cartel's monopoly power.

In Figure 1, the second major reason for cartel disintegration is behavioural problems within the cartel. Even though cartelisation may be profitable for the cartel as a whole, cartels still face the problem of assigning rights to these monopoly profits. To achieve the cooperation of its members, the cartel finds itself unable to achieve the joint profit maximising equilibrium. Experimental economics is able to construct hypothetical collusive situations with differing returns for collusion. The following generalisations follow from this literature:
(1) In experiments involving three or more players, the joint profit maximising solution occurs infrequently;[26] (2) *Ceteris paribus*, in repeated as opposed to one period games, collusion is more likely;[27] (3) In repeated games, reputational effects affect the likelihood of collusive outcomes.[28] Furthermore, from repeated game experiments with reputational effects, one might expect that cartel disintegration is more likely in the early years of a cartel's life than after a period during which players establish reputations.[29]

A third cause for cartel disintegration rests with primarily non—economic

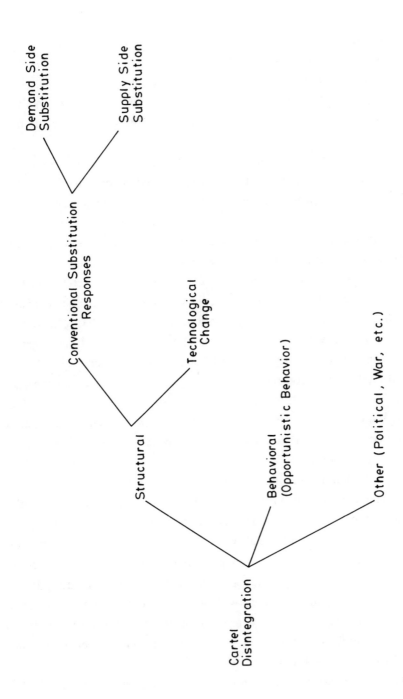

Figure 1. Taxonomy of Cartel Disintegration

causes such as wars. The numerous European cartels found that World War II dissolved cartel agreements. For example, German rearmament in the mid 1930s ultimately forced German producers of chemicals, steel, lights and other products to cease sharing patents and limiting production. In other instances, political events such as government changes have led to key cartel members exiting from the cartel.

Table 4 contains the assignment of the 54 cartels into the taxonomy of Figure 1. In some instances, the literature suggests that more than one cause is attributed to a cartel's disintegration. Interestingly, primarily political reasons account for the demise of 27 of the 54 cartels. World War II brought to an end 12 cartels (tea, rubber, steel, copper, aluminium, sugar, sulphur, phosphate, potash, coke, nitrogen, and magnesium). Once disbanded for a significant period, the possibility of recartelisation appears low. Only the sulphur cartel reemerged shortly after the war. Other reasons for cartel disintegration include changes in governmental policies and cartel reorganisation (e.g. sugar V, VI, VII; nitrogen II; magnesium I; and coffee III). In the case of the latter, cartel disintegration due to these causes might be better labelled "cartel reorganisation".

Conventional substitution responses rank as the second most common cause of cartel disintegration. Eighteen of the 54 cartels succumbed to conventional supply and demand substitution responses. While the written descriptions of these cartels do not always yield a clearcut assignment to demand side or supply side substitution responses, it would appear that expansion by the competitive fringe is more common than reductions in overall market demand.

While technological change has only been important in four of the 54 cases, it was decisive in these cases. The second rubber cartel was rendered impotent with the invention of synthetic rubber. Likewise, the development of substitute alloys vitiated the second zinc cartel's monopoly power. In the sulphur industry, the phenomenal growth of by—product supply from the natural gas industry left the traditional Frasch sulphur producers with a sharply diminished market share. Likewise, the development of by—product nitrogen from steel production undermined the original Chilean nitrate cartel, and forced the reorganised cartel (Nitrate II) to include steel producers.

Finally, behavioural reasons for a cartel collapse appear prominent in 14 of the 54 cartels. In these instances, it appears that cartelisation had resulted in positive monopoly rents and yet disagreement over market shares lead to the cartel's collapse. It is noteworthy that in four cases (tea II, wheat II, steel I, copper II, and copper III), the written accounts suggest that the cartel's monopoly rents had been reduced appreciably by conventional substitution responses. At this point, intracartel differences over production levels lead to its dissolution even though it appears collusion was still profitable.

## 5. IMPLICATIONS FOR OPEC

Before attempting to analyse the implications of these findings for OPEC, we first summarise the findings. As Table 1 suggests, cartelisation can be quite profitable. Moreover, for some products cartel organisations existed over substantial time periods. Prominent examples include rubber, aluminium, and mercury.

The evidence suggests that simple characterisation of cartels as "unstable and short lived" are not terribly useful generalisations. Even though the average cartel life was 7.3 years, there was wide variation around this mean. Furthermore, statements that chiselling and cheating ultimately lead to the demise of all cartels seems inconsistent with our analysis which showed that cartel disintegration was caused by a multiplicity of causes with war, a non—economic cause, the most prominent. Attempts to categorise the causes of cartel disintegration suggest that political upheavals have played a surprisingly important role. Conventional substitution responses and technological change have likewise played important roles. Behavioural explanations, based on intracartel disputes, appear important in some cases but are not the dominant explanation as suggested by Adelman's statement.

Even during the life of a cartel, there appears to be wide variation in the market power of cartels. Greater monopoly profits appear obtained with a high cartel market share, a cartel with a few dominant producers, and an organisational form capable of punishing cheaters and regulating output. But even with a cartel satisfying these characteristics, the resulting Lerner index of monopoly power is subject to considerable unexplained variation. Efforts to reduce this unexplained variation by the inclusion of additional explanatory variables and refined measuring of the Lerner index are not likely to significantly alter this conclusion.

If the average cartel's life expectancy is 7.3 years and the average Lerner index is .31, is OPEC an average cartel? Our estimates place OPEC's Lerner index at .70 for the period 1971 to 1986. Only two cartels, the first rubber cartel (1923–1928) and the second mercury cartel (1954–1970) enjoyed a higher average

Table 4. Causes of Cartel Disintegration

| Cartel | Structural | | | Behavioural | Other | |
|---|---|---|---|---|---|---|
| | Demand Side Substitution | Supply Side Substitution | Technological Change | | War | Political Misc. |
| Coffee II | x | | | x | | |
| Coffee III | | | | | | x |
| Tea I | | | | x | x | |
| Tea II | | | | | | |
| Cocoa I | | | x | | | |
| Wheat I | | x | | x | | |
| Wheat II | | x | | x | | |
| Rubber I | | x | | | | |
| Rubber II | | | x | | x | |
| Steel I | | x | | x | | |
| Steel II | | | | | x | |
| Copper I | x | x | | | | |
| Copper II | | x | | x | | |
| Copper III | | x | | x | | |
| Copper IV | | | | | x | |
| Copper V | | x | | | | |
| Lead I | | | | | | x |
| Zinc I | | x | | | | |
| Zinc II | | | x | | | x |
| Bauxite I | | x | | | | |
| Tin I | | | | | | x |
| Tin II | | | | x | | |
| Tin III | | | | | | x |
| Tin IV | | | | | | x |
| Aluminium I | x | | | | | |
| Aluminium II | | | | x | | |
| Aluminium III | | | | | x | |
| Aluminium IV | | | | | x | |

| Cartel | Structural | | | Behavioural | Other | |
| --- | --- | --- | --- | --- | --- | --- |
| | Demand Side Substitution | Supply Side Substitution | Technological Change | | War | Political Misc. |
| Mercury I | | | | x | | |
| Mercury II | x | x | | | | x |
| Mercury III | x | | | | | |
| Sugar I | | x | | | | |
| Sugar II | | x | | | | |
| Sugar III | | | | x | | |
| Sugar IV | | | | x | | x |
| Sugar V | | | | | | x |
| Sugar VI | | | | | | x |
| Sugar VII | | | | | | |
| Sulphur I | | x | | | | x |
| Sulphur II | | | | | | x |
| Sulphur III | | | | x | | |
| Sulphur IV | | | x | x | | |
| Uranium I | | | | | | |
| Platinum I | | | | x | | |
| Platinum II | | x | | x | | |
| Phosphate I | | | | x | | |
| Potash I | | | | | | |
| Coke I | | | | | | |
| Nitrogen I | | | x | | | |
| Nitrogen II | | | | | | x |
| Nitrogen III | | | | | x | |
| Magnesium I | | | | x | | x |
| Magnesium II | | | | | | |

Lerner index. Moreover, if one dates OPEC's emergence as an effective cartel to 1971, its age in 1987 is 16 years, which is also well above the mean for other cartels.

If OPEC appears exceptional by these two indicators of performance, does it have the characteristics of a strong cartel? Relatively, the answer is no. On the organisational index measure, OPEC does not have a strong organisational index mechanism to regulate output and punish cheaters. A grade of 6 for the organisational index may even be overly generous. The Herfindahl index of intra–cartel concentration is 1500, which is hardly a tight–knit, small group. Furthermore, the market share of the cartel in non–communist world supply has averaged 56 percent over this period. In sum, OPEC would appear to be a rather ordinary cartel in terms of characteristics, but superb in terms of performance.

Is there an explanation for this conundrum? If one separates OPEC's performance in the 1970s from that in the 1980s, there would appear to be a reasonable explanation. During and towards the end of the 1970s, OPEC's monopoly power eclipsed. By 1980, OPEC's Lerner index reached .84, placing it in a rather unique position vis–a–vis other cartels. Griffin and Steele provide detailed accounts of the conditions prevailing in the 1970s which enabled OPEC to record such successes.[30] A prevailing view among OPEC producers during the 1970s was that both the price elasticity of oil demand and the supply elasticity from non–OPEC countries was extremely price inelastic. Accordingly, OPEC thought it could raise price with impunity. Furthermore, as growing GNP increased oil demand, OPEC would experience ever increasing production volumes as production from non–OPEC countries stabilised or declined. Given this view of the world, there was little reason for any one OPEC country to greatly expand production at that time, since by waiting to produce in the future, the value of oil in the ground was perceived to have a higher present value. There are numerous explanations of why OPEC formed this perception of the world, but several factors deserve comment. First, OPEC did not appreciate the distinction between short and long run elasticities. The long run elasticity of demand is tied to turning over the stock of energy conserving capital and this takes time. Likewise, the adjustment to the long run supply schedule for non–OPEC involved significant delays in the leasing, seismographing, drilling, and equipping new wells. Second, governmental price control policies in the 1970s in the US and Canada impeded these conventional substitution responses, by masking the effects of higher OPEC prices.

The sharp decline in worldwide oil demand beginning in 1980 and the steady increase in production from non–OPEC sources as shown in Figure 2 taught OPEC that long run conventional substitution responses were at work limiting its monopoly power just as they have worked on other cartels. The adjustment from the short run to the long run may have taken longer for oil than for other commodities, but their effects have been nonetheless real. By 1986, when OPEC prices tumbled to $10 per barrel before stabilising at $18, OPEC production had fallen to 17 million barrels per day, leaving OPEC with only 42% of free world oil consumption. In contrast, OPEC production in 1973 stood at 31 million barrels per day, which represented a 66% market share. It is also interesting that by 1987, the Lerner index has fallen to .42, assuming that competition would result in a price of $7.50 per.[31]

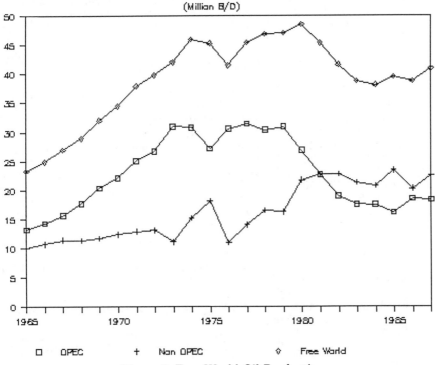

Figure 2. Free World Oil Production

In sum, the OPEC of the 1980's shares much more in common with other cartels than the OPEC of the 1970's. Accordingly, the following observations appear relevant: First, the possibility of cartel disintegration cannot be summarily dismissed. Second, if there is an important lesson for OPEC from the experience of other cartels it is that it is as vulnerable from political events as it is from traditional substitution responses and incentives for cheating. OPEC as it is currently constituted must be viewed as a fragile alliance. Third, though monopoly profits are diminished, they still significantly exceed profits under competitive resource extraction. Therefore, as long as cartelisation remains extremely profitable, new OPECs can be expected to ignite from the ashes of old cartel agreements. The turbulence that has described price fluctuations over the last several years is likely to be a good guide to the future.

## NOTES

* The author wishes to thank Albert LaMore for untiring and conscientious research assistance. This research was supported by a grant to the Center for Free Enterprise from the Tenneco Foundation. Thanks are extended to both groups; they are not responsible or endorse the views herein.

1) Griffin, J.M. (1985), "OPEC Behavior: A Test of Alternative Hypotheses", *American Economic Review*, pp.954–63.
2) Friedman, M. (1974), "FEO and the Gas Line", *Newsweek*, March 4, p.71.
3) Adelman, M.A. "Is the Oil Shortage Real?", *Foreign Policy*, (Winter, 1972–1973), p.71.
4) For example, see "OPEC's Scramble to Avert Price Collapse Depends on Curbing Runaway Output", *Wall Street Journal*, Dec. 8, 1987.
5) Smith, Adam (1937), *An Inquiry into the Nature and Causes of the Wealth of Nations*, Modern Library, New York.
6) Hexner, E. (1946), *International Cartels*, University of North Carolina Press, Chapel Hill, pp.1–18.
7) Smith, R.A. (1961), "The Incredible Electrical Conspiracy", *Fortune*, pp.132–37, 170–80.
8) Voigt, F. (1962), "German Experience with Cartels and Their Control During Pre–war and Post–war Periods", in J.P. Miller ed., *Competition, Cartels, and Their Regulation*, North Holland, Amsterdam, pp.169–208.
9) Larson, D.A. (1970)," An Economics Analysis of the Webb–Pomerance Act", *Journal of Law and Economics*, vol. 13, pp.461–500.
10) Caves, R.E. and M. Uekusa (1976), *Industrial Organisation in Japan*, Brookings Institution, Washington, D.C.
11) Hexner, *International Cartels*, p.17.
12) Stocking, G.W. and M.W. Watkins (1946), *Cartels in Action*, Twentieth Century Fund, New York.
13) Scherer, F.M. (1980), *Industrial Market Structure and Economic Performance 2nd Edition*, p.173, Rand McNally College Publishing Col, Chicago.
14) Voigt, *German Experience*, pp.169–208.
15) Eckbo, P.L. (1976), *The Future of World Oil*, Ballinger, Cambridge.
16) Lerner, A.P. (1934), "The Concept of Monopoly and the Measurement of Monopoly Power", *Review of Economic Studies*, pp.157–75.
17) Friedman, J. (1986), *Game Theory with Applications to Economics*, Oxford University Press, New York.

18) If $S_i$ is the percentage share of the ith cartel members of total cartel production, the Herfindahl index is measured as follows: HERF $= \Sigma S_i^2$. For additional discussion, see Scherer, *op. cit*, pp.274–80.

19) Hexner, E. (1945), *The International Steel Cartel*, University of North Carolina Press, Chapel Hill.

20) Stocking, *Cartels*, pp.56–117.

21) Stocking, *Cartels*, pp.304–62.

22) Klein, L.R. and R. Summers (1966), *The Wharton Index of Capacity Utilization*, Economics Research Unit, University of Pennsylvania, Philadelphia.

23) See W. Labys and J.F. Hewheler (1974), "Survey of Commodity Demand and Supply Elasticities", UNCTAD Research Division, Research Memorandum No. 48. Also see sources in bibliography for individual cartel studies.

24) Pindyck argues that most cartels fail due to structural responses outside the cartel. See R.S. Pindyck (1988), "Cartel Theory and Cartel Experience in International Minerals Markets" in R.L. Gordon et al. (eds), *Energy, Markets and Regulation: Essays in Honor of M.A. Adelman*, M.I.T. Press, Cambridge.

25) Schumpeter, J.A. (1950), *Capitalism, Socialism and Democracy*, 3rd Edition, Harper, New York.

26) Dolbear, F.T. and L.B. Lave, et al. (1968), "Collusion in Oligopoly: An Experiment on the Effect of Numbers and Information", *Quarterly Journal of Economics*, pp.240–59.

27) Alger, D. (1986), *Investigating Oligopolies Within the Laboratory*, Washington: Bureau of Economics, Federal Trade Commission.

28) Roth, A. and F. Schoumaker (1983), "Expectations and Reputations in Bargaining: An Experimental Study", *American Economic Review*, pp.362–72.

29) Phillips, O.R., R. Battalio, and J. Holcomb (1986), "Duopoly Behavior With Market History", Texas A&M Economics Department mimeo.

30) Griffin, J.M. and H. Steele (1986), *Energy Economics and Policy*, Academic Press, Orlando.

31) This estimate of the long run marginal cost is obtained by assuming prices equaled costs in 1972 and that real costs escalated by 2% per year. This accords reasonably with other estimates; see R.S. Pindyck (1977), "Gains to Producers from Cartelization Exhaustible Resources", *Review of Economics and Statistics*.

## REFERENCES

Fisher, F. and P. Cootner (1972), "An Econometric Model of the World Copper Industry", *Bell Journal of Economics and Management Science*, pp.570–91.

Fisher, L.A. and A.D. Owen (1981), "An Economic Model of the U.S. Aluminium Market", *Resources Policy*, pp.150–60.

Joskow, P. *Journal of Legal Studies*.

Labys, W.C. and J.F. Hewheler (1974), "Survey of Commodity Demand and Supply Elasticities", UNCTAD Research Division, Research Memorandum No. 48.

LeCraw, D.J. (1977), "The Uranium Cartel", *Business Quarterly*, pp.77–83.

Oualid, W. and L. Ballande (1938), *International Raw Material Cartels*, League of Nations, Paris.

Peck, M.J. (1961), *Competition in the Aluminium Industry 1945–1958*, Harvard University Press, Cambridge.

O'Carroll, L.T. (1987), "Modelling the Aluminium Industry", Reynolds Metal Co., October 20.

Pindyck, R.S., "Cartel Theory and Cartel Experience in International Minerals Markets", mimeo.

Prain, R. (1975), *Copper: The Anatomy of an Industry*, Mining Journal Books Limited, London.

Rieber, M. (1985), "International Commodity Agreements", *Resources Policy*, pp.87–98.

Sarkar, G.K. (1972), *The World Tea Economy*, Oxford University Press, Bombay.

Stocking, G.W. and M.W. Watkins (1946), *Cartels in Action*, Twentieth Century Fund, New York.

Wallace, B.B. and L.R. Edminster (1930), *International Control of Raw Materials*, Brookings Institution, Washington, D.C.

Woods, D.W. and J.W. Burrows (1980), *The World Aluminium Bauxite Market*, Praeger Publishers, New York.


### Commodity Information Sources and Data

Commodity Research Bureau, *Commodity Yearbook*, New York, Various Years.

Metallgesellschaft, A.G., *Metal Statistics*, Frankfurt am Main, Various Years.

U.S. Department of the Interior, *Minerals Yearbook*, Bureau of Mines, Washington, D.C., Various Years.

United Nations, *FAO Production Yearbook*, Rome, Various Years.

CHAPTER 8

# THE IMPLICATIONS FOR FUTURE CONTINGENCY PLANNING OF THE 1979 GASOLINE SHORTAGE

Leslie E. Grayson, *University of Virginia*
Robert K. Morris, *Rochester Telephone Company*

## 1. INTRODUCTION

This paper examines the origins and management of the 1979 oil crisis in search of policy implications for the next oil shortage. Deliveries of gasoline were insufficient to meet demand during the first eight months of 1979; gasoline represented half of all refinery output.[1]

Nationally, gasoline deliveries were about 10% above historical levels for each of the first three months of 1979. (See Exhibit I). However, the deliveries dropped to near historical levels for April and May, then five percent below historical levels for June and July. By August, deliveries had returned to levels consistent with the three previous years. Obviously, apparent demand would not have dropped below historical levels in the summer months alone if the decline were only part of a long term consumer downtrend: the more likely cause was, instead, (a) the consumers' reaction to higher prices, (b) their flight from longer waiting lines, and (c) their frustration with stockouts — all matters of the moment.

Where in the supply system did the shortage begin? Despite the loss of 251 thousand barrels per day (mbd) from Iran between 1978 and 1979[2], total US imports grew by about 500 mbd between the first halves of 1978 and 1979. Net inventory accumulation for crude oil, gasoline, heating oil, and other intermediate oils explained the product shortages the end users experienced in 1979's second quarter.[3]

The theses of this paper are that: (1) a domestic event, accumulation of stocks during shortage conditions, worsened the problem, and (2) encouragement

207

*L. R. Klein and J. Marquez (eds.), Economics in Theory and Practice: An Eclectic Approach, 207–225.*
© *1989 by Kluwer Academic Publishers.*

of a gasoline buildup before the next shortage occurs, rather than reliance on allocation rules at the time of a shortage, should be the government's policy focus.

There were reasons why a stock buildup should not have happened. Firms are normally risk averse: by neglecting sales to build stocks they risked losing market share, and accumulation was seen as speculation rather than investment. If, for example, the prime rate was the effective cost of capital, then the present value of delaying the sale of a barrel for one year would have exceeded that of its immediate sale in only five of the years 1973–1981.[4]

Yet in 1979 stocks were built. In late 1978 gasoline stocks were close to the 1979 minimum operating (MOI) of 210 million barrels (mmb) (see Exhibit II). (The MOI is "the inventory level below which operating problems and shortages would begin to appear in a defined distribution system".)[5] Consumption in the latter half of 1978 had been high, and in reaction stocks had been drawn down to these low levels. Coupled with the prospects of a long term disruption in the Mideast[6] and oil price decontrol later that year, these low inventories persuaded suppliers to panic and begin an upward price spiral. The problem is that stockbuilding leads to price increases which lead to stockbuilding which lead to price increases and so on[7] and this is what happened in 1979–80.

In 1979–80 the market did not operate in a political vacuum. The purpose of gasoline allocation was to preserve competition and to ensure "equitable" distribution of the product.[8] Controls had two major effects.

First, supplier/purchaser relationships, volumes, and prices were frozen at a fixed point in time. The "base period" idea assumed that historical relationships were the most reliable key to equitable continuity. However, suppliers were required to offer historical volumes to their outlets; the purchasers could then resell on the spot market.

Second, special allocations granted in exception to the general allocation procedures (such as upward certification and base period adjustments for unusual growth) had the perverse effect of decreasing the amount of product available to most historical purchasers. This unfavoured majority often received only a percentage of their historical volumes after all the special allocations were made.

## 2. ANALYSIS OF GASOLINE DELIVERIES BY MAJOR REGIONS

Did certain regions fare better than others during the shortage? As Table 1 indicates, between Petroleum Administration for Defense (PAD) districts gasoline supply availabilities did vary widely.[9] The first shortages were felt in the East (PAD I). Vulnerability to the flow of imports was not the explanation — total imports, we have seen, did not drop in 1979 and gasoline is almost entirely a domestic product, anyway. Then, apparently, the PAD III states of Texas, Oklahoma, and Louisiana shipped more refined product to PAD I to moderate its shortage, and soon PAD II (Midwest and Plains states) lost part of its shipments from PADs I and III. On the average, PADs IV (Mountain) and V (West Coast) seemed to be least susceptible to the disruption.

Table 1. Number of Refineries vs. Percentage of States per PAD that Suffered at Least 10% Shortfall for 1 Month or 6% Shortfall for 2 Months

| PAD | Refiners | 10% – 1 Mo. | 6% – 2 Mos |
|-----|----------|-------------|------------|
| I   | 19       | 33%         | 39%        |
| II  | 17       | 47          | 47         |
| III | 17       | 17          | 0          |
| IV  | 12       | 20          | 40         |
| V   | 12       | 43          | 57         |

Source: Cabot Consulting Group report

If there is some inequitable pattern of regions that suffered, it should be reflected in the gains or losses in market share for the refiners serving them. Exhibit III lists both the top 20 firms' regional market concentrations in early 1979 and their total changes in gasoline deliveries between the first halves of 1978 and 1979. Regression analysis was performed using regional concentrations as the independent variables and delivery changes as the dependent variables. Only four of the five PAD concentrations were included in the model as the five concentrations necessarily sum to 100%; thus, the interpretation of each coefficient is relative to PAD V which was excluded. An $R^2$ of .68 was obtained. For the full equation, $F = 7.34$ (df $= 4, 15$; $p \leq .05$):

$$\text{Percent Change in Deliveries} = 24.427 - 0.186 \ (\text{PAD I}) - 0.137 \ (\text{PAD II})$$
$$- 0.643 \ (\text{PAD III}) - 0.483 \ (\text{PAD IV})$$

The coefficients for PADs I and II are not significant; however, the $p$–levels for the coefficients of PADs III and IV are significant at .001 and .10, respectively. The equation suggests that PADs I and II are most disruption proof whereas PADs III and IV are more susceptible to changes in deliveries. The large number of suppliers in the East and Midwest insulate these areas from fluctuations in the available supplies of individual companies. Conversely, the supplier concentrations in PADs III, IV, and V reduce the number of companies available to make up for reductions in deliveries. Thus, these PADs would be less protected.

In contrast, the ranking of the PADs according to supply availability in Table 2 indicate V (+0.9%), IV (−3.9%), II (−6.6%), I (−10.5%). Therefore a firm focused on regions with more abundant supply was not necessarily better situated to hold or gain market share than one concentrated in regions better situated with lower supplies. Comparisons based on regional changes only in production or net receipts from other PADs revealed new rankings also different from those of the coefficient magnitudes.

Table 2. Indicators of Gasoline Available from Production, Pipeline Shipments, and Primary Stock Percentage Changes, 1978−1979 for Months and Averages
(excludes gasoline imports, tanker and barge shipments)

|          | April  | May    | June   | July   | Apr−July Avg |
|----------|--------|--------|--------|--------|--------------|
| PAD I    | −5.7%  | −12.8% | −11.0% | −12.3% | −10.5%       |
| PAD II   | 0.4    | −6.6   | −10.7  | −9.3   | −6.6         |
| PAD III  | −4.9   | −4.3   | −18.1  | −12.1  | −9.9         |
| PAD IV   | 3.6    | 7.3    | −15.9  | −0.7   | −3.9         |
| PAD V    | 5.3    | −2.1   | 5.4    | −4.9   | 0.9          |
| National | −1.6   | −6.8   | −10.3  | −10.0  | −7.2         |

Source: Shriver Associates, *Evaluation of the Gasoline Allocation Program*

This suggests other causes for company gains or losses. A case−by−case analysis reveals the exceptions that actually caused market share changes. Two of the losers, for instance − Conoco and Shell − lost key refineries to accidents before the shortages.[10]

As indicated in Table 1, the probability of a PAD faring well did not seem related to the number of top twenty refiners serving it.[11] The regression correlations using the number of refiners as the independent variable and the shortfall percentages as dependent variables were both under .20. Flexibility in selecting alternative major suppliers evidently did not help PADs I and II during the shortage.

## 3. ANALYSIS OF GASOLINE DELIVERIES IN KEY STATES AND WASHINGTON, D.C.[12]

The District of Columbia's supply position was strong at the beginning of 1979;

then in February its deliveries declined eight percent, rallied slightly in March, April, and May, then plummeted to a twelve percent loss in June and July. Recovery appears to have begun in August.

As shown in Table 3, Exxon, the leading supplier, held a historical market share for the period January to August of 30.1 percent. In January, Exxon delivered 4,700 barrels less gasoline than it had during its prior three—year monthly average. Other suppliers were able to compensate for that loss, which represented one percent of total January deliveries by all suppliers. As the spring and summer months approached, however, other suppliers were not able to compensate for Exxon's and other suppliers' losses. The two exceptions were Amoco and Mobil.

Table 3. Deliveries in Washington, D.C. by Significant Suppliers

| Significant Suppliers | Historical Market Share | Actual Deliveries: Jan—Aug (thousands of barrels) | | Change | Percent Change |
|---|---|---|---|---|---|
| | | 3—year Avg | 1979 | | |
| Exxon | 30.1% | 955.0 | 804.5 | (150.5) | (15.8) |
| Amoco | 23.1 | 734.2 | 898.9 | 164.7 | 22.4 |
| Texaco | 6.6 | 209.8 | 154.2 | (55.6) | (26.5) |
| Sun | 6.3 | 200.7 | 150.6 | (50.1) | (25.0) |
| Shell | 6.2 | 196.8 | 181.1 | (15.7) | (7.9) |
| BP | 6.0 | 191.8 | 123.0 | (68.8) | (35.9) |
| Mobil | 0.8 | 25.5 | 153.6 | 128.1 | 502.7 |
| | | | | +253.1 | |

Chi—squared for deliveries for 1979 (observed data) versus 3—year average (expected data) equals 757 (df = 6; $p$ < .001).

Source: Cabot report (Chi—squared calculations were done by the authors.)

In New York State overall deliveries during 1979 were almost the same as the historical average, although some suppliers increased and others decreased deliveries. The most severe months were June and July, when the state experienced a four percent decline in the quantity of gasoline deliveries. Why was New York, then, considered a state which had problems, if (as shown in Table 4) it received normal deliveries into the state? Two reasons can account for the problems; neither can be measured by available data.

First, deliveries are not necessarily equivalent to supplies demanded. Although supplies were equal to historical averages, consumers might have demanded greater than average amounts of gasoline. This would lead to gasoline lines. Secondly, the available data do not track distribution within a state. New York might have had adequate supplies, but some local areas might have had less than adequate supplies. No measurement tool exists to prove or disprove either of these hypotheses. Only the appearance of lines of motorists at gasoline stations in Manhattan reflected insufficient supplies to meet demand at the existing price.

Table 4. Deliveries in New York State by Significant Suppliers

| Significant Suppliers | Historical Market Share | Actual Deliveries: Jan–Aug (thousands of barrels) | | Change | Percent Change |
|---|---|---|---|---|---|
| | | 3–year Avg | 1979 | | |
| Mobil | 16.0% | 15,388.8 | 15,127.1 | 261.7 | 1.7% |
| Others | 10.3 | 9,915.8 | 12,390.0 | 2,474.2 | 25.0 |
| Texaco | 9.9 | 9,521.8 | 8,025.9 | (1,495.9) | (15.7) |
| Exxon | 8.8 | 8,420.8 | 7,829.7 | (591.1) | (7.0) |
| Shell | 8.0 | 7,624.2 | 6,199.3 | (1,442.9) | (18.9) |
| Gulf | 6.6 | 6,350.5 | 6,653.4 | 302.9 | 4.8 |
| Amoco | 6.5 | 6,268.4 | 6,572.8 | 304.4 | 4.9 |
| | | | | (186.7) | |

Chi–squared for deliveries for 1979 (observed data) versus 3–year average (expected data) equals 1,201 (df = 6; $p$ < .001).

Source: Cabot report (Chi–squared calculations were done by the authors.)

The impression that California, as a whole, suffered shortages resulted largely from media coverage of gasoline lines in Los Angeles and other urban areas in southern California. Table 5 indicates that, on an overall basis, California did not receive less than historical levels from major suppliers. Nonetheless, local supply problems probably resulted from sharp decreases in deliveries by refiners below the top twenty. Ranking second in market share, "others" delivered about 9.5 million barrels of gasoline less from January to August of 1979 than they averaged in the previous three years. Alternatively, or in addition, the lines might have resulted from increases in demand to a level sufficiently above increases in supply.

The increase in demand may well have been exacerbated by the media. Television news is "made" in the District of Columbia, Manhattan, and Southern California. All three areas experienced moderate shortages and corresponding lines for gasoline purchases. The nightly reporting of these lines may have created incremental demand in two ways: (1) by making the shortage appear worse and more national than it actually was, and (2) by motivating shortage–fearing

Table 5. Deliveries in California by Significant Suppliers

| Significant Suppliers | Historical Market Share | Actual Deliveries: Jan–Aug (thousands of barrels) | | Change | Percent Change |
|---|---|---|---|---|---|
| | | 3–year Avg | 1979 | | |
| Chevron | 15.6% | 28,389.4 | 29,982.2 | 1,592.8 | 5.6% |
| Others | 14.6 | 26,557.2 | 17,081.3 | (9,475.9) | (35.7) |
| Shell | 14.0 | 25,551.8 | 25,287.5 | (264.3) | (1.0) |
| Arco | 11.3 | 20,569.7 | 23,160.6 | 2,590.9 | 12.6 |
| Union | 10.5 | 19,235.8 | 22,409.9 | 3,174.1 | 16.5 |
| Mobil | 7.7 | 14,060.2 | 15,147.4 | 1,137.2 | 8.1 |
| Tosco | 7.6 | 13,911.2 | 16,671.2 | 2,760.0 | 19.8 |
| | | | | 1,484.8 | |

Chi–squared for deliveries for 1979 (observed data) versus 3–year average (expected data) equals 4,963 (df $= 6$; $p < .001$).

Source: Cabot report (Chi–squared calculations were done by the authors.)

consumers to line up more frequently for gasoline and drive with fuller tanks than they would have done under normal conditions.

On the other hand, the deliveries for 1979 versus the historical averages suggested a change had occurred in these areas. Using the three–year average as the expected values, chi–squared analyses indicate significant differences in deliveries for Washington, D.C., New York, and California (see Tables 3, 4, and 5 for the chi–square statistics). Chi–square considers differences not direction. However, the numbers suggest that deliveries for the period were increased overall by 1484.8 and 253.1 thousand barrels for California and Washington, D.C., respectively. Conversely, New York experienced an overall shortfall of 186.7 thousand barrels during the same period.

## 4. THE DISTRIBUTION LAG AND THE SHORTAGE TIMING[13]

Exhibits IV and V indicate the distribution times that prevailed under stable conditions. Liftings ceased at Iranian ports on December 26, 1978. The time lag between the cutoff and product shortages at the retail outlets is a function of the time it takes for a "dip" to move from the foreign crude oil loading docks through the refining and distribution chain down to the retail outlets.

Although it takes a specific period of time for first crude and then product to be moved through the system, this does not necessarily mean that a shortage at the retail outlets will require this length of time in order to appear, after a cutoff. Actually, the time at which the shortage on the consumer level is experienced is a function of inventory and distribution decisions made by the refiner. This may result in the consumer feeling the shortage before the reduction in supply caused by the drop in crude had physically moved through the system.

It is a standard practice for a pipeline to move various products in a routine cycle by product type. Because the product cycle remains basically unchanged, shippers and terminal operators can predict the entry and exit of product from a particular pipeline. This element of predictability is essential to the smooth functioning of a pipeline system and product distribution in general.

During a shortage, some of this predictability is lost. As a result, temporary disruptions can actually reduce long term capacity. The maximum allowed volume a refiner can enter into the pipeline is generally based on an average of the volume moved in the precedidng twelve months. Thus it is in the interest of the refiner to ship volume continuously to maintain a high base period average.

The problems with predictability during a shortage are worst when dealing with demand as divorced from supply. Table 6 compares for January–August 1979 the DOE estimates of gasoline supplied with two forecasts of gasoline demand assuming 3.5 percent real annual growth in GNP and personal income, in August 1978[14] and June 1979,[15] respectively, for this period. If the methodologies were consistent, then in August 1978 DOE underestimated demand by 444 mbd below the probably more accurate June 1979 figure. The underestimate can, in part, be accounted for by the gasoline usage model presented in Appendix A. This model incorporates major influences of demand which are not altered in the short run by increases in price. For example, vehicle travel is largely fixed due to the exigencies of the work force and place and delivery of goods and services. Short run price increases will have no significant impact on this demand.

Table 6. Estimates of National Gasoline Shortage

| August 1978 Demand Forecast** | June 1979 Demand Forecast*** | Gasoline Supplied to Wholesale Market (mbd)* |
|---|---|---|
| 7,138 | 7,294 | 7,738 |

Sources: *  US Department of Energy/Energy Information Administration, *Weekly Petroleum Report*, November 2, 1979 (based on average of January–August 1979)

** US Department of Energy, *Motor Gasoline Supply and Demand Through 1980*, August 1978 (based on average for all of 1979)

*** Short Term Petroleum Forecasting System, runs of June 30, 1979

Similarly, the miles per gallon (mpg) of existing vehicles cannot be increased immediately in response to price increases or shortages in gasoline deliveries. Development of more efficient vehicles and the usage of these vehicles is a long term response. Predictions not considering the time lag required for decreases in vehicle travel and increases in fleet mpg (in response to price increases) to occur will perforce underestimate demand.

Finally, with regard to distribution, it is worth asking whether this country was particularly vulnerable to the effects of an overseas disruption. For the years 1973 to 1979 three independent variables of obvious importance were examined:

(1) US stocks less Minimum Operating Inventory (MOI)/US demand per day

(2) OECD stocks/IEA demand per day

(3) US refinery utilisation rate

Using a binary indicator as a dependent variable and to distinguish years of shortage and upward price spirals (first trial with 1973, 1974, 1978, and 1979; second trial with only 1973 and 1978) from years of stability, regressions were run. No correlations above .46 were found between stock levels and/or refinery utilisations versus actual disruptions. Disruptions have been no easier to predict than region or company vulnerability.

No simple lessons emerge from these correlation analyses. Regulations with equitable distribution as their goal must first analyse what conditions cause inequitable results for various firms, regions, and other categories. If this analysis proves so complex that regulators cannot fully explain the causes they use as regulatory assumptions, then the rules and their impact may be no less complex or inexplicable.

## 5. POLICY IMPLICATIONS

What contingency plans, then, should the government try to develop for the next oil crisis? Greater attention to distribution incentives seems to have been the missing insight in 1979. The obvious alternative to regulations as a means of providing these incentives is represented by the assertion that the free market can best regulate reactions to the next disruption. One policy suggestion has been to exempt profits from taxation during shortage conditions. Companies would see a windfall in selling off stocks before the shortage ended rather than in building them in anticipation of higher prices prevailing after the shortage. In short, the moratorium would create the incentive.

The difficulties would be two–fold. First, even if Congress passed such legislation to prepare for the next shortage, firms could not secure a guarantee that a future Congress would not alter the terms of the act. Refiners would remain risk averse and keep stocks low. Second, Congress would have to determine which gains to exempt. Certainly exemption for all profits is politically impossible, so speculative stocks beyond seasonal demand would have to be defined — an enormous bureaucratic task.[16]

## 5.1 Strategic Petroleum Reserve

Perhaps, then, the reason the Strategic Petroleum Reserve (SPR) has survived so long has been that it is a physical project, not an administrative trigger. The SPR's intent to sell to meet all demand at near—market prices during a shortage distinguishes it from a crisis stock—builder, as many firms may become again.

Currently the drawdown policy is that, if a shortage is determined by the Department of Energy, SPR barrels would be auctioned. There would be no auction price floor, so conceivably firms might be able to buy oil cheap from the SPR without incurring the carrying costs of inventory speculation. It has been suggested that the SPR instead use a standing price at the world market price plus one year of carrying costs;[17] this should avoid discouragement of prudent stock buildups in stable times (since no relief bargains, as are possible now in a shortage, could be anticipated) and better pre—empt panic at the first hint of disruption (since the SPR as an ever—available surge capacity would have been demonstrated through the drawdown all along).

If standing availability is not possible for the SPR, an option system may be the best drawdown policy. Call options would be sold by the government on SPR oil for a certain period, say three months. Should another shortage appear imminent, the option price would rise. The target price of a barrel would be the market price plus a carrying—cost premium. Market forces, more than political timing, would determine the reserve's availability.[18]

## 5.2 Policy Implications of the Changed Oil Industry Environment and Structure

Earlier it was shown that in the 1970s there was little correlation between stock levels and refinery utilisation rates versus the actuality of a disruption. Is it likely that in the future there will occur a disruption large enough to trigger a shortage and an upward price spiral? Regressions run for 1973–85 yielded no significant correlations, but for 1978–85 the R—squared with international stocks—over—demand as an independent variable reached .94 and with refinery utilisations .66:

Disruption = −4.294 + 0.048 (International Stocks–over–Demand)

Disruption = 4.910 − 0.054 (Refinery Capacity Utilisation Rate)

(Yes=0, No=1)

For this analysis 1978 and 1979 were listed as the years prone to disruption and assigned a dependent variable value of zero. It is assumed that if there had been other such years, OPEC would have latched onto some Mideast crisis then, too, as pretext for another "world shortage".

There are explanations for these higher correlation coefficients. One is that the sample is small and the disruption years few and clustered at one end of the period. (However, the t–statistics for both indicated an under–five percent probability of these fits being attributable to chance rather than a real relationship). Another is that between the first and second crisis the world market had grown much more flexible as well as less dependent on contract relationships − hence the levels of world stocks and refinery utilisations became relevant to all producers and customers in the oil arena. An obvious third reason is that since 1980 demand has dropped, leaving higher stocks and lower refinery utilisation until the two influences are eventually adjusted downward and upward, respectively, to tempt the next shortage.

Exhibit VI suggests that the threshold of shortage lies somewhere in the range of 94 to 109 days for world stocks–over–demand and/or 80 to 84 percent for refinery utilisation rates. In mid–1986 the latter variable measured 87 percent; because there was still only negligible upward pressure on prices then, the world stocks ratio (109 days at the end of 1985) seems to be the primary variable. Other ratios may be considered as well, such as that of the SPR to US oil imports (6 percent in December 1980, 33 percent in December 1985),[19] which reinforce the primacy of adequate reserves for price stability or reduction.

The difficulty with developing a predictive threshold is similar to that of selecting a policy trigger where market perspectives are involved. It implies a commitment based on market assumptions that the government cannot fully understand or anticipate. Perhaps this problem in deciding which conditions cause vulnerability to disruption argues all the more for the market presence of the standing auction proposed for SPR allocation.

## 6. CONCLUSION

Another shortage is likely in the early mid–1990s. It is naive to think the government then will be able to resist media and public pressures indefinitely in support of the free market – at some point regulations will be used again. Many of those implemented in 1979 were unsatisfactory because there were insufficient data on the shortage at the time, inadequate time under emergency conditions to make comprehensive analyses, and immense political pressure on lawmakers and regulators to focus on the equitability aspect of the problem. To prepare for the next shortage, therefore, the regulations of DOE (whose crisis role should be minimised) should be flexibly conceived and written. And, although SPR drawdown tests are now conducted periodically, the reassuring continuity of a standing auction system should be considered.

NOTES

1) Cabot Consulting Group, *Performance of the US Petroleum Distribution System under Shortage Conditions: Implications for Contingency Planners*, Contract No. DE–AC01–70PE–70051, pp.6–8. L.E. Grayson was consultant in the preparation of the report. The following companies have kindly cooperated in the study: Arco, Chevron, Sohio, Texaco, Union, and, most helpfully, Exxon.
2) *Monthly Energy Review*, DOE/EIA, February 1986, p.42.
3) Philip K. Verleger, Jr. (1982), *Oil Markets in Turmoil: An Economic Analysis*, Ballinger, Cambridge, Mass, pp.90–100.
4) *Ibid.*, pp.200–202.
5) National Petroleum Council (1984), *Petroleum Inventories and Storage Capacity*, June, pp.19, J–2, J–3, J–4.
6) Glen Toner (1987), "The International Energy Agency and the Development of the Stocks Decision", *Energy Policy*, February, pp.40–58. L.E. Grayson was consultant to the International Energy Agency, Paris, Summer, 1984.
7) M.S. Robinson (1982), "The Crude Oil Price Spiral of 1979–1980", Shell International, London.
8) Based on Cabot, chapter 4.
9) R. Shriver Associates, *Evaluation of the Gasoline Allocation Program*, Contract No. DE–AC01–79PE–70037, pp.70–71.
10) Based on DOE official interviewed on May 28, 1986, Washington, D.C.
11) Cabot, pp. 33, 53, 64, 66, 70.
12) Based on Cabot, chapter 2.
13) Based on Cabot, chapter 3.
14) US Department of Energy/Energy Information Administration, *Motor Gasoline Supply and Demand Through 1980*, August 1978, pp.8–11 and US Department of Energy/Energy Information Administration, *Model Documentation Report: Short Term Integrated Forecasting System*, January 1986, p.8.
15) Cabot, pp.142–43.
16) Verleger, pp.206–07.
17) M.A. Adelman (1982), "Coping with Supply Insecurity", *The Energy Journal*, January–March, pp.1–17.

18) George Horwich and David Leo Weimer (1984), *Oil Price Shocks, Market Response, and Contingency Planning*, American Enterprise Institute, Washington, pp.128–32.

19) US Department of Energy/Office of Petroleum Reserves (1986), *Strategic Petroleum Reserve Annual/Quarterly Report*, February 15, p.17. For additional insight into the role of inventories, see Toner (1987), pp.40–58.

## APPENDIX A: GASOLINE MODEL VARIABLES AND FORMULAS

Let motor gasoline demand be expressed as an identity:

$$G = GVMT/GMPG \,, \qquad\qquad (A1)$$

where      $G$ = total gasoline demand (millions of gallons)

         $GVMT$ = monthly gasoline powered vehicle travel (millions of miles)

         $GMPG$ = monthly gasoline powered vehicle miles per gallon

           (weighted fleet average)

Both $GVMT$ and $GMPG$ are averages rather than monthly measurements, except for certain compilations of panel data or vehicle travel surveys.

The following relationships for these variables are posited:

$$GVMT/Days = Exp[a + b \ln(PRMG/GMPG) + c \ln(YD72)$$
$$+ \, d \ln(JQINDM)] \qquad\qquad (A2)$$

If this equation is expressed in daily rates to correct for varying lengths of months,

$$GMPG = Exp[d + e \ln(PRMG) + f \ln(MGTIME)] \,, \qquad\qquad (A3)$$

we may substitute equation (A2) into (A1):

$$G/Days \text{ per Month} = Exp[a + b \ln(PRMG) + c \ln(YD72) + d \ln(JQINDM)$$
$$- (b+1)\ln(GMPG)] \qquad\qquad (A4)$$

Equation (A4) may be divided by 42 on each side to convert units into barrels from gallons. Variables introduced are:

         $PRMG$ = average real retail motor gasoline price, all grades

         $YD72$ = real personal disposable income (in 1972 dollars)

      $JQINDM$ = industrial production index, all manufacturing

      $MGTIME$ = integer representing time periods since December 1984

$PRGM/GMPG$ = real fuel costs per mile of gasoline powered travel

The proxy used for $GMPG$ is $PGMPG = (VMT/G)$, where $VMT$ equals total highway vehicle travel (million of miles). It is assumed that $PGMPG$ is generally proportional to $GMPG$, where $k$ is the factor. The estimating equations are:

$$k \; GMPG = Exp[p + q \ln(PRM) + r \ln(MGTIME) + s \; DPRE$$
$$+ t \; DPRE \; x \; \ln(MGTIME)] \qquad (A5)$$

and

$$G/(Days \; x \; 42) = Exp[a - (b + 1)\ln(k) + b \ln(PRGM) + c \ln(YD72)$$
$$+ d \ln(JQINDM) - (b + 1)\ln(PGMPG)]/42 \qquad (A6)$$

where

DPRE = dummy variable for period 1975–1979, used to correct for apparent shift in rate of change in mpg due to medium run price effects after the Iranian revolution.

All model variables that include price, total motor gasoline demand, and mpg are deseasonalised for estimation purposes using the Census Bureau X–11 program's seasonal factors (0.974–1.019) for price, 0.933–1.059 for demand, and 0.916–1.080 for proxy mpg).

Source:    US Department of Energy/Energy Information Administration, *Model Documentation Report: Short Term Integrated Forecasting System,* January 1986, pp. 8, 12–14.

Exhibit I. Total US Gasoline Deliveries (first eight months of 1979)

| Month | 3–Year Avg | 1979 | Volume Change | Percent Change |
|---|---|---|---|---|
| January | 205,371.8 | 229,190.6 | 23,818.8 | 11.6% |
| February | 196,404.0 | 218,739.4 | 22,335.4 | 11.4 |
| March | 226,367.5 | 241,609.5 | 15,242.0 | 6.7 |
| April | 224,531.5 | 227,056.5 | 2,525.0 | 1.1 |
| May | 234,032.3 | 241,611.3 | 7,579.0 | 3.2 |
| June | 239,804.2 | 228,364.8 | (11,439.4) | (4.8) |
| July | 237,569.0 | 226,588.3 | (10,908.7) | (4.6) |
| August | 246,196.0 | 243,917.7 | (2,278.3) | (0.9) |
| Total | 1,810,276.3 | 1,857,078.1 | 46,801.8 | 2.6 |

Source: EIA–25, January–August 1979

Exhibit II

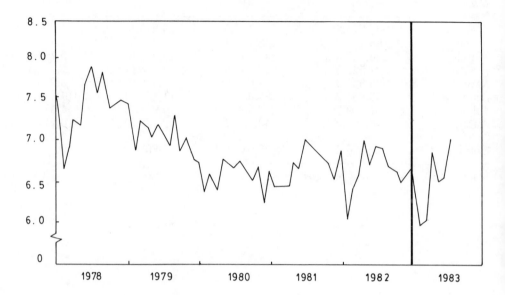

Demand on Primary System for Motor Gasoline – Total US

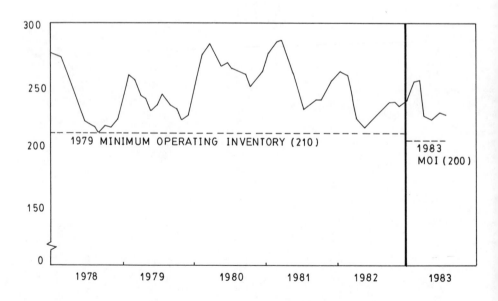

Stocks of Motor Gasoline – Total US

Source: National Petroleum Council, *Petroleum Inventories and Storage Capacity,*
June 1984.

Exhibit III. US Gasoline Deliveries Vs. Market Concentrations

| Company | Percent Change in Gasoline Deliveries (1979 vs. 3–year avg) | PAD Concentrations (by percentages)* | | | | |
|---|---|---|---|---|---|---|
| | | I | II | III | IV | V |
| Amoco | 5.2 | 35 | 51 | 8 | 5 | 1 |
| Arco | 2.3 | 36 | 12 | 14 | 1 | 38 |
| Ashland | 1.2 | 32 | 67 | 0 | 1 | 0 |
| BP | 9.0 | 100 | 0 | 0 | 0 | 0 |
| Chevron | 8.9 | 26 | 6 | 12 | 5 | 51 |
| Citgo | (8.7) | 56 | 29 | 15 | 0 | 0 |
| Coastal | (40.2) | 0 | 0 | 100 | 0 | 0 |
| Conoco | (0.8) | 19 | 34 | 22 | 12 | 14 |
| Exxon | 11.8 | 51 | 10 | 24 | 3 | 13 |
| Getty | 4.4 | 50 | 39 | 6 | 4 | 0 |
| Gulf | 8.6 | 45 | 25 | 24 | 1 | 6 |
| Hess | 6.9 | 100 | 0 | 0 | 0 | 0 |
| Marathon | 25.6 | 23 | 74 | 3 | 0 | 0 |
| Mobil | 1.4 | 43 | 27 | 10 | 1 | 20 |
| Phillips | (9.6) | 27 | 43 | 21 | 7 | 2 |
| Shell | (2.9) | 30 | 29 | 13 | 0 | 27 |
| Sun | (2.5) | 45 | 47 | 7 | 0 | 0 |
| Texaco | (13.5) | 37 | 20 | 23 | 4 | 17 |
| Tosco | 18.5 | 1 | 15 | 12 | 0 | 71 |
| Union | 15.6 | 20 | 26 | 6 | 1 | 48 |

* Due to rounding errors not all company PAD concentrations will add up to
  100%
Source: Cabot Consulting Group report

Exhibit VI. Conditions for Potential Shortage

| Years | US Stocks over Demand | OECD Stocks over IEA Demand | Refinery Capacity Util. Rate | Shortage Yes/No (1/0) |
|---|---|---|---|---|
| 1973 | 17 | 76 | 91 | 1 |
| 1974 | 21 | 88 | 85 | 1 |
| 1975 | 25 | 91 | 83 | 0 |
| 1976 | 22 | 86 | 88 | 0 |
| 1977 | 32 | 93 | 89 | 0 |
| 1978 | 30 | 87 | 87 | 0 |
| 1979 | 34 | 94 | 84 | 1 |
| 1980 | 39 | 109 | 75 | 1 |
| 1981 | 48 | 112 | 67 | 0 |
| 1982 | 46 | 112 | 66 | 0 |
| 1983 | 52 | 110 | 69 | 0 |
| 1984 | 57 | 109 | 77 | 0 |
| 1985 | 55 | 109 | 80 | 0 |

Source: *Monthly Energy Review*, February 1986; National Petroleum Council, *Petroleum Inventories and Shortage Capacity*; National Petroleum Refiners Association official, June 16, 1986, Washington, D.C.

224

Exhibit IV. Overview of Gasoline Supply and Approximate
Time Required for Distribution

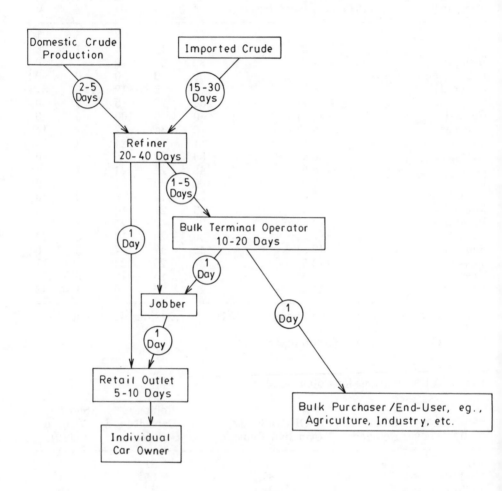

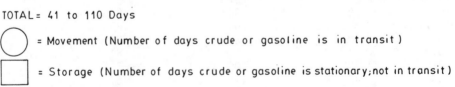

TOTAL= 41 to 110 Days

◯ = Movement (Number of days crude or gasoline is in transit )

☐ = Storage (Number of days crude or gasoline is stationary; not in transit )

Source: Based on interview by the senior author, May 1,
1980, Houston, TX.

225

The transportation response time for a supply interruption or rapid demand change may range from two days up to three weeks depending on the location and mode of transportation used. The table below describes typical times required between supply source and destination to respond to a change in requirements.

Typical Transportation Time, Refinery to Consumer

| Transportation Mode | Origin | Destination | In Transit | Heading | Total | Cycle Times In Days |
|---|---|---|---|---|---|---|
| Colonial P/L | Houston, Texas | New York Harbour | 12 | 2 | 14 | 10 |
| Plantation P/L | Baton Rouge, La. | Washington, DC | 15 | 2 | 17 | 7 |
| Buckeye P/L | Linden, N.J. | Pittsburgh | 5 | 2 | 7 | 5 |
| Tanker | Houston | New York | 5 | 2 | 7 | 13 |
| Tanker | Caribbean (Aruba) | New York Harbour | 5 | 2 | 7 | 13 |
| Barge | Baton Rouge | Pittsburgh | 10 | 1 | 11 | 22 |
| Barge | Baton Rouge | Memphis | 5 | 1 | 6 | 12 |
| Local | - | - | - | 2 | 2 | - |

("Lag" Times – Days: In Transit, Heading, Total)

o Tankers provide the fastest, direct transportation mode to handle Gulf to East Coast supply changes. However, for larger volumes, tankers are difficult to relocate from previous trade.

o Pipeline response time from the Gulf to the upper East Coast is 14-17 days, but fixed capacity provides assurance of supply.

o Barges can respond to changes in the upper Ohio River area faster than pipeline supply from the Gulf via Colonial and Buckeye pipelines.

o Exchange supply, when available, provides the fastest response but no assurance of supply. Exchange arrangements can never provide a full response to a supply interruption or demand change where demands are handled, in part, by the transported supply from another region. However, they can dampen the effects of regional supply interruptions until the transported supply mode can respond.

Source: Based on interview by the senior author, May 1, 1980, Houston, TX.

CHAPTER 9


INTERNATIONAL TRADE, INVESTMENT,
AND AMERICAN CITIES AND REGIONS


Norman J. Glickman, *University of Texas, Austin*


## 1. INTRODUCTION

In this chapter I set out some working hypotheses about the role of cities in today's changing international division of labour (IDOL), within the context of more general structural change[1]. In doing so, I examine the complex ways in which cities have evolved over time, how they are centres for political and economic struggle, and how public policies affect metropolises. I discuss the following major points:

1. There has been a vast transformation of the world economy in that energy price changes, new investment and migration patterns, and the interpretation of markets have had profound and uneven effects on national economies. In recent years, economic growth, profits, and wages have stagnated in many developed countries, while there have been diverse effects on industries, occupations, and cities. Employment fell in traditional manufacturing and shifted to the high technology and service sectors.

2. The "third industrial revolution" (involving electronics, biotechnology, and, significantly, information processing) helped produce two contradictory urban trends. First, it encouraged de–urbanisation and the dispersion of the population. This is so because technology and the maturation of product lines promoted both standardised work and dispersed job sites, and because changing business strategies and organisation allowed firms to seek less urbanised locations. Hence, decline occurred in traditional manufacturing regions and there has been a continuing decentralisation of jobs and population. At the same time, an opposite tendency produced agglomerations

227

*L. R. Klein and J. Marquez (eds.), Economics in Theory and Practice: An Eclectic Approach, 227–247.*
© *1989 by Kluwer Academic Publishers.*

of corporate headquarter functions in a few large cities. These centres of administrative activities maintain control over regions that specialise in production processes in smaller cities.

3.  As a result of economic change, there have been pressures by groups and classes (e.g., income, race, regional, industrial, and occupational) which have lost out and who demand policies to cushion themselves from decline. In an era of slow growth, with many groups bringing simultaneous pressure on the State, fiscal problems result. For instance, firms petition the State to increase their profitability through tax cuts, deregulation of markets, decreased enforcement of health and safety regulations, and reduced social welfare benefits. Corporations have attempted to roll back previously won wage and working conditions directly through bargaining and indirectly through appeals to the State on the grounds that high wages are the prime cause of inflation and low productivity. Workers, on the other hand, fight to maintain their living standards and economic security through extension of social legislation and urban programmes. With slow economic growth, the State cannot meet all demands simultaneously. These problems are made more difficult to solve in a more internationalised economy, as external pressures add new dimensions to political conflict.

4.  Economic programmes trying to reestablish faster growth have geographical side effects that often aid growing areas and suburbs at the expense of declining regions and central cities. Urban policies, on the other hand, generally try to ameliorate the problems of large cities and declining areas. Therefore, a policy dilemma has resulted that the State cannot easily solve.

In what follows, I expand on these points with emphasis on the situation in the United States.

## 2. SOME PHENOMENA

### 2.1 National and International Economic Change

The worldwide economic picture has changed significantly in the last twenty five years. The 1970s saw sharp decreases in economic growth and increases in inflation. In non—socialist industrialised countries, for example, the average annual Gross Domestic Product (GDP) growth fell from 5.1% to 3.0% from the 1960s to the 1970s and to 2.3% in the 1980s. Inflation rates more than doubled during the 1970s, but declined during the 1980s, in part because of the fall in commodity prices and austere monetary policy. There have been extraordinary increases in international trade, with the world's exports increasing more than twelve times between 1963 and 1981 (Deardorff and Stern, 1983).

To understand changes in the IDOL, it is useful to divide the world into three types of countries : 1) *core* countries that make up the leading industrial producers of the Organisation for Economic Cooperation and Development (OECD) and that house most corporate centres; 2) *semi–periphery* nations, consisting of the middle–income OECD nations and newly industrialised countries (NICs) that are dependent on core nation capital investment; and 3) the poor countries and oil exporters of the *periphery* (Wallenstein, 1974).[2]

Two stages of international trade, capital investment, and migration patterns can be set out (Glickman and Petras, 1981). During the 1950s and 1960s, core countries imported labour from the periphery and semi–periphery, capital intensive exports were sent from the core to the semi–periphery and periphery, most trade and foreign investment was intracore, and the core imported low cost energy from the peripheral oil nations. After about 1974, however, new trends emerged. As economic growth declined, most labour importation ended, foreign direct investment (FDI) increased from the core to a small number of NICs, more labour intensive imports came into the core from the NICs, and core countries imported high price energy. Although cut–offs of labour importation into the core were accompanied by capital exports to NICs, FDI went to a largely different set of countries than those that were previously labour exporters. Thus, a *triangular* relationship of labour–capital exchange took place: labour was imported from one set of semi–periphery and periphery countries, but capital exports went to NICs, few of which had been labour exporters.[3] The search for low–cost labour in the NICs was mostly in assembly operations, especially in the semiconductor, textile, clothing, and shoe industries. Relocation of auto, chemical, steel, and rubber operations from developed nations were often for marketing purposes or to supply other overseas operations. Importantly, while assembly functions decentralised, control activity remained in the core. During the 1980s, some NICs challenged the developed world, successfully exporting autos, steel, and computers.

A good example of worldwide industrial dispersion can be seen in the automobile industry. Hill (1983) describes the transition from a US dominated industry in the 1960s to one now characterised by massive foreign investment by American carmakers and increasing competition from Japanese and European producers. As a result, fierce global competition emerged and the US share of sales dropped sharply. There has been integration of worldwide auto operations, efforts to penetrate European markets by American firms, and penetration of the US market by the Europeans and Japanese. The results have been dramatic: between 1978 and 1982, US firms' auto sales declined by 32% while imports rose from 18% to 28% of the domestic market. Employment fell by nearly 300 thousand workers. Most recently, there has been massive foreign investment by American car companies (about $58 billion between 1980 and 1985) and simultaneous demands for protection at home. Global integration of operations came about, involving geographically separate engineering, design, production, assembly, and other operations. Ford's "World Car" is an example of this strategy. Nearly identical cars were assembled in a multitude of places using components produced in a variety of countries.[4] Firms are thus able to take advantage of local production conditions to maximise worldwide profits.

Castells (1985) shows a similar globalisation of the semiconductor industry. Research and management functions, oriented as they are to intellectual labour, locate near universities and cities where "quality of life" factors are high. But the other processes — mask making, wafer fabrication, assembly, and testing — may have geographically distinct and separate patterns. Therefore, labour–intensive assembly functions have been locating in NICs such as Hong Kong, Singapore, and Korea, where wages are low. By 1976, "offshore" assembly plants employed twice the number of people working in similar domestic operations. The same lines of geographic development can be seen in the assembly processes of many other industries.

These patterns emerged because of improvements in communications technology and changes in business organisation, resulting in the establishment of a "Global Factory" (Barnet, 1980). A large number of people have been brought into this internationalised system of production, exchange, and finance. For assembly activity, work can be done nearly anywhere in the world using largely interchangeable, low–skilled workers. Thus, firms have looked for sites with low wage, stable, and unorganised labour, both within developed nations and in "safe" LDCs (usually those with totalitarian regimes).[5] Crucially, the speed of capital shifts increased as firms have become better able to disperse production worldwide because of the information revolution (Castells, 1985; Bluestone and Harrison, 1982).

Two spatial phenomena are directly connected to recent global economic change. First, the evolving IDOL has meant that cities have developed new functions. In particular, a few "world cities" (Friedmann and Wolff, 1982) have evolved to organise and manage the far–flung operations of multinational corporations. Cities such as New York, Tokyo, London, and Paris house concentrations of corporate headquarters, high–level corporate services (accounting, law, etc.), banking, research, and government. Supervision of production facilities lower in the urban hierarchy takes place in these con-urbations. Smaller cites assume roles as production, service, and consumer centres (Noyelle and Stanback, 1984; Pred, 1977; Cohen, 1981). The higher a city is in the hierarchy, the more control it will have over its own economic destiny. Therefore, we see both a *spatial diffusion* of economic activity and a pronounced *territorial hierarchy* (Castells, 1985). Second, foreign direct investment has affected regional development. During the early postwar era, most investment was in the core regions of developed nations because of uncertainty about alternative sites and the desire to be near consumer markets. Later, multinational corporations (MNCs) decentralised investment, particularly in assembly operations (Glickman and Woodward, 1989).[6]

### 2.2 International Trade and the US Economy

Within these global patterns, the US economy changed as well. During the 1970s, the economy stagnated, there was a fall in the rate of profit (Nordhaus, 1974; Lovell, 1978), more overseas investment (OECD, 1981), slower productivity growth (Denison, 1979), and stagnation. For example, the GNP growth rate fell from 4.7% per annum (1961–1965) to 2.2% (1973–1981). Between 1980 and 1986 it fell further, to 1.8% per year. Inflation reached 13% in 1980, declining under the deflationary monetarist measures of the early 1980s and the deepest postwar recession.

US direct investment abroad increased substantially, while direct foreign investment in the US exploded in the 1970s.[7] US assets abroad were $260 billion at the end of 1985, four times the 1970 level. There was also a major shift towards investment in the NICs: 7% of US FDI went to these countries in 1960–1968 compared with 19.4% between 1973 and 1978. By 1977, production by US parent companies and majority–owned foreign affiliates overseas was $161 billion, more than one–twelfth of domestic GNP (Howenstine, 1983).[8] Inward FDI grew from $13 billion in 1970 to $209 billion in 1985. Much inward FDI was by oligopolistic firms seeking access to the large US market in order to exploit their "ownership advantage"[9] in such high technology sectors as machinery and chemicals (Dunning, 1981; Schoenberger, 1983).

Trade of US goods and services grew rapidly, as exports increased from $29 billion in 1960 to $348 billion in 1982. (Belli, 1983). Imports and exports were both about 8% of production in 1969; however, exports rose to 16% and imports increased to nearly 20% of domestic output by 1982. Most significant has been the penetration of US manufacturing goods markets and the decline of the US as a world trade leader.[10] By 1980, nearly three–quarters of all goods produced in the US were in active competition with imports from other countries (Reich, 1983). The US had net exports of some high–tech items,[11] corporate and financial services, and agricultural products. Also, imports are strong in traditional manufactured markets that were previously US dominated. Major import industries are autos (21% of domestic consumption), consumer electronics (52%), calculators (43%), textile machinery (46%), and cutlery (90%) (Magaziner and Reich, 1982). Significant balance of trade problems resulted from declining competitiveness. The 1987 trade deficit was $171 billion.

Foreign trade and investment has had differential effects on occupations and segments of the labour force. Frank and Freeman (1978) show that about 85% of the job loss attributable to US investment abroad has been in blue–collar occupations. Sectors affected adversely by imports have been more heavily unionised and have employed more blue–collar, female, and minority workers. Export industries tend to have more highly educated, young, and managerial employees. Thus, increased imports and outward FDI have negatively affected lower skilled workers. Glickman (1988) confirms these occupational, gender, and racial effects for US overseas investment for 1977–1986.

## 2.3 IDOL and US Spatial Change

Changes in the IDOL have produced many notable effects on American cities and regions. First, the decline in sales of heavy manufacturing goods in international markets (e.g., transportation equipment, nonelectrical and electrical machinery, chemicals) has exacerbated unemployment problems in the Industrial Heartland of the Northeast and Midwest. Simultaneously, other regions have gained from trade: agricultural sales abroad have helped farming regions in the 1970s, and some of the large cities that lost manufacturing jobs have gained service positions (particularly in corporate headquarter functions). These corporate service jobs are concentrated in the Northeast and other large metropolitan areas (Stanback and Noyelle, 1984).[12]

Second, there has been an uneven pattern of foreign direct investment among

US regions. In 1981, employment in nonbank US affiliates of foreign firms was concentrated in the Mideast (23.4%), Southeast (14.9%), and the Great Lakes (16.2%)[13]. But, the fastest employment growth between 1974 and 1981 was in the Southwest (20.1% per year compounded), the Rocky Mountains (16.1%), and Far West (12.8%) regions. McConnell (1980) argued that locations outside the Industrial Heartland are fast becoming the preference for foreign multinationals. In this sense, foreign affiliates are following the decentralisation patterns of US firms. Glickman and Woodward (1989) show that there was significant dispersion from regions with considerable inward DFI directed to those areas that had little in the early 1970s. Their analysis points out that the spatial distribution of foreign firms is becoming similar to that of domestic companies, increasingly favouring the South and West.

Third, international migration (illegal and legal) has had a distinct regional character. Most migrants come from the Caribbean Basin, Central America, and (more recently) Asia. Many Hispanic workers (often employed in secondary agricultural and service jobs) reside in the Southwest (e.g., California, Texas) and parts of the Northeast (New York, New Jersey). In all, the greater openness of the US economy meant that international forces had more significant effects on urban and regional development than previously.

Returning to the automobile and semiconductor examples of Section 2.1, the regional consequences of the industries' transformations have been important. Historically, car assembly and production have been regionally concentrated in Michigan. In 1963, for example, 36% of auto employment was in that state. With the globalisation of the auto industry, that figure fell to 26% by 1977.[14] Semiconductors have been concentrated in California, Arizona, and Massachusetts, where three–fourths of employment is located. Areas such as "Silicon Valley" near San Jose and the Route 128 area around Boston dominate research and management locations. Assembly operations not located abroad are in low–wage areas of western and southern states.

## 2.4 Urban and Regional Change in the United States

Besides the effects of the IDOL, there have been other important spatial ramifications of structural change. On an interregional basis, sharp reversals of long term regional patterns took place during the 1970s: the growth of jobs and population was greater in non–metropolitan regions than in metropolitan areas for the first time. Cities with large manufacturing bases lost jobs and population[15] to the suburbs (first the inner suburbs, then the outer suburbs, and, finally, the exurbs and other non—metropolitan areas) and to the Sunbelt.[16] These phenomena represent more than spillovers across metropolitan boundaries, but encompassed growth far from metropolitan areas as well during the 1970s. Part of the non—metropolitan change is due to energy and resource development, and a portion is a result of recreation— and retirement—related employment. However, much non—metropolitan employment growth is also in assembly operations (often in branch plants of large companies) that have relocated from large cities. Most big cities have lost population, independent of region. There has been much continuing migration to the Sunbelt[17], including the return flows of Blacks who moved to the North two generations ago.[18]

The relative importance of industrial location factors changed. With the decline of manufacturing (particularly heavy manufacturing), the traditional location determinants (transportation availability and cost, agglomeration economies, energy, and, to a lesser extent, labour) have less significance or have changed in character. Firms have become more communications and technology oriented. Both manufacturing and service firms, for example, are able to decentralise routine operations to low wage regions (domestically and internationally) and need little unskilled labour near their home office locations. Technological advances in transportation and communication allow greater decentralisation, as firms have become more footloose (Markusen, 1983; Malecki, 1979); also, financial reorganisation makes decentralisation more feasible. Firms, particularly those that hire many white—collar workers, increasingly demand "quality of life" factors. These reasons help explain why many small and medium sized cities with pleasant living conditions and low taxes have been growing rapidly.

There has been, as a result of these factors, a polarisation of the urban system. Cities with concentrations of corporate command functions have a good deal of independence from the rest of the urban system, while areas that specialise in traditional production of provide consumer services are dependent upon corporate centres for investment and finance. Even within metropolitan areas, there is considerable economic segregation, what Friedmann and Wolff (1982) call the "citadel and the ghetto". The gleaming towers of Manhattan coexist with the poverty of nearby Harlem and Bedford—Stuyvesant, although there is little employment for these neighbourhoods' residents on Wall Street. Economic and spatial segmentation can also be seen in Silicon Valley, where the homes of researchers and managers are located away from production line workers (Samenian, 1984).

## 3. SOME TENTATIVE EXPLANATIONS OF ECONOMIC AND POLITICAL CHANGE

Having discussed the IDOL and its effects on the US, I want to try to tie several things together: the economic slowdown and responses to it, the changing nature of the State, the role of people's movements and corporate initiatives, and fiscal problems at the local level. I provide some tentative explanation in this section.

Three elements of the international postwar corporate system that were put in place in the 1940s and 1950s came back, in a dialectical manner, to haunt the American economy in the 1960s. These were: 1) *Pax Americana*, consisting of the Bretton Woods Agreement and other economic and defense measures, aimed at maintaining American postwar hegemony; 2) *a limited capital–labour accord*, an informal agreement between "Big Capital" and "Big Labour", to share productivity gains in key industries and to pass on higher costs to others; and 3) *a limited capitalist–citizen accord* to provide economic security through social legislation (social security, medical care, etc.) and the reduction of cyclical unemployment through demand management (Bowles, Gordon, and Weisskopf, 1983). Much of this unwritten "social contract" was confined to certain sectors, classes, and interest groups. The whole arrangement was predictated on the ability to reward those inside (and, to a lesser degree, outside) the accords by distributing the fruits of economic growth. Wolfe (1981, p. 10) said of the early postwar political situation: "A bipartisan coalition was formed to pursue economic expansion at home through growth and overseas through empire. ... Politics would concern itself with the means – growth – and the ends, or purpose, of social life would take care of themselves."

However, there were exogenous and endogenous forces at play that destroyed this very delicate set of arrangements. Significantly there came the decline in US economic dominance and the end of the *Pax Americana* in the 1960s. This occurred because of the drain put on the economy in the late 1960s by the support for the military in Vietnam and by competition with the countries that the US had been trying to build up both for markets and for geopolitical purposes (e.g., Germany, Japan, and stable LDCs). The growth of social programmes and the unwillingness to raise taxes to pay for both the war in Southeast Asia and the War on Poverty strained the US fiscal and political capacity. The rise of OPEC and the greater strength of raw material producers also weakened US hegemony. The US economic leadership declined drastically as it was increasingly challenged in its own domestic markets as well as in world markets that it formerly dominated. As a result, stagflation set in, and latent problems in various strata of society surfaced — in production lines, welfare lines, and bottom lines. With fewer resources available to keep the accord together, the agreement came unglued.

Federal policies reinforced many of America's problems. For instance, by encouraging the outflow of FDI through the tax laws and by other means, domestic jobs were lost. Glickman and Bannister (1988) show that 3.4 millions jobs were lost between 1977 and 1986 due to US investment abroad. Beginning in the 1970s, American firms were increasingly competing with their own foreign subsidiaries. Corporations, as part of a conscious business strategy, reduced (when practical) production in the United States in many processes and industries (e.g., the assembly operations in the auto industry). Tax and regulatory policy made these corporate strategies easier to carry out. Reagan–era monetary policy, in trying to battle inflation, created high real interest rates and many international trade problems. The resulting overvalued dollar has made foreign investment cheap and exports expensive for American firms. By the time the dollar began to fall in 1985, much production which had been sourced offshore stayed there or was shifted to LDC's whose currencies had not risen relative to the dollar. At this writing, little overseas production had returned to this country.

The domestic "growth coalitions" (Wolfe, 1981; Mollenkopf, 1983) aimed at increasing economic growth both nationally and locally fell into disarray. These alignments of corporate, labour, and community leaders failed partly because so many people were not in the coalition to begin with: secondary workers, women, minorities, consumer groups, environmentalists, and others had been largely powerless from the outset. During the 1960s, these groups put pressure on the State for a bigger piece of the pie. Wage bargaining by workers got much more aggressive, since the cost of unemployment was very low due to unemployment compensation and tight labour markets. Women and minorities also became more important economic and political forces. These internal factors, plus the US decline in the international sphere, contributed to the fall in the profit rate and to some of the productivity growth rate decline. Also, even within the growth coalitions, primary workers began negotiating more aggressively on workplace issues (e.g., speedups, work safety), thereby putting further pressure on profits.

Workers were less willing to put up with bad working conditions and began to revolt on the production line (Aronowitz, 1973). Finally, there were additional costs placed on the system by the pressures of environmentalists, consumers, and others.

The profit squeeeze of the late 1960s early 1970s inevitably brought a counterattack by corporations. As a result, the "people's movements" for greater social welfare (Piven and Cloward, 1971) of the 1960s were superseded by what can be called "corporate movements" in the 1970s and 1980s. Faced with poor earnings, business took the offensive at the negotiating table, mounted strong anti—union drives, and pushed for restrictive macroeconomic policy in order to reduce wage pressure. At the local level, fiscal limitations efforts (such as California's Proposition 13) received heavy corporate backing. Politically, the corporate movement reached its peak with Ronald Reagan's election in 1980 and the passage of the 1981 tax and domestic spending reductions. The deep recession of 1981—1982 served to discipline the work force and to gain wage and shop floor "give backs". Lax workplace and environmental safety enforcement were major components of the Reagan Revolution. The deregulation of financial markets and laid back anti—trust enforcement helped spur takeovers and speculative activities.

In light of the corporate offensive, much of the increased international and interregional mobility of capital can be seen both as a way to increase profits by relocating to lower cost areas (in the conventional, neoclassical economist's view) and as a way of combating labour's gain; in the latter sense, this is a way of "zapping" the labour movement (Bluestone and Harrison, 1982). Therefore, the movement of branch plants to nonmetropolitan areas in the 1970s can also be seen as part of an anti—labour strategy (since nonmetropolitan areas are generally non—union). Relocation to low—wage areas is not only national but international, as indicated earlier.

In addition, the work process was changed to reduce the demand for skilled and semi—skilled labour. This was accomplished by automation, the re-organisation of work, and other methods. A good deal of this "deskilling" occurs when firms relocate operations to low—wage regions and take advantage of new (and non—union) employees to restructure work. This reduces the necessity of employing high—skilled, expensive, and independent labour. It helps tip the bargaining scales in favour of management and to increase profits.

## 4. CHALLENGES TO THE STATE

In response to some of the effects of structural change, the State was called upon to do several, often contradictory, things: to take measures to increase profits and economic growth; to institute class–based social policies to aid displaced workers; to initiate urban and spatial measures to help depressed areas, and so forth. (Friedland, Piven, and Alford, 1979; Glickman and Alford, 1982). Since all of these could not be accomplished simultaneously in a slow growth era, several kinds of conflict resulted.

On one level, the State has been subject increasingly to *external* pressures as trade relations grow more complicated. Assaults have come from other nations (e.g., trade wars, protectionist pressures), multinational corporations (who pressure for subsidies by threatening to relocate offshore), migrant workers and their employers, and international organisations (the Common Market, LAFTA, etc.). All these groups petition the State to protect their interests.[19] Corporations seek to break down national boundaries and use their full power globally. National governments, as a result, find themselves bargaining with footloose MNCs and, as a result, are less able to formulate effective policy.[20] Pressures build to protect jobs and social services for workers displaced by global shifts. These tugs bring out ideological conflicts between free trade and protectionism (e.g., the "voluntary quotas" for imported Japanese cars). International conflicts over a variety of products (e.g., steel, wine, pasta) give significant trouble to nation–states.

Besides these external pressures, the State is faced with *internal* conflicts. These have taken several forms, mostly over distributive shares. For example, the corporate ascendancy of the last decade has resulted in sharply lower business tax rates, an increasingly regressive tax code, and real reductions in social spending. This has led to greater tax burdens placed on consumers and workers. Displaced auto, steel, and textile workers seek protectionism, training, and social benefits. Geographically, there are also built–in conflicts between economic policies that help expanding areas and urban policies that try to cushion declining cities (Luger, 1983; Glickman, 1984). Stagflation deepened these conflicts: as the economy performs poorly, there is more competition among interest groups and classes to try to fight for their shares of the pie. Fiscal strains result from these internal pressures on the State, especially when the economic pie is growing slowly.[21]

In addition, *region*–based demands add another dimension to the problems of the State. That is, coalitions of capital and labour fight for preferences for localities; these groups often transcend class and other alignments, coming together for limited purposes under emergency situations. Examples include a coalition of the Chrysler Corporation, the United Auto Workers Union, and the City of Detroit that brought pressure for the 1980 federal loan guarantee to Chrysler.

Just as firms put pressure on the State for tax breaks to increase profitability at the national scale, they also do so to increase profitability at the local level. President Reagan's New Federalism, the devolution of other federal programmes to the states, enterprise zones, and cuts in social spending are ways of aiding corporate growth. For instance, dispersing the powers of the federal government to the states means that lobbyists for social causes must go to 50 state capitols, where their power is diluted and where corporate power is felt most strongly (Peterson, 1982). Also, one can view tax revolts at the state and local level as corporate/wealthy—led attacks on the social wage; this weakens local tax bases and makes localities more vulnerable to further pressure from firms that induce cities to give greater tax breaks.

These international and domestic pressures result in an increasingly impotent State, since governments cannot deal effectively with internal pressures that often lead to fiscal stress. Nor can the State effectively make successful arrangements with the many pressure groups negotiating with it. The combination of internal and external pressures makes decision making very difficult.

Several elements are important to recall at this juncture: 1) pressures by corporations on the State to do things to increase profitability; 2) corporate strategies to increase profits, including speedups, increases in supervision, less workplace autonomy, mergers, and, significantly, threats to relocate; and 3) pressures by labour, consumers and environmentalists to maintain social and quality of life programmes. These aspects make the State (at both national and local levels) less able to operate effectively. The international dimension reduces even more the effectiveness of State policy because firms can withdraw capital investment. Capital mobility is a tool used by firms to gain advantage over labour and to extract concessions from the State. And, as we shall see next, it makes urban policy more difficult to carry out.

## 5. URBAN POLICY

Urban policy (UP) is formulated to correct for market failure brought on by spatial imbalances and to spur economic development. For example, in order to provide space and funds for urban revitalisation, urban policy has consisted of programmes such as urban renewal (in the 1950s and 1960s, particularly) and housing. Other things have been done by national governments to reduce the cost of doing business in cities, including infrastructure grants, loans, small business development efforts, transportation, and water and sewer programmes. An increasing number of programmes are undertaken by localities themselves: write–downs of land, infrastructure provision for business, subsidised loans, and grants aimed at attracting firms in the spatially competitive environment noted earlier.

Another portion of urban policy consists of income transfers and public services, including Aid to Families with Dependent Children, housing allowances for low–income people, Supplemental Social Insurance, and other income and service programmes. These programmes are often not targeted to places, but to people, and certainly have important urban effects. Some urban programmes come about through categorical grants to localities and states, others through less restrictive block grants. The trend since the Nixon Administration has been towards the latter.[22]

Most of the money for these urban programmes is targeted to social transfers rather than places. In fact, about $18 is spent on social transfers (including retirement) to every $1 expended on urban programmes. Funds for place– - targeted urban programmes have been cut sharply, by 27 percent in real terms between 1978 and 1984 (Glickman, 1984) and have fallen further since then. Means–tested social programmes for the poor were cut by one–sixth during the early Reagan years – about $75 billion (Bawden and Levy, 1984).

But, in addition to these nominal urban programmes, what I call "the *real* urban policy" includes the indirect urban consequences of economic policy: accelerated depreciation allowances, investment tax credits and so forth. (Glickman, 1984). The incentives put in place by these programmes are very powerful aids to industrial relocation even though they are not intended for these purposes. For instance, these tax programmes try to increase investment by lowering the cost of capital and increasing cash flow. However, in doing so, they also encourage investment in new assets over the replacement of existing assets and favour equipment over structures. This has meant that the investment that results from these tax write–offs takes place in growing (often sunbelt) areas, rather than declining regions. Moreover, there are other non–urban policies that affect the spatial division of labour: the allocation of R&D expenditures, defense appropriations and bases, and other spending to growing, non–union, low–wage areas (Luger, 1983). These non–urban portions of urban policy constitute the most important part of the real urban policy.

Therefore, we have three parts of urban policy: "place programmes", "people programmes", and non–urban tax/expenditure policies. Most of these programmes tilt towards growth areas that have low wages and "good business climates". Regions that have strong unionism, higher wages, and so forth are being left behind, especially for footloose, assembly operations. Therefore, economic policy aimed at increasing investment and production also aids corporations in a spatial sense since capital movements disrupt organising efforts by workers. As a corollary, the efficiency of most local or national urban development programmes is lessened by the mobility of capital. In effect, cities have far less leverage over local business activity because firms are so easily able to move. Therefore, municipalities find it more difficult to formulate and carry out development policies because of the capital mobility and the conflict of urban policies with national economic programmes.

For localities, slower economic growth and a more internationalised economy have led to frantic attempts to attract industry through local tax incentives particularly tax abatements and industrial development bonds for new factories.[23] Theses local programmes have become fundamentally "defensive" in nature since local economic development officers say, "If we don't offer these benefits, our town will be perceived as having a bad business climate". This is a "negative–sum" game for communities, as subsidy funds are transferred to the corporate sector. As soon as subsidies run out or depreciation allowances are taken, firms are free to move on, since they have not put much capital into their plants. Firms can then play off cities to get better tax deals and create a "reserve army of places" (Walker, 1978). Increasingly, tax incentives are being given when there are threats by existing firms to move elsewhere.[24]

Related is the "capital versus community" theme of Bluestone and Harrison (1982): firms are able to exert their power over communities and impose other social costs related to plant closings. The role of conglomerates (which have a "portfolio of firms" to maximise total profits) has become more important in the movement of capital as a way of opening new markets, disciplining labour, and taking external control of regional activity.

Fiscal problems have been occurring at the local level, not just in New York and Cleveland, but in growing areas since older areas are "stuck" with old private capital or old public infrastructure and because of conscious disinvestment decisions on the part of corporations. The New York Municipal Assistance Corporation ("BIGMAC") and other (unelected) agencies are instituted to force reductions in services and wages on the public. However, fiscal problems in fast growing areas (e.g., San Jose and Houston) are also due to the overextension of local capital infrastructure and the refusal of local firms to endorse public spending on infrastructure or services needed for social reproduction.

## 6. CONCLUSIONS

I want to close with a brief set of conclusions about the relationship between the IDOL and cities. Despite the rise of conscious and concerted efforts to control and direct growth, the ability of cities to determine their own economic destinies has been sharply limited by increases in capital mobility and by the changes in trade and foreign investment patterns. The ability of firms to rapidly shift productive activities globally makes cities' futures less secure than previously.[25] Moreover, cities continue to be the centres of political struggle over the distribution of income, as they house both modern corporate headquarters and wretched slums. The urban growth coalitions, as Mollenkopf (1983) tells us, have become weaker due to the splits between citizens groups and firms. A hypothesis put forward here is that firms have been using the possibility of international relocation to extract concessions from workers and cities. In doing so, they are able to tilt economic and political power in their favour.

In the end, cities find themselves less able to deal with their economic problems. Friedmann and Wolff (1982, p. 327) described the dilemma as follows:

> A major loser is the local state. Small, isolated without financial power, and encapsulated within the world economy, it is barely able to provide for even the minimal services its population needs. And yet, instead of seeking alliances with neighbouring cities and organised labour, it leaves the real decisions to the higher powers on which it is itself dependent, or to the quasi—independent authorities created by state charter that manage the infrastructure of global capital—system—wide facilities such as ports, airports, rapid transit, water supply, communications, and electric power.

The internationalisation of economies, then, provides many difficult questions for urban planners:

— How can they control or influence the economic restructuring taking place at the local level, when it is often directed by external forces?

— How can they mediate local conflicts over land use, job creation, and the environment?

— What new political strategies and institutions can they develop to gain a measure of autonomy in this ever—changing environment?

These questions must be answered by planners and local activists if cites are to regain political power.

## NOTES

1) Structural change (or economic restructuring) involves long term shifts in the composition of demand, production, and occupational patterns; new technology; a changing international division of labour; shifts in relative prices; and evolving location patterns (both migration and industrial spatial restructuring)

2) Core countries include Northwest Europe, North America, Japan, and Australia. The semi—periphery consists of lower income OECD countries such as Ireland and the NICs (including the Republic of Korea, Taiwan, Brazil, and Singapore). The NICs have specialised in labour—intensive goods such as clothing, shoes, toys, and electronics; many, however, became more capital intensive in the late 1970s, increasing exports of items such as steel to core nations.

3) Pre—1974 importation of labour from Northern Europe took place largely because of labour shortages in industries such as construction, textiles, metal working, health care, and consumer services. The major exporters came from the southern tier of Europe and North Africa and from the Caribbean Basin. In Europe, many institutions were established to recruit and transport labourers for employers. After 1974, investment in NICs such as Brazil, Hong Kong, Korea, and Singapore, none of whom had been a major labour exporter previously, received much FDI.

4) For instance, by 1980, 12% of US Big Three cars were produced by their Latin American affiliates, up from 5.5% only seven years earlier (Trachte and Ross, 1983, as cited by Castells, 1985).

5) This industrialisation of a few Third World countries has led to rapid urban growth in major cities of these NICs. Although this chapter concentrates on the developed world, the impact on NICs must be kept in mind.

6) Among the studies of the regional location of direct foreign investment, see Dickens and Lloyd (1976), Howenstine (1983), McDermott (1977), McConnell (1980), Little (1978, 1983) and Glickman and Woodward (1989).

7) Although investment abroad by American firms increased, other countries' investment grew even more quickly. Between 1961 and 1967, the US had 61% of all FDI made by 13 major investing countries (OECD, 1981). By 1974—1978, the US share dropped to 30%, while Japan and West Germany increased their combined shares from 9.6% to 29.9%. The share of foreign direct investment by the 13 countries made in the US was only 1.4% in 1961—1967, but grew to 24.5% by 1974—1978. By 1983, inflows of capital to the US ($82 billion) were far greater than outflows ($50 billion).

8) Viewed in another way, foreign production was three times the value of exports in 1960; by 1977, it was more than five times exports. 25% of outward FDI was in petroleum; other major industries in which US firms had large foreign investments were paper, rubber, textiles, wholesale trade, and finance.

9) "Ownership advantage" refers to the ability to exploit superior technology, innovation, and product differentiation abroad.

10) The US share of exports of industrialised capitalist countries declined from 21% in 1965 to 16% in 1983. During the same period, the US absorbed an increasing share of the world's imports (20% in 1983 compared with 17% in 1965).

11) According to the 1977 *Annual Survey of Manufactures*, the most export-intensive manufacturing sectors were electrical and nonelectrical machinery, instruments, transportation, and tobacco products. All but the last (which is small absolutely) have high-technology characteristics.

12) Corporate headquarter activity has been greatest in New York, Los Angeles, Chicago, and San Fransicso. Cities gaining *Fortune 500* corporate headquarters between 1959 and 1976 were Houston and Minneapolis (Noyelle and Stanback, 1984).

13) About one-fourth of the book value of property, plant, and equipment was in the Southeast, with Louisiana, Florida, South Carolina, and Georgia being the largest in that region. Among the states, California, Texas, and Alaska had the largest foreign investments (Belli, 1983).

14) Auto production has been spatially concentrated in other countries as well. Regions such as the Piedmonte (Italy), Niedersachsen (FRG), Ile de France (France), and the West Midlands (UK) have been major centres of auto production (Hill, 1983). The secondary effects of the decline in auto production have been felt in related industries such as steel and tires. This change in location has been a major factor in serious fiscal problems in auto dominated cities such as Detroit and Flint.

15) For example, between 1970 and 1980, population declined by 18% in St. Louis, 24% in Cleveland, and 21% in Detroit (Tabb, 1984).

16) Garnick (1983) reports that metropolitan area population grew at nearly four times the rate of nonmetropolitan regions between 1959 and 1969. In the next decade, nonmetropolitan areas grew faster. But this reversal of long term trends was not uniform; in the more urbanised parts of the country (New England, the Mideast, the Great Lakes, and the Far West), nonmetropolitan areas grew faster in the 1960s and slower in the 1970s compared with metropolitan areas. For less urbanised regions, metropolitan areas grew faster in both decades. During the 1980s, however, there was a return to older patterns: metropolitan areas grew faster than nonmetropolitan areas.

17) Houston and Phoenix grew by more than 25% during the 1970s, for instance.

18) It is critical to understand that often-made "Frostbelt-versus-Sunbelt" categorisation is simplistic. There are sections of the Sunbelt that have continued to stagnate (e.g., Mississippi) while states such as Texas (at least until the mid 1980s oil bust), Florida, and Arizona have boomed. Similarly, there was solid growth in parts of New England and other Frostbelt areas.

19) Or at least, not to interfere with their self-perceived prerogatives.

20) Unions also cannot bargain effectively with MNCs because labour is rarely organised internationally. Therefore, firms can play off workers in different countries and reduce wage costs (Bluestone and Harrison, 1982).

21) Although states and localities in the aggregate have run budget surpluses

(deficits are generally not permitted by law), there are fiscal problems in many large central cities, intensifying the battle among cities for jobs and tax bases. Fiscal stress is particularly severe in cities with traditional manufacturing bases and large minority populations. Infrastructure is decaying and services have been cut. Fiscal problems make attracting employment more difficult for cash–poor cities.

22) Reasons given for devolution are the desire for greater local autonomy and an interest in reducing federal social expenditures. In actuality, the result has been considerably less money going to needy cities and the poor.

23) At the same time, there are moves to create a positive environment for research based employment (e.g., ties with universities) in order to attract "high tech" firms.

24) Essentially, location decisions that were formerly among the best kept corporate secrets have become among the most public as firms await bids from hard–up cities. In recent years, International Harvester has played off Ohio and Indiana, the Microelectronic and Computer Technology Corporation considered bids from 57 cities, and there has been international bidding for auto plants (e.g., Austria vs Spain). The implications of these tax losses for local fiscal cities are obvious and serious (Harrison and Kanter, 1978).

25) This is not to say that cities ever had complete control over their own economic development. My argument is that increased capital mobility and internationalisation of the economy result in more external influence.

## REFERENCES

Aronowitz, S. (1973), *False Promises*, McGraw–Hill, New York.

Barnet, R.E. (1980), *The Lean Years*, Simon and Schuster, New York.

Bawden, L. and F. Levy (1982), "The Economic Well–Being of Families and Individuals", in J.L. Palmer and I.V. Sawhill (eds.), *The Reagan Experiment*, Urban Institute Press, Washington, D.C.

Belli, R.D. (1983), "Foreign Direct Investment in the United States: Highlights from the 1980 Benchmark Survey", *Survey of Current Business*, 63, No. 10, pp.25–35

Blackbourn, A. (1972), "The Location of Foreign Owned Manufacturing Plants in the Republic of Ireland", *Tijdschrift voor Economische en Sociale Geografie*, 6, pp.438–43.

Blackbourn, A. (1978), "Multinational Enterprises and Regional Development: A Comment", *Regional Studies*, 12, pp.125–27.

Bluestone, B. and B. Harrison (1982), *The Deindustrialization of America*, Basic Books, New York.

Bowles, S, D.M. Gordon, and T.E. Weisskopf (1983), *Beyond the Wasteland*, Doubleday, New York.

Castells, M. (1985). "High Technology, Economic Restructuring, and the Urban–Regional Process in the United States" in M. Castells (ed.), *High Technology, Space, and Society*, Sage Publications, Beverly Hills.

Cohen, R.B. (1981), "The New International Division of Labor, Multinational Corporations and Urban Hierarchy" in M. Dear and A.J. Scott (eds.), *Urbanization and Urban Planning in Capitalist Society*, Methuen, London.

Deardorff, A.V. and R.M. Stern (1983), "Current Issues in Trade Policy" (mimeo).

Denison, E.F. (1979), *Accounting for Slower Growth: The United States in the 1970s*, The Brooking Institution, Washington, D.C.

Dicken, P. and P.E. Lloyd (1976), "Geographical Perspectives on United States Investment in the United Kingdom", *Environment and Planning*, 8, pp.685–705.

Dunning, J.H. (1981), *Economic Analysis and the Multinational Enterprise*, George Allan and Unwin, London.

Frank, R.F. and R.T. Freeman (1978), *The Distributional Consequences of Direct Foreign Investment*, Academic Press, New York.

Friedland, R., F.F. Piven, and R.R. Alford (1979), "Political Conflict, Urban Structure, and the Fiscal Crisis" in D.E. Ashford (ed.), *Comparing Public Policies: New Concepts and Methods*, Sage Publications, Beverly Hills.

Friedmann, J. and G. Wolff (1982), "World City Formation: An Agenda for Research and Action", *International Journal of Urban and Regional Research*, 6, pp.309–44.

Garnick, D.H. (1983), "Shifting Balances in Metropolitan and Nonmetropolitan Area Growth", Paper presented at the 1983 Meetings of the Regional Science Association, Chicago, Illinois.

Glickman, N.J. (1984), "The Economy and the Cities: In Search of Reagan's *Real* Urban Policy", *Journal of the American Planning Association*, August, pp.471–78.

Glickman, N.J. and R.A. Alford (1982), "The State in an Internationalized Economy" (mimeo).

Glickman, N.J. and E.M. Petras (1981), "International Capital and International Labor Flows: Implications for Public Policy", Philadelphia: *Working Paper*, 53, Department of Regional Science, University of Pennsylvania.

Glickman, N.J. and G.J. Bannister (1988), "The Regional Effects of U.S. Direct Investment Abroad", Austin TX, *Working Paper*, 47, Lyndon B. Johnson School of Public Affairs, University of Texas.

Glickman, N.J. and D.P. Woodward (1989), *The New Competitors: How Foreign Investors are Changing the U.S. Economy*, Basic Books, New York.

Harrison, B. and S. Kanter (1978), "The Political Economy of States Job–Creation Business Incentives", *Journal of the American Institute of Planners*, 44, pp.424–25.

Hill, R.C. (1983), "The Auto Industry in Global Transition" (mimeo).

Howenstine, N.G. (1983), "Gross Product of US Multinational Companies, 1977", *Survey of Current Business*, 63, No. 2, pp.24–29.

Kemper, N.J. and M. De Smidt (1980), "Foreign Manufacturing Establishments in the Netherlands", *Tijdschrift voor Economische en Sociale Geografie*, 71, pp.21–40.

Law, C.M. (1980), "The Foreign Company's Location Investment Decision and its Role in British Regional Development", *Tijdschrift voor Economische en Sociale Geografie*, 71, pp.15–20

Little, J.S. (1978), "Locational Decisions of Foreign Investors in the United States", *New England Economic Review*, January/February.

Little, J.S. (1983), "Foreign Investor's Locational Choice: An Update", *New England Economic Review*, January/February.

Lovell, M.C. (1978), "The Profit Picture: Trends and Cycles", *Brookings Papers on Economic Activity*, Issue No. 3, pp.769–88.

Luger, M. (1984), "Federal Tax Incentives as Industrial and Urban Policy" in L. Sawers and W. Tabb (eds.), *Sunbelt–Frostbelt: Regional Change and Industrial Restructuring*, Oxford University Press, New York.

Magaziner, I.C. and R.B. Reich (1982), *Minding America's Business*, Vintage, New York.

Malecki, E. (1979), "Location Trends in R&D by Large US Corporations, 1965–1977", *Economic Geography*, 55, pp.309–23.

Markusen, A.R. (1983), "Sectoral Differentiation of Regional Economies", paper presented at the Regional Science Association meetings.

McConnell, J.E. (1980), "Foreign Direct Investment in the United States",

*Annals of the Association of American Geographers*, 70, pp.259–70.

McDermott, P.J. (1977), "Overseas Investment and the Industrial Geography of the United Kingdom", *Area*, 9, No. 3, pp.200–207.

Mollenkopf, J.H. (1983), *The Contested City*, Princeton University Press, Princeton.

Nordhaus, W. (1974), "The Falling Share of Profits", *Brookings Papers on Economic Activity*, Issue No. 1, pp.169–208.

Noyelle, T. and T.M. Stanback (1984), *Economic Transformation of American Cities*, Allanheld and Rowman, Totowa, New Jersey.

OECD (1981), *International and Multinational Enterprises: Recent Direct Investment Trends*, OECD, Paris.

Peterson, G.E. (1982), "The State and Local Sector" in I. Sawhill and J. Palmer (eds.), *The Reagan Experiment*, The Urban Institute Press, Washington, D.C.

Piven, F.F. and R. Cloward (1971), *Regulating The Poor*, Pantheon, New York.

Pred, A. (1977), *City Systems in Advanced Economies*, John Wiley, New York.

Reich, R.M. (1983), *The Next American Frontier*, Times Books, New York.

Samenian, A. (1984), "The Urban Contradictions of Silicon Valley: Regional Growth and the Restructuring of the Semiconductor Industry" in L. Sawers and W. Tabb (eds.), *Sunbelt/Snowbelt: Urban Development and Regional Restructuring*, Oxford University Press, New York.

Schoenberger, E. (1983), "The Logic of Foreign Manufacturing Investment in the United States: Implications for the US Economy" (mimeo).

Tabb, W. (1984), "Urban Development and Regional Restructuring, An Overview" in L. Sawers and W. Tabb (eds.), *Sunbelt/Snowbelt: Urban Development and Regional Restructuring*, Oxford University Press, New York.

Trachte, K. and R. Ross (1983), "The Crisis of Detroit and the Emergence of Global Capitalism", presented at meetings of the American Sociological Association (mimeo).

Walker, R. (1978), "Two Sources of Uneven Development Under Advanced Capitalism: Spatial Differentiation and Capital Mobility", *Review of Radical Political Economics*, 10, No. 3, pp.28–37.

Wallerstein, I. (1974), *The Modern World System*, Academic Press, New York.

Watts, H.D. (1980), "The Location of European Direct Investment in the United Kingdom", *Tijdschrift voor Economische en Sociale Geografie*, 71, pp.3–14.

Wolfe, A. (1981), *America's Impasse*, Pantheon, New York.

World Bank (1980, 1983), *World Development Report*, The World Bank, Washington, D.C.

# INDEX

# Advanced Studies in Theoretical and Applied Econometrics

1. Paelinck, J.H.P. (ed.): *Qualitative and Quantitative Mathematical Economics.* 1982
ISBN 90-247-2623-9
2. Ancot, J.P. (ed.): *Analysing the Structure of Econometric Models.* 1984
ISBN 90-247-2894-0
3. Hughes Hallet, A.J. (ed.): *Applied Decision Analysis and Economic Behaviour.* 1984
ISBN 90-247-2968-8
4. Sengupta, J.K.: *Information and Efficiency in Economic Decision.* 1985
ISBN 90-247-3072-4
5. Artus, P. and Guvenen, O. (eds.), in collaboration with Gagey, F.: *International Macroeconomic Modelling for Policy Decisions.* 1986    ISBN 90-247-3201-8
6. Vilares, M.J.: *Structural Change in Macroeconomic Models.* Theory and Estimation. 1986    ISBN 90-247-3277-8
7. Carraro, C. and Sartore, D. (eds.): *Development of Control Theory for Economic Analysis.* 1987    ISBN 90-247-3345-6
8. Broer, D.P. (ed.): *Neoclassical Theory and Empirical Models of Aggregate Firm Behaviour.* 1987    ISBN 90-247-3412-6
9. Italianer, A.: *Theory and Practice of International Trade Linkage Models.* 1986
ISBN 90-247-3407-X
10. Kendrick, D.A.: *Feedback, A New Framework for Macroeconomic Policy.* 1988
ISBN Hb: 90-247-3593-9; Pb: 90-247-3650-1
11. Sengupta, J.K. and Kadekodi, G.K. (eds.): *Econometrics of Planning and Efficiency.* 1988    ISBN 90-247-3602-1
12. Griffith, D.A.: *Advanced Spatial Statistics.* Special Topics in the Exploration of Quantitative Spatial Data Series. 1988    ISBN 90-247-3627-7
13. Guvenen, O.: *International Commodity Market Models and Policy Analysis.* 1988
ISBN 90-247-3768-0
14. Arbia, G.: *Spatial Data Configuration in Statistical Analysis of Regional Economic and Related Problems.* 1989    ISBN 0-7923-0284-2
15. Raj, B. (ed.): *Advances in Econometrics and Modelling.* 1989 ISBN 0-7923-0299-0
16. Aznar Grasa, A.: *Econometric Model Selection.* A New Approach. 1989
ISBN 0-7923-0321-0
17. Klein, L. and Marquez, J. (eds.): *Economics in Theory and Practice.* An Eclectic Approach. Essays in Honor of F. Gerard Adams. 1989    ISBN 0-7923-0410-1